FLEET STREET REMEMBERED

Also by Tony Gray

Fiction

Starting from Tomorrow
The Real Professionals
Gone the Time
Interlude (from an original screenplay
by Lee Langley and Hugh Leonard)
The Last Laugh

Non-fiction

The Irish Answer
The Record Breakers (with Leo Villa)
Psalms and Slaughter
The Orange Order
Buller (with Henry Ward)
No Surrender: The Siege of Londonderry, 1689
Champions of Peace: The Story of Alfred Nobel,
the Peace Prize and the Laureates
The White Lions of Timbavati (with Chris McBride)
Some of My Best Friends are Animals
(with Terry Murphy)
Operation White Lion (with Chris McBride)
The Road to Success: Alfred McAlpine, 1935–85

Fleet Street Remembered

TONY GRAY

HEINEMANN : LONDON

William Heinemann Ltd
Michelin House, 81 Fulham Road, London sw3 6rb
LONDON   MELBOURNE   AUCKLAND

First published 1990
Copyright © 1990 Tony Gray

A CIP catalogue record for this book
is available from the British Library
ISBN 0 434 27788 6

Typeset by Hewer Text Composition Services, Edinburgh
Printed and bound in Great Britain
by Mackays PLC, Chatham.

For Pat, for everything

Contents

Part One:
THE
FLEET STREET
STORY

by Tony Gray

Introduction

Long before this book is published the last of the national dailies will have moved from EC4, and 'the street', as it was known to three generations of newspapermen, will be no more than a memory.

For almost a century, from the time when Alfred Harmsworth, later Lord Northcliffe, launched the first popular morning newspaper, the *Daily Mail* in 1896, Fleet Street was a unique centre of journalistic and allied entrepreneurial and promotional talents; there has never been anything even remotely like it in any other country.

Around the turn of the century a number of factors combined to create a growing, insatiable, nation-wide appetite for a daily ration of news and opinion and gossip and scandal and speculation about the rich and the famous, the wicked and the wild, at a time before the radio, the cinema and television had begun to compete for a share of the public's fickle attention. These included the achievement in the United Kingdom of almost universal literacy, the rapid development of the high-speed rotary press and the hot metal linotype machine, the proliferation of the telephone as a means of instant communication, the swift progress of the techniques of photography and half-tone reproduction and the growth of a new cult of stars of the stage, screen, society and sport.

That they happened almost simultaneously in a small, wealthy, densely populated island already equipped with a highly efficient road and rail network enabled daily newspapers to be delivered on every doorstep in the land in time for breakfast. The arrival on the scene – traditionally the centre of London's print industry – of a succession of colourful and eccentric press barons and a galaxy of brilliant journalists, whose names soon became almost as well-known as those of the celebrities about whom they wrote, provided the principals for the cast of this new branch of the entertainment industry.

The term 'the street' embraced the whole area around Fleet Street, right down to the Thames Embankment near Black-friars Bridge, as far north as Holborn and Gray's Inn Road, as far west as the Law Courts. It included all the pubs and clubs and drinking dens in the district, a Grand Duchy far more than a district really, with its own capital, El Vino, in Fleet Street itself, almost opposite the end of Fetter Lane; a superficially convivial community composed, like the Serengeti, of various species of prey and predator and every bit as perilous.

With the national newspapers now scattered as far apart as Battersea and Wapping, Kensington and the Isle of Dogs, as a result of the belated introduction of the new computerised print technology, the street – the street of ink, the street of fame, the street of shame, the street of adventure as it has been variously called – will soon be no more than yet another office development area. And while there have been plenty of books about Fleet Street, including a few farewells, they have all tended, naturally enough, to reflect only whatever aspect of that infinitely diverse jungle happened to be readily observed from each author's own particular lair.

In an effort to pin down as many differing facets of the Fleet Street experience as possible before it is too late, I have assembled this anthology of memories from Fleet Street and ex-Fleet Street hands from many branches of the business; editors and proprietors, columnists and foreign correspon-dents, reporters and sub-editors. Like any anthology, it is completely personal; a varied cross-section of personalities and opinions which I hope will convey something of the splendid diversity of the Fleet Street experience.

I should perhaps make my own position clear and admit at this stage that my particular slice of the Fleet Street experience was limited to three bewildering years on the *Daily Mirror* in the early sixties. I had been plucked from the editorship of an obscure weekly illustrated tabloid published by the *Irish Times* Group in Dublin by an old school friend, James Gordon Pettigrew who ran the William Hickey column in the *Daily Express* in the fifties and subsequently the John Rolls gossip column in the *Mirror*, and I was flown over to London for a series of interviews. When, out of the blue, I was offered the job of features editor of the *Daily Mirror*, then the top-selling daily newspaper in the world, at a salary slightly higher than that of the Prime Minister of the Republic of Ireland, plus a weekly expense allowance which was roughly double my basic salary in Dublin, I immediately assumed that someone had spotted a hint of potential journalistic genius in me that I had never suspected to exist.

It was several months before it gradually dawned on me that I had simply been picked as a minor pawn in one of the innumerable power games that were going on in the *Mirror* Group and all over Fleet Street at that time, and indeed all the time. It then occurred to me that I had been chosen because I obviously knew enough not to make a complete idiot of myself straight away, but not enough even to attempt to insert myself into any of the incipient niches that were being industriously developed. I was abruptly sacked within three years when the *Mirror* decided to invite Harold Keeble to join their staff. Mine happened to be the only conveniently placed office on the editorial floor which could immediately be vacated without any harmful effect upon the newspaper, since from the moment of my arrival I had contributed nothing whatever of value to its conduct or its character, apart from the dubious pleasure of my company, usually baffled by what was going on around me and frequently suffering from the after-effects of unaccustomed, overlong, delicious expense-account luncheons.

It was not altogether my fault; the change in pace from a Dublin backwater where I had been in charge of a paper that sold – not really sold, or even made freely available, merely printed – about 30,000 copies once a week to my new situation as head of the features department of a paper then selling five million copies a day, with Hugh Cudlipp as overlord, was so cataclysmic that I was only beginning to adjust to it when the axe fell.

When later I relived some of my memories of this period in a novel I called *The Real Professionals*, James Drawbell, himself one of the undisputed, genuine Fleet Street real professionals, was kind enough to say of it: 'This is an important, revealing novel . . . a picture of a wasteland. I recommend it as Exhibit A in the next Press Inquiry if there are enough newspapers left to justify another investigation.'

He was wrong about one thing, just as Cecil King had been equally wrong when he predicted, in the sixties, that soon there would only be three national newspapers left. They couldn't have foreseen, of course, what profound changes the new computer technology would bring about – the unthinkable total collapse of the powerful printers' unions; the even more incredible dispersal of the national newspapers to warehouses in Wapping and former department stores in Kensington and other unlikely locations, where the reporters and special correspondents would sit in front of TV monitor screens feeding their stories into computers which would regurgitate them in any type-face imaginable without the aid of linotype men, compositors, sterotype men or even, it sometimes seems, without being scanned by the eagle eye of a sub; and, what would perhaps have seemed most unlikely of all, the appearance, for the first time since the turn of the century, of a couple of new titles which genuinely represented new newspapers and not mergers, or rejigs of old ones.

Nor could they have foreseen the complete disappearance of what was, for varying periods for all of us, the epicentre of our entire world, Fleet Street – the Fleet Street of the Press Club, of El Vino, and Winnie's, and the Stab, and Barney Finnegan's and Gerry's bar in the Cock, and the Clachan, and Mooney's Irish House, and the Forum, and the Wig and Pen, and all the others I've forgotten.

It is not really fair to myself to say that my experience of Fleet Street was limited to the period from 1959 to 1961, when I worked on the *Mirror*. After that I worked for a couple of years in ITN and then for Associated Rediffusion, both situated on the corner of Kingsway opposite Bush House, and continued to spend most of my spare time in Fleet Street drinking and chatting with my ex-colleagues and friends from the other newspapers. And even when I left television to write books full-time, I continued, between books, to work as a freelance for several of the Fleet Street papers, and I have kept in touch with many of the people who appear in this anthology over the years.

When I started to research this book, I went up to the British Newspaper Library in Colindale convinced that there must be a book which would give me, in about 50,000 words, an impartial, concise summary of what happened in Fleet Street from the appearance of the first *Diurnal Occurrences* in 1641 to the arrival of the new technology and the flight to Wapping in 1986, but I couldn't find one. In fact, I don't believe there is one.

There are plenty of books on various aspects of Fleet Street, the power of the press, pressures on the press, the lives and times of the press barons and so on. There are plenty of books about specific newspapers, like Denis Hamilton's four volume history of *The Times*, Hugh Cudlipp's highly entertaining books on the *Mirror* group, Alistair Hetherington's excellent *The Guardian Years*, and that splendid history of the *Sunday Times*, *The Pearl of Days* by Harold Hobson, Phillip Knightley and Leonard Russell. More recently there have been plenty of books about the new barons and about all the troubles caused by the print unions, such as Simon Jenkins's brilliant *Newspapers: The Power and the Money* and *The Market for Glory*, Harold Evans's *Good Times, Bad Times*, David Goohart's *Eddy Shah and the Newspaper Revolution* and Linda Malvern's very detailed day-to-day account of the final show-down, *The End of the Street*. On the subject of Reuters, there is a fascinating account by John Lawrenson and Lionel Barber, *The Price of Truth: the Story of the Reuter Millions*. And of course there are plenty of autobiographies dealing with the professional careers of editors like Stafford Somerfield, Bob Edwards, Arthur Christiansen and many others.

However, apart from Francis Williams's *Dangerous Estate: The Anatomy of Newspapers*, which gives exactly the kind of detached, overall view of the entire proceedings I was looking for, I could find nothing. Also Francis Williams's story ends in the mid-fifties, before Fleet Street's troubles had really started.

So, while I continued to search through all the books on newspapers I could find in all the local libraries, sampling every volume on every list of recommended reading at the end of each book that I consulted, I decided, for my own information, and in order to make sense out of all the recollections and anecdotes of the journalists I intended to contact, that I would sit down and write the sort of historical sketch I had been trying to find. Then having done so, still without finding anything even remotely comparable, I thought it might be a good idea to include it in this book as an introduction to all these Fleet Street memories.

Before the
Northcliffe Revolution

Caxton, a cloth merchant, who had learned the new craft of printing in Cologne, set up the first printing press in Britain at Westminster in 1476. It didn't occur to anybody at the time that the press could be used for anything more controversial than running off cheap copies of documents already available in manuscript form, for example bibles previously and laboriously hand-copied in the monasteries.

By the early 1620s, however, the first English newsbooks, based on the Dutch *corantos*, began to appear. They consisted mainly of items of foreign news, not that the British public was particularly interested in foreign news, but because the continental newspapers already existed and items from them could be filched and translated to fill the spaces between government proclamations and other paid-for advertising matter. However, the men who printed and distributed these early newspapers soon discovered that the odd items of local news of murders, robberies and other villainies which they had included to fill any blank spaces with which they were left proved far more popular with the public than Government proclamations or foreign news.

Right from the beginning, the official attitude towards the printing press was that it should only be used to reflect the views of the Crown and the Establishment. It was only after the bloodless revolution of 1688 that a general dislike of censorship of any form began to develop and firm parliamentary control over the press was allowed to lapse.

There had been a news sheet called *Diurnal Occurrences* in 1641 which probably must be regarded as the first English newspaper, and a twice-weekly paper the *London Gazette* from 1665 which became the official Government vehicle for the dissemination of information. It was not until the appearance of the *Daily Courant* in 1702, however, that England had a daily newspaper recognisable as such, although within ten years of the relaxing of the controls on the press, about twenty papers with two or four pages were appearing weekly or twice-weekly in London and the provinces. Some of these were so openly critical of the Government that in 1712 the first of a series of Stamp Acts was introduced to stem the mushroom growth of independent papers by making them too expensive for the ordinary people to buy. At this period journalists were widely regarded as hacks in the pay of politicians or engaged in the treasonable activity of arousing the mob against their betters. The press on the other hand saw itself as an indispensable link between public and parliament and the public's principal safeguard against abuses on the part of the ruling classes.

Initially the stamp duty was set at a penny for each full sheet – normally folded so as to make a four-page paper – and a halfpenny for a half-sheet. The sheets all had to be physically stamped at Somerset House in the Strand, which was another reason why Fleet Street became the centre of the newspaper industry. The first reason was the fact that Fleet Street had become the traditional headquarters of London's print industry.

How this came about is interesting enough in itself. From the beginning of the Middle Ages, Fleet Street – named after a tributary to the Thames which has long since been buried deep under buildings and roadways – occupied a singularly strategic position as the main artery between the commercial centre, which occupied the site of the old Roman city of London and the headquarters of the Crown, Court and Church at Westminster.

It was a natural development that monastic foundations such as the Whitefriars, the Blackfriars and the Knights Templar should move into the vicinity of the seats of temporal power, and as the various Inns of Court then grew up, initially as appendages of the Church, but later in secular form, Fleet Street became London's main legal thoroughfare. Susie Barson and Andrew Saint were very interesting on this subject in their introduction to the English Heritage *Farewell to Fleet Street* exhibition, held at the Barbican in 1988.

Lawyers by their very nature tend to generate vast quantities of paperwork and so, long before printing had arrived on the scene, the street was busy with clerks and scriveners making copies of all the documents required. When printing came along, it was natural that the printers would set up their presses in this area.

Wynkyn de Worde, Caxton's successor, and Thomas Berthelet, who was appointed the King's printer in 1530, were among the first to set up their presses in Salisbury Square, in the courtyard of the London residence of the bishops of Salisbury. Oliver Goldsmith worked for a time in Samuel Richardson's printing works in Salisbury Square and Edward Lloyd, who founded *Lloyd's Weekly* in 1842 and later the *Daily Chronicle* which survived into our own times as the *News Chronicle*, held a lease from Richardson dating back to 1770.

The Sign of the Sun, near St Bride's Church, is a relic of the earliest days of printing; Wynkyn de Worde's presses were set up 'at the Sign of the Sun'. Not only Fleet Street itself, but all the streets and alleys off it, and a large part of the Strand were dominated from the seventeenth century by booksellers, printers, publishers, stationers and binders. It was for this reason that Samuel Johnson lived in Gough Square to the north of Fleet Street when he was compiling his dictionary and that the taverns and coffee houses of Fleet Street were always popular with what might be loosely described as the intelligentsia.

The monks, who in a sense started it all by bringing an unusual degree of literacy into the area, are commemorated in such place names as Blackfriars, Whitefriars Street, and Carmelite Street as well as the Temple.

When the Government of the period decided to impose a stamp duty on the newspapers and news sheets, this was done, as mentioned above, by stamping each sheet individually at Somerset House in the Strand. Over the years the duty fluctuated, rising as high as four pence at one period. In addition a tax of one shilling was placed on all advertisements, raised in Pitt's time to three shillings. This made newspapers extremely expensive; certainly they cost the equivalent of much more than £1 relative to today's prices. But loopholes in the legislation were found by some printers; others merely ignored it and distributed unstamped papers.

It would be pointless to list the names of all the newspapers that appeared in London between the beginning of the eighteenth century and the beginning of the twentieth. They were mostly owned by small syndicates of businessmen, many of them subsidised wholly or partly by one or other of the political parties, and the majority of them focused round a printer. The *Morning Chronicle* appeared in 1769; the *Morning Post* in 1772 (it survives in the title of the *Daily Telegraph*); the *Morning Herald* in 1780; the *Observer* in 1791; the *Globe* in 1803; the *Sunday Times* in 1822; the *Standard* in 1827; the *Daily News* was founded by Charles Dickens in 1846; the *Pall Mall Gazette* was founded in 1865 and eventually incorporated in the *Evening Standard*; the *Daily Chronicle* was founded in 1871; the *Daily Graphic* was founded in 1890, and later incorporated in the *Daily Sketch* which was itself absorbed into the *Daily Mail* only a few years ago; and the *Westminster Gazette*, founded in 1893, was absorbed by the *Daily News*, which was itself absorbed by the *News Chronicle*, which was finally sold off to the *Daily Mail* in 1960. These were among the best known, leaving *The Times* aside for the moment.

There were also many weekly reviews and there is no doubt that Addison and Steele's *Spectator* of 1711 with the enormous circulation for those days of 4,000 copies, Daniel Defoe's *Review* and Jonathan Swift's articles in the *Examiner* all paved the way for one aspect of modern journalism. The freedom of the press, however, was by no means yet universally acknowledged; in one year alone, 1711, fourteen journalists and printers went to jail for various forms of sedition, and between 1715 and 1759, over seventy warrants were issued against unnamed newspaper personnel.

For years Parliament could only be covered by smuggling in

reporters and publishing their reports when Parliament was in recess and therefore not in a position to call them to account for themselves before the Bar of the House. In 1763 John Wilkes challenged as illegal a general warrant to arrest everybody on the staff of his paper the *North Briton*, from the office boy to the proprietor and including the editor, Wilkes himself. The charge was for reporting Parliament and he won the case in open court. He followed this up in 1771, when he had himself become a magistrate, by rejecting a warrant to arrest a printer for reporting some of the proceedings of the House and in turn charged the Commons messenger with false arrest.

Thereafter no newspaperman was ever harassed for reporting or even criticising parliamentary debates and from 1771, the House of Commons allowed reporters to take notes of its debates, and the Lords followed suit a few years later.

Throughout this period and indeed right up to the middle of the nineteenth century, a great many newspapers were subsidised out of the Government's Secret Service Funds; by the placing of government advertisements, mostly proclamations, and by offering various purely nominal but highly paid posts to editors who supported the Government of the day. Walpole was accused of spending £50,000 on the Secret Service, in other words on bribing the press.

In the meantime, *The Times* had been founded in 1785 by John Walter, a former coal merchant and Lloyd's underwriter who had lost a fortune as a result of the activities of American privateers who sank the ships he had insured. Looking for some means of paying off his creditors, he became interested in the possibilities of logography, a new printing process by which complete words and syllables could be cast in type, instead of the former technique using single letters. The system had been invented to print lottery tickets but Walter believed it could be adapted for general printing. Events proved him wrong and he found himself stuck with a printing press, so he decided to start a newspaper.

The Times appeared (initially, and for three years, under the title of the *Daily Universal Register*) on 1 January 1785. It consisted of one sheet folded to make a four-page paper and was exactly similar to London's other eight morning papers of the period. Walter used his logographic equipment to print posters for his newspaper.

Initially *The Times* paid the Post Office 60 guineas (£63) a year to deliver the continental newspapers, still the primary source of foreign news coverage, plus another 100 guineas (£105) or more to the guinea men, the postal clerks who translated the stories in the continental newspapers. According to *The Times* bicentenary supplement 'it was to break the Post Office monopoly, incompetence and malevolence in diverting the mail to those papers which had agreed to grease the postal palm that *The Times* set up its own network of correspondents and couriers – the start of its foreign news service.'

When John Walter's second son, John Walter II, took over the paper he immediately began to transform it into the greatest newspaper in the world. He began by appointing the paper's first foreign correspondent Henry Crabb Robinson who reported the retreat of the British forces from Corunna and the fall of Danzig.

The circulation steadily increased but the old hand-presses were capable of printing only 250 sheets an hour. Walter had heard about a new German steam-press. In deepest secrecy, similar to that which marked Murdoch's move to Wapping nearly two centuries later, and for the same reason – even in Walter II's day the printers were violently opposed to innovations of any kind – he smuggled the press into *The Times* building piece by piece, assembled it in a spare room and ran off an entire edition while the printers were standing by for what he had told them was going to be a special late edition. This first Koenig steam-press could print 1,100 sheets an hour and with the help of two British technicians Walter had upped its performance to 4,000 sheets an hour within a few years of its introduction in 1814.

Walter eventually grew tired of 'living over the shop', as

Louis Heren, former deputy editor of the newspaper, put it in his book *The Power of the Press?* and moved to a country house in Berkshire. He appointed Thomas Barnes editor and gave him full editorial independence, but only after the poet Robert Southey had turned down the job.

It was under Barnes that *The Times* acquired the epithet 'The Thunderer' – the phrase came from one of his leading articles which urged the country to 'thunder for reform' – and soon after he took over he created a sensation by sending a reporter, John Tyas, to cover a public meeting in Manchester calling for parliamentary reform. The meeting, held in St Peter's Fields and now known as Peterloo, was regarded by the magistrates as subversive and the yeomanry attacked a crowd of 80,000 people, killing twelve and wounding 420. Hundreds were arrested including *The Times* reporter who spent the night in jail writing his report. This report appeared in the paper unsigned, using the editorial 'we' throughout which left the impression that it was *The Times* newspaper rather than an individual who had been so affronted. The cause of parliamentary reform became a national issue overnight and Barnes found himself a powerful force in the land, with his newspaper a real Fourth Estate (the concept comes from a phrase of Edmund Burke; the other three estates were the Lords Spiritual, the Lords Temporal and the Commons). It was now in a position to state its own terms for its continued support of any government; over such matters as full civil rights for Catholics, for example.

Barnes and his successor John Delane, the newspaper's two outstanding editors between 1816 and 1897, developed *The Times* international news service, the most comprehensive in the world, long before Havas or Reuter had thought of the idea of a news agency.

In the first quarter of the nineteenth century *The Times* was spending £10,000 a year on its 'Extraordinary Express' from India alone. This was far more than any other newspaper could afford, and its arrangement for world news coverage included the permanent maintenance of a fast cross-channel steamer between Boulogne and Dover and a special fast train between Dover and London. Agents were posted in Alexandria to receive despatches brought there by camel trains from the Middle East and north Africa and to transfer them to fast steamers. A special courier service was installed between Marseilles and Boulogne and by travelling day and night these couriers could do the journey in seventy-four hours. They were paid £100 a year plus £1 per hour while travelling, with a bonus of £2 for each hour saved.

A pigeon post set up between Paris and Boulogne in 1837 could average four hours against the fourteen hours taken by the couriers, so they were superseded for the Paris–Boulogne section of the journey. By 1844 the new electric telegraph had arrived – it was first used to announce the birth of Queen Victoria's second son – and news could now be transmitted and received almost simultaneously.

Reporters on assignments outside London were provided with fast coaches and were expected to write their stories as they bowled along towards London.

When the British Empire was being built up in the second half of the nineteenth century, much depended on the rapid communication of political, diplomatic and above all financial news from Hong Kong, Singapore, India and Africa. Until the development of the telegraph and the telephone, *The Times* communications network was unchallenged.

Delane succeeded Barnes at the age of 23. It was he who declared *The Times* policy in a leading article: 'We hold ourselves responsible to the people of England for the accuracy and fitness of what we think proper to publish.' It was he who sent Thomas Chenery, later to become editor, to Constantinople, and William Howard Russell, the first professional war correspondent, to accompany the British forces to the Crimea. Delane even insisted on going to the Crimea to see for himself the conditions under which Russell had said the men were suffering. The result was a campaign which led to wide-ranging reforms in both the War Department and in the medical services, as well as forcing the Government to resign.

In the first fifteen years of Delane's editorship the circulation rose from 20,000 to 60,000, three times the combined circulation of all the other London papers, occasionally peaking to 70,000 as, for example, on the morning when it carried Russell's on-the-spot report of the Charge of the Light Brigade.

The Times network of foreign correspondents supplied it with information in advance of all the other newspapers and often in advance of the Government's own sources until Reuter developed his highly successful news agency in the 1850s.

In the light of future events it was highly significant that the basic business launched in 1849 by Julius de Reuter – he acquired a European baronetcy in 1871 – was the supply of financial information. He had left his native Germany in 1848 after a revolutionary piece of writing by him had attracted the hostile attention of the authorities. While in voluntary exile in France, he worked for the French news agency Havas. Charles Louis Havas had started the first successful news agency, using carrier pigeons.

After a year, Reuter set himself up in competition with his employer working from a Paris flat with a staff of one, his wife Ida Maria. He soon spotted a gap between the end of the Belgian cable and the start of the German one at Aachen so he moved there and rented pigeons to carry the stock market prices between Brussels and Berlin; his birds did the trip in two hours, seven better than the mail train.

When the German telecommunications engineer Siemens announced that he was planning to run a telegraph wire alongside the railway line between Brussels and Aachen, Reuter sent his wife to Siemens to beg him not to do it, as the telegraph line would put the firm of Reuters out of business. Legend has it that Siemens suggested that Reuter move to London, then the centre of the European financial communications network with an underwater cable between France and England planned to coincide with the Great Exhibition of 1851.

Reuter moved to London and was soon making a handsome

profit by providing the City of London with stock prices from the various European bourses by telegraph. For an immigrant German Jew in London in the middle of the nineteenth century, however, financial success did not necessarily mean social recognition and it was to gain prestige (as well as meet the growing demand for foreign news following Gladstone's repeal of the stamp duty on newspapers in 1855) that Reuter expanded into news gathering. At a period when most of the newspapers were financed and run by political parties, Reuters news agency very quickly acquired a reputation for objectivity which has been its major asset over the years. As the Government encouraged the installation of international cables to link up the furthermost outposts of empire, Reuter followed up the network with an ever-expanding news and share price service. He had very soon signed up most of the London and provincial newspapers as subscribers to his service.

Of all the other newspapers then in existence James Perry's *Morning Chronicle* was popular with the Whigs in the early 1800s and Henry Heatherington's *Poor Man's Guardian* – which employed such writers as Hazlitt and Dickens – was an unstamped opponent of the 'taxes on knowledge' in the 1830s. The *Morning Herald* and the *Daily News* had, like *The Times*, good foreign coverage from their own correspondents.

William Cobbett's *Political Register* founded in 1802 was more of a review like today's *New Statesman* than a newspaper and William Hone's *Reformist Register* of 1817 satirised the Government using parodies of the Prayer Book. The *Manchester Guardian* was founded in 1821 by John Edward Taylor, son of a Manchester Unitarian minister and financed by eleven middle-class Reformers. It stood for parliamentary reform and civil and religious liberty.

The reduction of the stamp duty in 1836, the abolition of the advertisement duty in 1855, the abolition of the newspaper stamp duty the same year and of the paper duty in 1861 all came about as a result of the growing power and pressure of the confident Victorian middle-class. They saw an expanding press as a spokesman for their interests as against the landed gentry on the one hand and the militant new working-class on the other. The seditious libel laws under which earlier generations of newspapermen had been arrested and jailed were seen as counter-productive, providing valuable publicity for those who were prosecuted, and the stamp duty had proved to be unenforceable. By 1836 the predominantly radical unstamped press had a combined circulation far greater than that of the legal, stamped press.

The Companies Act, which came into force the year after the repeal of the Newspaper Stamp Tax, made it easier for companies to be formed. Thus, before the turn of the century the press had become an attractive investment for speculators and more and more family newspapers were going public as a safety measure.

When the stamp duty was abolished altogether in 1855, the *Manchester Guardian* became a daily, dropped its price from two pence to a penny and gradually assumed the status of a national newspaper, though it did not drop the *Manchester* from its title until 1959, or move its headquarters to London until 1964. Described as Britain's nonconformist conscience, it tried to combine social awareness with good writing, and under the 57-year editorship of C. P. Scott employed writers of the calibre of John Masefield, Arnold Toynbee, J. M. Synge and W. T. Stead. It always attracted a highly literate readership, about a third of them graduates, most of them interested in books, music and the theatre.

The *Daily Telegraph and Courier*, as it was initially called, was first published on Friday 29 June 1885, price two pence. It carried advertisements on the front page of a four-page broadsheet and its founder was Lieutenant-Colonel Arthur Sleigh, an army officer. It was printed by J. M. Levy of Peterborough Court, which is a small turning off Shoe Lane, Fleet Street. When Lieutenant-Colonel Sleigh found himself unable to pay off his printing debts, Levy's son Edward, who had become a Christian and had changed his name to Lawson (and later became the first Lord Burnham), took over the paper, and reduced its price to a penny at a time when *The Times* still cost 7d and the other national dailies 5d each. Its circulation immediately rose to 27,000 and it soon became Britain's favourite middle-class daily.

By 1875 it had a circulation of 190,000, the bulk of its readers being London commuters living near the main rail networks. Before the seventies came to an end, the *Daily Telegraph* was selling 250,000 copies, the first break-through to something approaching mass circulation and at that time the highest in the world. Only twenty years earlier *The Times* with only 50,000 copies a day had more readers than any other daily newspaper in the world.

It had not of course escaped the attention of newspaper proprietors that the London Stock Exchange was becoming a matter of great importance to many readers. In 1884 the *Financial News* was founded (it had originally been called the *Financial and Mining News*), followed four years later by the *Financial Times* with its motto 'Without Fear and Without Favour'.

In 1893 Douglas MacRae, proprietor of the *Financial Times* and a former printer by trade, had the brilliant idea of having it printed on pink paper. It distinguished it from all the others and, at the same time, pink paper was far cheaper. For years the two financial papers remained roughly on a par as regards circulation, profits and reputation.

The real inspiration, if that's the right word, for the modern popular mass circulation papers came not from the dailies but from the late nineteenth century Sundays and weekly newspapers, such as *Titbits* and *Answers*. One of the pioneers of one aspect of modern popular journalism was W. T. Stead, a *Manchester Guardian* contributor who founded and ran the *Pall Mall Gazette* in 1865. While Stead never achieved anything like the circulation of the modern tabloids, he pioneered many of their practices. He was the first journalist to break the wall of anonymity which had cloaked the face of Victorian reporting, the first editor, in fact, to name names. He was also the first editor to go in for 'shock' campaigns. His first was directed at the horrors of slum housing and he kept it on the boil with extravagant phrases like 'these fever dens' until a Royal Commission was appointed to inquire into the dwellings of the poor. Stead also managed to get what today would be called a 'scoop' interview with General Gordon of Khartoum when the latter was passing through Southampton on his way back to the Sudan. As a result his newspaper started a popular demand for the relief of Khartoum and created a crisis that split the Cabinet.

Stead believed that the press lords had a much larger part to play in running the country than the politicians would acknowledge and argued that the editors received their mandate afresh from their readers every morning, while the politicians only got theirs every five years or so.

In 1885 Stead exposed what he described as London's 'white slave traffic' (juvenile prostitution) under the general head-line: THE MAIDEN TRIBUTE OF MODERN BABYLON. This was a personal investigation into vice in London, seemingly carried out with the support of the Archbishop of Canterbury, Cardinal Manning and General Booth of the Salvation Army. Stead concluded the series in typical tabloid fashion by purchasing a 13-year-old girl Eliza Armstrong from her mother for £5. Having satisfied himself that she was *virgo intacta* and that he could have had his will of her, so to speak, if he had so chosen, he handed her over to the Salvation Army. He made only one mistake, a technical one: he omitted obtaining her father's consent to this unconventional transaction and as a result spent two months in jail. His end was appropriate for so colourful a character: he went down with the *Titanic*.

Stead's partner, George Newnes, formerly a fancy goods salesman and proprietor of a vegetarian restaurant, produced the weekly paper *Titbits* in October 1881. It was an early *Reader's Digest*, a rag-bag of easily digested odds and ends, and it was an instant popular success. It soon had a sale of 900,000 and was offering prizes which included a house in Dulwich and free insurance for life.

One of the first contributors to the highly successful *Titbits* was a young journalist Alfred Harmsworth, the son of a Dublin schoolmaster turned barrister at that time living in Hampstead. Young Alfred had been thrown out of the house – for seducing a parlourmaid – by his mother, the redoubtable Geraldine, after whom the old *Daily Mirror* headquarters in Fetter Lane was named. Known as the Adonis of Hampstead, Harmsworth was a highly successful free-lance; one of his first publications was a booklet he had written himself on 'A Thousand Ways to Earn a Living'.

He studied the success of *Titbits* and of T. P. O'Connor's *Star*, which favoured entertainment at the expense of information and presented people in the public eye as they really were, by the invasion of their privacy if necessary. In June 1888, Harmsworth produced his own answer to *Titbits*. It was called *Answers* – its full title was *Answers to Correspondents on Every Subject Under the Sun* – and it improved on the Newnes formula by inviting readers to request their own titbits of information.

It was soon getting itself talked about because of the intriguing questions it raised. Can fish talk? Do dogs ever murder other dogs? Can a clergyman marry himself? It also offered curious facts such as the information that if all the hair were shaved off all the men in London and collected in one pile it would amount to the equivalent of three and a half tons of hay. Above all, it ran competitions. How many people cross London Bridge in twenty-four hours? What will be the exact value of all the gold in the Bank of England at a certain hour on a certain day? And the prize for the correct answer? £2 a week for life.

Within two years its circulation was pushing at the million mark. Harmsworth followed up its success with *Comic Cuts, Chips, Forget Me Not, Home Chat* and a whole stable of cheap, popular periodicals, commonly known as penny dreadfuls. Another periodical of the same type, *Pearson's Weekly*, appeared around the same time. It was important only in that both its proprietor Arthur Pearson and Alfred Harmsworth were now thinking along the same lines; they were both planning popular national daily newspapers.

On the other hand, George Newnes, who in a way had started it all with his *Titbits*, preferred to use the profit he had made on his popular periodicals for the honour and prestige of being associated with a newspaper with the limited snob appeal of the *Westminster Gazette*; he was happily losing £10,000 a year on it until it was absorbed by the *Daily News* in January 1928.

In the meantime, the Sunday press had been developing along similar lines to the popular weekly publications of Newnes, Harmsworth and Pearson. From the beginning of the nineteenth century, the Sunday newspapers had much bigger circulations and a far wider readership than the dailies. They included the *Weekly Dispatch*, the *Political Register* and the *Black Dwarf*. From the outset they were commercial enterprises within the new mainly metropolitan popular culture and they all contained a generous ration of crime and scandal as well as general and foreign news.

In 1839 the *Northern Star* was launched in Leeds as a militant Chartist organ – the Chartists were an early socialist group with a broad, devoted following, championing the causes of universal suffrage, secret ballots, annual parliaments and the removal of property qualifications for membership of parliament. It had the largest readership of any newspaper published in the provinces and soon the largest Sunday circulation nationwide outside of the radical Liberal *Weekly Dispatch*, which survived the Northcliffe revolution and became the *Sunday Dispatch*.

In the 1840s the *News of the World, Lloyd's Weekly* and *Bell's Sporting and Police Gazette and Newspaper of Romance* appeared. Together the new Sundays had a combined circulation of 170,000 at a period when the combined circulation of the dailies was no higher than 60,000.

John Bell, who might be described as the father of the popular Sunday newspaper, founded nearly a dozen publications during the eighty-six years of his life between 1745 and 1831. In 1776 he founded *Bell's Weekly Messenger*, from which sprang *Bell's New Weekly Messenger* in 1832, which in turn was succeeded by the *News of the World* which today, with a circulation pushing the five million mark, tops the table of national dailies and Sundays. Bell's first weekly paper was produced in a shed in the garden of a house on the Strand which led down to the Thames. By 1803 he was selling 6,000 copies and the edition featuring Nelson's funeral topped 14,000.

His son, John Browne Bell, produced a new Sunday newspaper, the *New Weekly Messenger* from 2 Surrey Street off the Strand. Ten years later he brought out the first issue of the *News of the World*, which proclaimed itself as 'the Best as well as the Largest and Cheapest of all the newspapers published'. It cost 3d a copy, 5½d less than the average for the period, and Bell's initial determination to keep the price down despite the protests of newsagents who claimed that they were losing money selling it led to great problems. Later the fluctuating uncertainty of his sons and grandsons as to whether to maintain that firm pricing policy very nearly led to its extinction in the late 1880s.

At that stage, Henry Lascelles Carr 'burst out of South Wales', as the famous *News of the World* editor Stafford Somerfield (1960–70) puts it in his book *Banner Headlines* – and as indeed other talented Welshmen like the Cudlipp brothers and the Berry brothers were to burst out of Wales and dominate the Fleet Street scene subsequently. Lascelles Carr had been running the *Western Mail* and, with a small group of relatives and friends, he made a bid for the ailing *News of the World* when it came on the market in 1891. Between them, the Carrs and the Jacksons, who were related, with their family solicitor George Allardice Riddell, ran the paper very successfully for nearly eighty years until they were eventually taken over by Rupert Murdoch in 1968. Ironically, Murdoch had originally been brought in by Carr to help him fight off a threatened take-over by the Czech socialist millionaire Robert Maxwell.

Carr bought new presses capable of printing 25,000 copies an hour, secured new premises in Whitefriars Street, off Fleet Street, leased the old premises to George Newnes and sold off the old presses for £900 worth of printer's ink. Money was a constant problem, but when the company could not pay in cash they paid with shares. The Phillips firm of South Wales sold them a boiler and took 512 shares in the company in lieu of the £200 it cost; by 1950, when they sold them, these shares were worth £73,000. Handbills for the paper claimed that it contained 'the brightest and best reports of the week's news, thrilling series, the latest fashion, society gossip, parliamentary intelligence, plus gardening notes. All for 1d.' They had at last decided upon a popular pricing policy.

For nearly ten years the fortunes of the paper fluctuated but by 1895 a circulation of 100,000 had been achieved and by 1904 the net profit was high enough to enable them to pay a dividend of 15 per cent free of tax plus a bonus of £1 per share. The anxious years were over. Three more presses were installed and the newspaper spread into Bouverie Street.

Another popular Sunday newspaper which followed the *News of the World* in 1850 was G. M. Reynold's *Reynold's Newspaper* (later *Reynold's News*), the organ of the radical Co-operative Movement. It survived until 1936. There were other radical Sundays, some financed by the trades unions, some by the militant Chartist movement, mainly by the working-class, in fact. They fostered a new class consciousness and focused attention on aspects of the coming class struggle in a way that the Establishment found a bit frightening. The first generation of radical papers had emerged during the Napoleonic Wars and the fact that they were eagerly read by the serving soldiers and the servants below stairs was regarded with alarm if not despondency by the ruling class.

The popular Sundays that emerged in the early and middle nineteenth century were truly popular in three ways: they were of and for the people; they owed their popularity to the skilful exploitation of the growing general interest in certain aspects of crime, scandal, romance and sport; and of course, in the purely market sense, they were products specifically designed for popular mass consumption.

The increasing industrialisation of the newspaper industry from 1870 onwards which followed the introduction of the Hoe rotary presses and their continuous increase in size and sophistication, and the introduction in 1892 of the Linotype machine and the whole 'hot metal' process – whose era coincided almost exactly with that of the great days of Fleet Street – enabled the big circulation Sundays to reach out towards the magic one million figure, achieved by *Lloyd's Weekly News* in 1896. But it also meant that they had to become less radical in tone, if only because the enormous cost of the new printing machinery meant that they had to be financed by display advertising or by capitalist financiers.

In order to secure the circulation they needed to attract the full-page display advertisements from the big new department stores, they not only had to sell their papers at a price so low that they became largely dependent on advertising for their revenue, but they also had to aim their bid for mass circulation at the increasingly prosperous literate lower-middle-class (not the militant working-class) because they alone had the disposable income – and the desire – to buy the articles advertised. As Cyril Freer put it in a 1921 book on advertising: for an average proposition, neither a Rolls Royce nor a three-penny fire lighter, 'you cannot afford to place your advertisements in a paper which is read by down-at-heels who buy it to scan the Situations Vacant columns.'

Costs in general were rising sharply. Although the figures are unreliable, estimates at the time reckoned that it cost Alfred Harmsworth nearly £500,000 to set up and launch his first national popular daily newspaper as against the £2,000 to £3,000 it had cost to establish a newspaper in the nineteenth century. Some of the working-class radical newspapers of the 1820s had been printed on machines costing no more than £10 or £15 to set up in a small print shop. Other costs were also rising, including staffing, both on the editorial and commercial side, to say nothing of wages paid to the compositors and printers and the ever-increasing cost of newsgathering and newsprint.

Still marshalling his resources in preparation for the launch of a new popular daily, Alfred Harmsworth floated *Answers* as a public company, Harmsworth Brothers Ltd in 1893 (it later became known as the Amalgamated Press Ltd). Then in 1894 he bought the Conservative Party's moribund London *Evening News* for £23,000. He reduced its price to $\frac{1}{2}$d and brought it down-market, soon pushing its circulation up higher than any other evening newspaper in the world. In his first year as proprietor of the *Evening News*, he made a profit of £25,000 – £2,000 more than he had paid for it.

Even at this early stage in his career, Harmsworth, like so many of the press barons who succeeded him, found it hard to resist the lure of politics. In 1895 he lost a safe Conservative seat in Portsmouth after buying a local paper to drum up votes and indulging in an American presidential-style election campaign razzmatazz. Leaving politics until he was in a position in which he was likely to be offered a place in the Lords, he and his younger brother Harold now got down to the serious business of producing England's first popular daily newspaper.

The *Daily Mail*, launched on 4 May 1896, cost $\frac{1}{2}$d and consisted of eight pages, standard broadsheet size, with classified advertisements on the front page. Sporting the Royal Arms in the middle of the title it also had two slogans: 'A penny newspaper for a halfpenny' and 'The busy man's journal'. On the first day it sold 397,215 copies – more than any other newspaper had sold in one day.

It applied the *Titbits/Answers* formula to daily journalism with the news parcelled up into short, easily digested paragraphs. Because it had classifieds on the front page, it didn't look all that different from *The Times* and so could be safely purchased by men who might read, but would never be seen carrying, penny dreadfuls like *Answers* and *Titbits*. It portrayed the various sections of the community as inter-dependent with the emphasis placed, as in today's Thatcherism, on the individual as master of his own destiny in a free opportunity society in which he could reap the rewards of his own initiative and industry and participate as a fellow consumer in the growing prosperity of industrial Britain.

Within four years, printing in Manchester as well as London, the *Daily Mail* had passed the million mark and Harmsworth's personal income was reckoned to have reached about £150,000 a year. Although he had to wait another five years for his title, the Northcliffe revolution, as it came to be called in retrospect, had started. This was the beginning of the legendary Fleet Street; from this period the term was used as a collective one to describe Britain's national newspapers.

The Heyday
of the First Barons

At the turn of the century the *Daily Mail* fired what might be regarded as the first shot in the circulation war by declaring an advertising rate per 1,000 copies sold. It claimed to present 'all the news in the smallest space' and the editorials were often reduced to one strong paragraph making one single, telling point. The Harmsworth brothers spent a lot of money on promotions of all kinds, for example prizes for firsts in the new and exciting field of aviation. The newspaper set out deliberately to appeal to the acquisitive instincts of its readers, and particularly its women readers, for consumer goods. This was the real significance of the Northcliffe revolution; it secured the freedom of the press from political subsidy through a combination of circulation and advertising revenue.

In the partnership as it developed, Alfred remained the impresario and his brother Harold became the entrepreneur. Their next target was the *Weekly Dispatch*, founded in 1801 as a radical/Liberal newspaper of opinion. It had been bought by the Irish barrister Robert Bell who began in 1815 to give more space to reports of sport, murder, rape and seduction than to foreign or political news. The Harmsworth brothers made it a Sunday and turned it into one of the best-selling Sunday newspapers in Britain. Alfred provided the ideas and Harold introduced the new and sophisticated accounting machines, bought the raw materials they needed at knock-down prices, diversified into timber companies and paper mills, installed the latest typewriters, telephones, filing systems and made the maximum use of the rapidly developing road and rail network to deliver their newspapers to every household in the country.

Arthur Pearson, who had begun his journalistic career writing pieces for *Titbits*, eventually became George Newnes's right-hand man. He went on to launch *Pearson's Weekly*, which

made him a great deal of money and in April 1900 he founded
the *Daily Express*, the first English newspaper with news on the
front page. It consisted of eight pages about the size of today's
Telegraph pages, divided into seven columns of small type with
mainly single column headlines, and its policy was impartiality. It was not the organ of any political party or clique and it
stood for the British Empire. Pearson believed in protectionism
and tariff barriers and became chairman of the Tariff Reform
League in 1903. Not long after founding his paper, he began to
ignore it for all his other interests, leaving it to his editor Ralph
Blumenfeld to run. Blumenfeld had been the London represen-
tative of James Gordon Bennett, the American newspaper
tycoon, but the *Daily Express* was never in those days more than
a dull, characterless paper. It was never taken seriously as a
'quality' paper, but proved quite incapable of taking the popular
line which made the *Daily Mail* such a sensational success.

In 1903 Alfred Harmsworth launched another new paper, the
tabloid *Daily Mirror*, 'a newspaper for gentlewomen', edited by
a woman, Mrs Mary Howarth, who was transferred from the
Daily Mail at a salary of £50 a month. Purchasers of the first
issue received a free gift of a gilt and enamel hand-mirror.

The Harmsworths spent a great deal of money promoting
the paper but it proved to be an instant, dismal flop. Within a
few months, Mary Howarth was back at her desk in the *Daily
Mail* and Alfred Harmsworth had put a man, Hamilton Fyfe,
into the *Mirror* as editor. Harmsworth commented that he had
learned two things from the experiment: that women couldn't
write and didn't want to read. Harmsworth may merely have
been a bit ahead of his time in launching a paper for women,
but he wasn't taking any chances; soon he had sacked most of
the women on the staff. The *Mirror* was then, according to
Cudlipp's *Publish and Be Damned*, turned round by a technician,
Arkas Sapt, who had discovered the secret of printing half-tone
pictures at speed on a Hoe Rotary press, and by Hannen
Swaffer, the newspaper's first art editor.

On 25 Jan 1904 (again according to *Publish and Be Damned*)

the new product, the *Daily Illustrated Mirror* appeared, printing picture pages at the rate of 24,000 an hour; its circulation immediately trebled to 71,000 and reached 140,000 within a month. I have very deliberately quoted Hugh Cudlipp's *Publish and Be Damned* because other authoritative books on Fleet Street give a quite different impression; for example, Simon Jenkins merely says that after the initial flop, Alfred Harmsworth turned it into a picture paper and sales slowly began to improve. It is only fair to add that before the advent of the ABC (Audit Bureau of Circulation) in the thirties, circulation figures quoted by the newspapers were often grossly unreliable. In any event, Alfred Harmsworth soon lost interest in the paper, and sold it to his brother Harold for £100,000. Apparently, Harold showed no great interest in it either, despite the fact that it had reached the magic million circulation by the time he acquired it in 1914, and in 1931 he hived it off to an independent company with its own directors. Perhaps the truth is that the *Daily Mirror*'s climb to security seemed slow after the meteoric successes of *Answers*, the *Evening News* and the *Daily Mail*, and perhaps it needed a new kind of proprietor with an eye to the only expanding market for newspapers and the goods they were advertising, the working-classes.

By 1905 Alfred Harmsworth was at the height of his powers. He bought the *Observer*, founded in 1791 by a small syndicate and as late as 1840 still receiving grants of Secret Service (i.e. Government) money. In the same year, 1905, Harmsworth was created Baron Northcliffe by the Conservative Cabinet.

In 1908 he rescued *The Times* from economic collapse. It was being outsold by the *Daily Telegraph* and the Conservative *Morning Post*; its circulation was down to 40,000 copies a day and it was making almost no profit. The Walter family had lost interest in their inheritance and were ready to sell. He paid £320,000 for it and promised the staff editorial independence but immediately began to interfere in all departments, obsessed with one thing: increasing its circulation.

His interference worked; in 1914, while it was still losing

money, he reduced the price from 3d to 1d and the circulation
rose to 150,000. By 1914 *The Times* had climbed back to
340,000. He had saved it.

However, the era was not a happy one, either for *The Times* or
for Northcliffe who distrusted what he called The Black Friars
– the members of *The Times* staff – by whom he now found
himself surrounded. The trouble was that Northcliffe's growing megalomania led to rows with the staff who felt that his
political views were a betrayal of all that *The Times* stood for.
When he took over *The Times* in 1908 the manager, Moberley
Bell, kept all the newspaper's worldwide accounts in a penny
notebook. Northcliffe replaced the editor, a man called Buckle,
by Geoffrey Dawson; he was succeeded by Wickham Steed,
another famous *Times* editor.

In the meantime, Northcliffe had met a young Welsh
reporter from Merthyr Tydfil, one of three sons of an estate
agent there. William Berry had started his career at fourteen in
a local paper and had left it to get a job in London aged 19. It
was when he was working for the Commercial Press Association that Berry attended a Harmsworth general meeting and
asked a few pertinent questions. Northcliffe was greatly
impressed and offered him a job immediately after the meeting,
which Berry refused.

In 1901, aged 22, he had launched the *Advertising World*,
reputedly writing every line of it himself, as well as doing all the
lay-out and production, and canvassing for advertisements for
it personally. Two years later he was also producing the
magazine *Boxing*, with his younger brother Gomer as manager.
By 1915 the Berry brothers were rich enough to pay £75,000 for
the *Sunday Times*. It had been started by Henry White, and had
grown out of White's first Sunday newspaper the *Independent
Whig* which he started in 1806 and edited until 1821. Then, in
an attempt perhaps to steal some of the readership of the very
successful *Observer*, he relaunched his paper under the title the
New Observer. Soon he changed its name once again to the
Independent Observer, a title which was incorporated in the title of
the *Sunday Times* when it first appeared on 20 October 1822. It

was a quality rather than a popular paper at the time it first appeared, in the sense that quality readers in the 1820s regarded any interest in sport or the theatre as extremely frivolous.

In its early days the *Sunday Times* had a very chequered history. White sold it to a lawyer named Harvey who sold it to a book publisher called Valby, who in turn sold it to another publisher by the name of Coburn whose list of authors included Samuel Pepys and John Evelyn. It was owned at one period by an English woman known as Princess Midas from the fortune she had made prospecting for gold in Australia. At another period it was owned by another woman, a member of the Sassoon family, whose husband Frederick Beere at the same time controlled the *Observer*. The *Observer* had been founded in 1791 and was financed for a time by the Tory party; later it was subsidised by the Whigs.

At the outbreak of World War I, the *Sunday Times* had fallen into the hands of a most unlikely quartet: a German financier, Hermann Schmidt; the munitions agent Sir Basil Zaharoff; Leander Starr Jameson, the South African nationalist who had sparked off the Boer War when he led a force of 600 Rhodesian police and volunteers to invade the Transvaal and who subsequently became Prime Minister of the Cape Colony; and Sir Arthur Steel-Maitland, an MP. Schmidt was interned in 1914, whereupon the paper went on the market and was bought by the Berry brothers; the editor was Leonard Rees and the contributors included James Agate, Ernest Newman, Desmond McCarthy and Dilys Powell. It had a very small permanent staff and was put together every weekend by casuals employed at the rate of two guineas (£2.10) per day. Nevertheless, with a circulation of only 30,000–50,000 as against the *Observer*'s 200,000–300,000 (the estimates vary by that amount), it was making money. And, although they paid a relatively high price for it – £75,000 as against the £5,000 Northcliffe had paid for the *Observer* in 1911 – by the time the Berry brothers had formed Allied Newspapers in 1923, the *Sunday Times* was contributing the biggest slice of profit to the entire enterprise, which now also included St Clement's Press which numbered among its very successful publications the *Financial Times*. They were now looking around for a prestigious daily to form the apex of their empire. They did not have very long to wait.

Lord Beaverbrook was born plain William Maxwell Aitken in Canada in 1879. He became a multi-millionaire before he was 30, and in 1910 made a pilgrimage to the land of his ancestors. He had already published a news sheet called *The Leader* in Canada when he was only fourteen and had established some connections with the *Daily Express*. He had received a knighthood in King George V's Coronation Honours List and had acquired a deep regard for the British Empire. He had also established connections with Bonar Law, the future Prime Minister, and almost as soon as he arrived succeeded in being elected as Conservative MP for Ashton-under-Lyne. He contributed to his own advancement by lending £25,000 to the Conservative *Daily Express*. At this stage, however, the *Express* needed more than loans to save it, and in 1916 he bought it for £17,500, plus about £40,000 in outstanding debts.

It has been said that one of the secrets of Northcliffe's success as a popular newspaper proprietor was that, apart from his ambition and enormous wealth, he viewed his papers very much as his readership did, a quality which Beaverbrook shared. When the latter took over the *Daily Express* he immediately became chief shareholder, proprietor, editor-in-chief and Principal Reader, the most meticulous one the newspaper ever had, as many of his editors discovered to their cost. He did not have anything like the immediate impact on the *Express* that Northcliffe had on his newspapers and it was not until the thirties that the *Express* topped the million mark.

By 1910 Northcliffe controlled an empire that included *The Times*, the *Observer*, the *Daily Mail* and *Evening News*, the *Sunday Dispatch*, the *Continental Daily Mail*, the *Daily Mirror*, the *Glasgow Record* and numerous magazines, penny dreadfuls and provincial papers. He had established his own printing press in

Whitefriars Street called the Geraldine Press after his mother, and he had acquired a newsprint factory at Grand Falls, Newfoundland and the Imperial Paper Mills at Gravesend. His brother Harold – created Lord Rothermere in 1919 – had been the hard business head of the partnership and a great deal of his energy had been expended on restraining Northcliffe's extravagance.

As mentioned earlier, Northcliffe had bought the *Observer* in 1905 for £5,000, and at that time the highly successful and influential editor J. L. Garvin had agreed to stay on, but only on condition that he retained editorial control and was given a share in the profits. When he and Northcliffe had a row over a matter of policy, as was inevitable, Northcliffe offered to let Garvin have the paper and gave him three weeks to find someone willing to put up the money. Garvin came up with one of the richest men in the world, William Waldorf Astor who already had acquired Stead's old newspaper, the *Pall Mall Gazette*. In 1911, he willingly bought the *Observer* for his son, Waldorf; he himself spent most of his time in Italy, leaving the conduct of the paper to the editor Garvin and to his politician son. When Astor accepted a Lloyd George viscountcy in 1917, and died in 1919, his son Waldorf had to go to the Lords and his seat in Parliament passed to his wife Nancy, the first woman MP to take a seat at Westminster.

By now Northcliffe was showing increasing signs of megalo-mania. After the Armistice he campaigned for the Kaiser to be brought to Britain for trial. He fully expected to go to Versailles as a delegate to the Peace Conference and when he was not chosen turned on Lloyd George whom he had been instrumental in putting in No. 10 Downing Street.

His last instruction to the *Daily Mail* was to put the best available man on to the task of writing his obituary. He died in 1922 with a loaded revolver under his pillow, convinced that the Germans were coming to get him. He had no legitimate children but his favourite nephew, Cecil Harmsworth King, his eldest sister's son, had spent his Oxford vacations working on the Northcliffe newspapers, mainly the *Daily Mail* and *The*

Times though he did one stint on the *Mirror* under Rothermere which he described later as 'the finest training in how not to run a newspaper'. Northcliffe left £6,000,000 and his brother Viscount Rothermere was reckoned to be worth £26,000,000 after his brother's death, though he managed to lose most of that by the time of his own death in 1940.

Northcliffe left *The Times* in his will to his wife Molly but the prestige and power of the paper soon brought the vultures hovering around. These included his own brother, Rothermere and members of the Walter family who still held an option to buy back *The Times* at its market value on Northcliffe's death. The Walter family was secretly being backed by another of Viscount Astor's sons, Major John Jacob (later Lord Astor of Hever) and by the managing director of *The Times*, Campbell Stuart, a Canadian. John Jacob Astor's motive was purely an attempt to gain prestige – at this period the Astors still had what seemed like unlimited wealth – and he topped Rothermere's final bid with one of £1,500,000 and remained chief proprietor of *The Times* for forty years until 1966.

At the time of Northcliffe's death in 1922, the controlling interest in Associated Newspapers Ltd – excluding *The Times* – passed to Rothermere. By now it included three national dailies, the *Daily Mail*, the *Daily Mirror* and the *Daily Sketch*, first published in 1909 and incorporating the old *Daily Graphic*. The *Sketch* had been sold to Rothermere by the first Sir Edward Hulton, along with his father's provincial newspaper empire. The same Sir Edward Hulton had already been pipped to the post by Rothermere in 1915; he was planning an illustrated Sunday newspaper to be called the *Illustrated Sunday Herald* when Rothermere heard about it, and came out first with the *Sunday Pictorial*, stable-mate of the *Daily Mirror*. Rothermere's empire also included the London *Evening News* and the entire Amalgamated Press magazine group with which he and Northcliffe had started out.

Rothermere was forever wheeling and dealing in newspaper and magazine groups. He sold the Amalgamated Press group to the Berry brothers, resold the Hulton provincial group at a profit, took 49 per cent of the shares in Beaverbrook Newspapers and sold them back to Beaverbrook in 1933 reputedly making £3,000,000 on the deal; by this time Beaverbrook Newspapers included the *Evening Standard*, which Beaverbrook had bought from Hulton in 1923. In 1931, as mentioned above, Rothermere hived off the *Daily Mirror* and the *Sunday Pictorial* to an independent company with its own directors.

Rothermere went to Germany to meet Hitler and on his return reported that 'under Herr Hitler's control the youth of Germany is effectively organised against the corruption of Communism' and went on to add that the British people should give 'full appreciation to the service which the National Socialist Party has rendered to western Europe'. He even defended the persecution of the Jews in Germany in the *Daily Mail* on the grounds that Germany had fallen under the control of 'alien elements'.

He tried to set up a political party, the United Empire Party, to contest half the seats in the next election with Beaverbrook as putative prime minister and a cabinet nominated by the press. This party was scuttled by Baldwin before it was properly launched.

He was offered the Crown of Hungary – by one faction anyway – after a visit there just before the war and claimed that he was the only press baron who might have become one of the crowned heads of Europe. He lost a lot of money towards the end of his life, partly through mismanagement and partly as a result of the Wall Street Crash of 1929, and when he died in 1940 he left only about £400,000 – not even enough to cover the legacies in his will.

In the meantime, the Berry brothers had been busy consolidating their growing empire. They had formed Allied Newspapers in 1923 and in 1926 had bought the Amalgamated Press from Rothermere creating one of the biggest publishing groups in the country. But they still didn't have a prestigious daily.

The opportunity came in 1928. The Tory-subsidised *Daily*

Telegraph was still owned by the descendants of the Levy-Lawson family, but like the Walter family when Northcliffe stepped in to save *The Times* in 1908, they had now lost all interest in it and were ready to sell. Edward Levy-Lawson, son of the original printer–proprietor, had been raised to the peerage as Lord Burnham in 1903, but he had done little to modernise the plant of his paper or to keep up with the changing times and had lapsed in his old age into a sort of adulatory conservatism which made for very dull reading. The *Telegraph*, which had been the best-selling daily in the world in the late 1870s, was down to 180,000 in 1918 and 84,000 in 1928. The second Lord Burnham, Edward Lawson's son, was glad to let William (by now Sir William) Berry have it.

Berry cut the price from two pence to one penny, doubled its circulation almost overnight and within a year had become Lord (later Viscount) Camrose, and his brother Gomer had become Lord (later Viscount) Kemsley. A third brother, who had never even left Merthyr Tydfil, became Lord Buckland.

In 1923, as already mentioned, Beaverbrook had added the *Evening Standard* to his stable by buying the magazine empire of Sir Edward Hulton – whose father had started as a printer in Lancashire – and then selling it again, at a profit. As his own commission on the deal, he retained the *Evening Standard*, the only newspaper left in the Hulton Group, which had once owned the *Daily Dispatch*, the *Sunday Chronicle* and the *Daily Sketch* as well as the *Evening Standard* and a whole string of provincial dailies.

Already by 1931 he was constructing a shining black glass and steel palace in Fleet Street to house the headquarters of his empire. It is one of the many ironies of Fleet Street that the firm he employed to build it was Trollop and Colls, and that the manager of Trollop and Colls at this juncture was a young man called Victor Matthews who, years later, with Nigel Broakes, was to form Trafalgar House, a property-developing amalgam which included the Cunard Steamship Company and the Ritz Hotel, an outfit which would ultimately buy the

Express newspaper group from Beaverbrook's son, Sir Max Aitken.

In 1937 Lord Camrose bought the ailing Conservative *Morning Post* with some 10,000 readers and incorporated it in his *Daily Telegraph*. In the same year the Berry brothers decided to split up, just as the Harmsworths had earlier done; Kemsley took the provincial papers, the *Daily Sketch* and the *Sunday Times*, and Camrose took the *Daily Telegraph* and the *Financial Times*.

By now yet another press baron had appeared on the Fleet Street stage, in the form of Julius Salter Elias. The *Daily Herald*, the one national paper to be successfully financed from within the working-classes, had been launched in 1908. It had begun life as little more than a strike sheet, but was relaunched as a left-wing daily in 1912, printed under contract by Odham's, a printing firm which had started to take over Newnes's and Pearson's old magazines. It survived the First World War, but only as a weekly, and was relaunched yet again as a national daily in 1919. It could get the circulation readily enough (mostly men, older than the average for the other popular papers and in the nature of things, less well-heeled), but it did not appeal to women which meant that it could not get the sort of display advertising that a mass circulation daily needed in order to survive. As editor George Lansbury once lamented: 'The more copies we sold, the more money we lost.'

Crippled by a lack of advertising revenue and without any solid financial resources, the *Herald* staggered from one financial crisis to another until in January 1922 it was forced to appeal to the Labour Party to save it. Eventually it was launched for a fourth time as the mouthpiece of the Labour Party and financed by the Trades Union Conference.

At this stage, Julius Salter Elias (later Lord Southwood) appeared on the scene. He had started out as an office boy in Odham's and by 1920 he had become managing director of Odham's Press Ltd, now a flourishing magazine empire. Odham's published *John Bull* and also the *Sunday People*, which

Elias took from 300,000 to 3,000,000 within three years. In 1929, as head of Odham's the printers and publishers of the *Sunday People*, Elias bought a controlling share in the *Daily Herald* – after the deal he held 51 per cent of the shares and the TUC 49 per cent – and he relaunched it for the fifth time as a genuinely socialist daily which could challenge the *Mail* and the *Express* as a popular paper.

Julius Salter Elias, son of a Hammersmith newsagent, was one of the great Fleet Street eccentrics. He regularly ordered twenty-four suits a year, invariably conservatively cut in navy blue, dark grey or brown; he never had less than fifty new pairs of shoes in his wardrobe and he had only been abroad once in his life, on a day-trip to Le Touquet. Normally he spent four weeks of every year in the Grand Hotel at Eastbourne. He listened to nothing on the radio apart from the religious programme 'Lift Up Your Hearts' and his whole life was devoted to Odham's and the *Sunday People*.

His special offers, while he was promoting the *People*, included the first free insurance scheme to come from a Sunday newspaper plus sensational new features such as Fleet Street's first 'true confessions' and 'intimate revelation' stories. He had also hoped to solve the perennial problem of the Sunday presses lying idle all week by securing a contract to print the *Radio Times* for the BBC. Unfortunately for him, Sir John Reith the BBC director-general was a man of almost painfully puritanical honesty. As he happened to have married into the Odham family he decided that for the BBC to give the contract for the printing of *Radio Times* to Elias would smack of nepotism and so it went elsewhere.

This was the period when the first big circulation war began to get out of hand and Julius Salter Elias was the man largely responsible. Vases, pens, dictionaries, cameras, leatherbound volumes of the works of Dickens and Shakespeare, the complete *Encyclopaedia Britannica* – all were toted around Britain in the wake of the *Daily Herald* circulation canvassers. The *Daily Express*, the *Daily Mail* and the *Daily Chronicle* all had to follow suit. Soon the country was awash with free gifts and the news in the papers began to matter far less than what they were offering in terms of loot. As Hugh Cudlipp once put it, the motto was: To hell with editorial enterprise – give them a grand piano instead.

The *Daily Herald* achieved its aim of a circulation of 2,000,000 but Elias was finding that he was being forced to spend £3,000,000 a year to hold on to his readership. He went down-market to keep the circulation high and lost out on advertising revenue. It was too early; the working-classes had not yet acquired the spending power that brought in the profitable display advertisements. On the other hand, Elias's rivals were having to spend the same kind of money to stay in business. In the decade between 1925 and 1935, the number of people employed on the national daily newspapers rose by over 70 per cent and very nearly half of that total were circulation canvassers of one sort or another.

When Beaverbrook withdrew from the race, in 1935, his newspaper was safely past the two million mark. Elias was elevated to the peerage as Lord Southwood and became a viscount in 1946.

The *News Chronicle* was the product of a merger in 1930 between Laurence Cadbury's Liberal *Daily News* and the *Daily Chronicle* owned by Pearson's Westminster Press. In 1936 Pearson sold full control of the *Chronicle* to the Cadbury family; the new paper had a combined circulation of 1,400,000 but nobody could decide whether the future lay with the Liberal Party or with Labour. In 1937 the *Chronicle* slid to fourth place and might have slipped even further if the war had not intervened to apply the brake of newsprint rationing.

Other newspapers were also grateful for the enforced truce in the circulation battle imposed by the outbreak of war. By 1937 a quarter of the national dailies published around the turn of the century had disappeared although the circulation of the surviving morning papers had gone up by 300 per cent; as Francis Williams put it, more people were reading fewer papers.

In 1934 the sales of the *Daily Mirror* were down to 730,000 and falling. The *Sunday Pictorial*, now run by Cecil King, Northcliffe's favourite nephew, who had become a director of the *Mirror* company in 1929, was also losing circulation. It had dropped from 2,416,981 in November 1925 to 1,336,000 in September 1937. The *Pictorial* was edited by Hugh Cudlipp (now Lord Cudlipp), one of the most brilliant journalists ever to hit the street. He had joined the paper in 1935 as features editor at the age of 21, and in 1937 he had become the youngest editor in Fleet Street's history.

The genius behind the *Daily Mirror* in the late twenties and early thirties was Harry Guy Bartholomew (known as Bart). He had joined the paper in 1904 when its circulation was 25,000 and his salary was 30 shillings a week. He had come from the engraving department of Northcliffe's *Illustrated Mail* (a short-lived experiment) and he knew exactly how pictures should be used to sell newspapers. But he also knew a lot more, as the *Mirror* people soon realised, and by 1913, at the age of 28, he was a director, pioneering the use of wired pictures. In 1923 he succeeded in reproducing perfectly clear, cabled pictures of Lipton's *Shamrock* racing off Rhode Island for the America's Cup.

One of his great moments – and one of the *Mirror*'s great moments – came in 1936 when Bart, by now editorial director, decided to break the news, as well as a gentlemen's agreement among the press lords not to spill the beans, on the subject of King Edward VIII's determination to marry the divorced Mrs Wallis Warfield Simpson. On this occasion he came back to the office in his pyjamas after the then chairman, John Cowley, was safely tucked up in bed and splashed the news all over the front page of the 3.53 a.m. edition. Bart took the editorial line that the decision could well be left to the country and published the first pictures of the lady for whom the King was prepared to give up his throne.

That, at any rate, is how it must have looked from the editorial chair of a popular tabloid. Certainly, Fleet Street had maintained silence for weeks despite the fact that the world's press was awash with stories of the Royal Romance. But the gaff was actually blown by the Bishop of Bradford, who made a sermon criticising the King which was reported in the *Yorkshire Post* and once the silence had been broken, all Fleet Street rushed it into print. The *Mirror* in common with the *Daily Mail* and the *Daily Express* backed the wrong horse; Geoffrey Dawson, editor of *The Times* and a friend of Baldwin's, took the Cabinet line that the King must abdicate. To the surprise of the popular papers, the abdication of this most popular of monarchs was accepted with total equanimity by the British public, who welcomed his shy and diffident brother George VI with open arms.

Despite the fact that it had miscalculated public opinion, the *Mirror*'s circulation increased more than that of any other daily newspaper during the crisis and by 1937 it was well past the million mark.

There was now a newcomer on the scene which while not strictly speaking a newspaper, nevertheless employed such brilliant journalists and photographers and had such an impact on the street that it deserves a mention in this book. *Picture Post*, a weekly news picture magazine, was launched in October 1938 by Edward Hulton (later Sir Edward), only son of the first Sir Edward who ran the Hulton empire until it became swallowed up in other empires, and Stefan Lorent, a brilliant Hungarian Jew who was its first editor. It folded in May 1957 – there was really no place for a news picture magazine once television got into its stride – but during the two decades of its existence it employed journalists like James Cameron, Anne Scott-James, Tom Hopkinson, Ted Castle, MacDonald Hastings, Katharine Whitehorn, Fyfe Robertson, Sydney Jacobson, Kenneth Allsop, and Robert Kee and photographers like Bert Hardy and Slim Hewitt, and throughout its existence, it was closely studied by all the newspapers in Fleet Street.

The Times and the *Observer*, both under the firm financial control of the Astor family and with brilliant editors (Geoffrey

Dawson and J. L. Garvin) were in good hands and were doing
well as World War II approached. When the Conservative
leadership split in 1939, the *Sunday Times* remained loyal to
Chamberlain. Although the *Daily Telegraph*'s circulation of
720,000 drooped a bit when the paper took what was then the
unpopular line against his Appeasement policy, its advertising
revenue made it totally secure. The *Sunday Pictorial* also took a
firm line on Appeasement, and both the *Mirror* and the *Pictorial*
argued forcibly for the inclusion of one of their regular
contributors, Winston Churchill, in the War Cabinet.

Right up until the moment when the Nazi troops overran
Poland, Beaverbrook's *Daily Express* had been assuring its
readers confidently that there would be no war, this year or
next, but this signal error of judgement didn't seem to upset the
readers. Maybe, as Beaverbrook is reputed to have remarked
to his editors: 'If we're right, everyone will praise our foresight.
If we're wrong, nobody will even remember what we said.'

Or maybe it was just that by 1939 it didn't seem to matter
what the *Express* said or did; its circulation went on climbing
steadily. Beaverbrook was then at the height of his very
considerable powers and he had found in Arthur Christiansen,
who had been editor since 1933, that rare combination, a
journalist sensitive enough to respond to every reaction from
his ever-growing readership using his technical ability to do
whatever was required of him brilliantly, and at the same time
possessed of a thick enough skin to be able to shrug off all slings
and arrows hourly hurled in his direction by the Beaver.

When the war broke out, Beaverbrook's *Daily Express* was
winning the circulation war hands down . . .

More Readers, Fewer Papers: the First Casualties

The war, when it came, meant very many different things to different newspapermen. To Fleet Street as an institution, it came like an interval between two acts of a drama. Over four years nothing of any great fundamental significance happened apart from the rows between the Cabinet and papers like the *Mirror*; the Cabinet thought that the *Mirror*'s outspoken criticism of the way in which the war was being fought was treasonable sabotage and Churchill threatened to close down the paper. But these matters were of more moment to the Fleet Street journalists still employed there than they were to the general public or to the Fleet Street journalists who had gone away to the war, and they had no real, lasting significance. The Government of any country with its back to the wall is likely to be highly sensitive to press criticism and the effects of all the exchanges between Cecil King and Churchill were transitory, despite all the space devoted to them in books about the period.

However, one event which was to prove of paramount importance to the national and indeed the provincial newspapers occurred right at the beginning of the war, though, understandably, none of the newspapers realised at the time how important it was going to be. In fact, with hindsight, it can now be said that without Reuters and without the Government's realisation that Reuters' objectivity and independence were an invaluable asset to a country at war, the national newspapers would never have acquired the large shares in Reuters which they did. They would therefore never have made the profits they did when Reuters started to make a fortune out of the currency trading which followed the collapse of the old Bretton Woods Agreement to hold the world's major currencies more or less at a par. It was this windfall which enabled them to finance the new technology and break out of Fleet Street to the new pastures. But all that still lay in the far future, in the eighties in fact. After its initial success, the Reuter news agency ran into a pack of trouble.

It started an international bank which collapsed ignominiously. It tried to develop an advertising agency which failed so disastrously that the manager responsible killed himself. So did the Baron Herbert Reuter, though his suicide note made it clear that it was his wife's untimely death and not the company's misfortunes which prompted him to do away with himself. The chief correspondent in Japan became involved in a political blackmail scandal which rocked the Far East, though the news service that Reuters were offering was still so reliable that the very word 'reuter' passed into a Chinese dialect as a synonym for truth. The whole story is told in fascinating detail in *The Price of Truth: The Story of the Reuter Millions* by John Lawrenson and Lionel Barber.

The British subscribers to the news service constantly complained that the reports were expensive and inadequate; and subscribers outside the UK – in Australia, for example – complained that the service was too British-orientated. The company narrowly averted a closely fought take-over bid by the Marconi Wireless Telegraph Company, and only with the aid of a vast influx of money which appeared to come from Starr Jameson, the maverick nationalist who had started the Boer War by leading a raid on the Transvaal, who had once been a major proprietor of the *Sunday Times* and who was chairman of the gold and diamond conglomerate known as the British South Africa Company.

For over twenty years, Reuters had enjoyed a unique carve-up of the world, along with Havas in France, Wolff in Germany and the Associated Press in America. Between them, they operated a 'news swap' agreement, under which the 'big four', as they were then known, had a guaranteed and unopposed monopoly of specified countries so long as the other members incurred no costs whatever for their news reports from those countries. In other words, they had all their raw material free and all their main markets assured. Alone among the big four, Associated Press, far from being a profit-making country like the others, represented a non-profit-making association of some 1,400 papers in the US which, towards the end of World War I, began to show signs of wanting to break away from the original big four and sell news coverage worldwide.

Reuters decided that the only way to meet this new American challenge was through a united British press front behind Reuters and against Associated Press. The Fleet Street national newspapers, divided then as they have been almost ever since, backed out of the deal but the Press Association, another agency which represented most of the British provincial newspapers, proved highly enthusiastic about the idea. On 31 December 1925, the Press Association took up 53 per cent of the shares in Reuters.

In the meantime, the United Press, the big commercial American news agency, had been expanding its activities across the world and Reuters were again feeling the pinch. In the years leading up to World War II, Reuters had to look to the Government for a subsidy to keep their news service going. During the phoney war and even more during and immediately after the Battle of Britain when a German invasion seemed imminent, the Government needed every possible means of keeping up morale. Censorship had already been introduced but the Government could not interfere with Reuters which controlled itself. So, under a 'gentleman's agreement', the Government paid a subsidy of £25,000 a year to Reuters, the biggest of any government pay-out apart from the BBC. Sir William Haley, later editor of *The Times* and before that, director-general of the BBC, became a director of Reuters. He ousted Sir Roderick Jones, who had been running it since the suicide of Baron Herbert Reuter, and managed to persuade the proprietors of the Fleet Street national newspapers to join the Press Association as co-owners of Reuters, though in fact, through their provincial holdings, they already owned nearly 25 per cent of the company.

Thus, securely financed by all of Britain's newspapers,

Reuters became effectively the British propaganda agency, operating from its brand new headquarters in Fleet Street, designed by Sir Edwin Lutyens, exactly opposite Beaverbrook's black glass palace.

In 1941 a Trust was formed which was originally intended to secure Reuters' future as an independent news agency, just as the *Guardian* Trust had secured the future of the *Guardian* and had preserved it from take-over attempts. At this period, Reuters' main business was the dissemination of news from all over the world, though notably from what had been the British Empire. In 1946, the Australian and New Zealand newspapers brought into Reuters.

Throughout the war, many of the brilliant young Fleet Street stars – writers, editors, columnists, reporters – were away, either fighting the war, running the many forces newspapers, or working, in one guise or another, for the Government's Department of Information. Not all the journalists, however, went to the war. While Hugh Cudlipp and the *Mirror*'s – perhaps Fleet Street's – greatest columnist Bill Connor (Cassandra) – were having a whale of a time following the 8th Army from Africa right up through Italy to Rome, the *Daily Mirror*, with Bart as chairman and Cecil Thomas as editor, managed to hit upon exactly the right formula and became the No. 1 Favourite with the Forces, and that term included not only the soldiers serving on the various fronts but also their wives and girl friends waiting for them back at home in blitzed, battle-scarred, beleaguered Britain.

Bart found a new and expanding market for readers among the working-classes – which naturally formed the bulk of the armed forces. Cudlipp, however, attributes the decision to go for this market to Cecil King who, in the late thirties, he says, announced one day that the only unexploited and expanding market for increased circulation lay with the working-classes and that if this meant embracing their socialist political views, then so be it. It's probably true: both Bart and Cecil King were consummate newspapermen and it is not beyond the bounds of possibility that the same idea occurred to them both at roughly the same time.

Bart was convinced that people preferred to look at papers rather than read them. He did not think that any story in the *Daily Mirror* should run to more than 100 words and he fervently believed that the mass-circulation papers were far more about display and presentation than about content. With these ideas he had taken the *Mirror* from 710,000 in 1934 when he became editorial director, to 1,200,000 at the outbreak of the war. Bart was robustly uninterested in politics but he knew all about illustrations and the strip cartoon Jane – about a vapid young thing who found the greatest difficulty in keeping her clothes on – was reckoned to be a contributory factor in the war effort. *Round-Up*, the US paper in the Far East, under the headline JANE GIVES ALL, commented in 1942: 'Well, sirs, you can go right home now. Smack out of the blue and with no one even threatening her, Jane peeled a week ago. The British 36th Division immediately gained six miles and the British attacked in the Arakan. Maybe we Americans ought to have Jane too.'

Arthur Christiansen of the *Express* was no more interested in politics than Bart but he was a superb journalistic technician. While he allowed the paper to become Beaverbrook's mouth-piece politically, he saw to it that it was always brilliantly edited, turned out smartly to appeal to its readership, and precisely attuned to the views of the man on the end of Rhyl Pier or on the top of the Birmingham No. 13 bus, the British equivalent of the viewpoint of the Kansas City milkman. He once said that he wanted to make the paper as interesting to the charwoman who cleaned out his office as it was to the Permanent Secretary of the Foreign Office, and he did this with news and features, brilliantly presented, not with strip cartoons, strip-tease, or any other stunts. Probably the greatest moment in his career had been his R101 scoop of 1930. He was then deputy editor in charge of the *Sunday Express* – the editor was John Gordon – and on a hunch that the unconfirmed reports of the disaster which had reached him were probably true, he stopped the presses to wait for confirmation. His hunch proved right and he was able to produce a Sunday morning edition at 8 a.m. carrying full news plus pictures of the airship crash long after the last copies of all the other Sundays had been printed and dispatched without any reference to it. Beaverbrook rang him at nine o'clock to say: 'You have secured a wonderful feat of journalism. I am proud to be associated with the newspaper on which you work. Goodbye to you.' Three years later, Christiansen became editor of the *Daily Express*.

When the war ended, the *Daily Express* was still leading the field, but only by a neck.

Newsprint rationing was eased a bit in 1949 though it was not until 1956 that it ended completely. When the newspapers started to expand in size again, they very quickly found that things had changed utterly during the war. Newsprint had actually dropped in price during the twenties and at the outbreak of war had cost only £11 a ton. By 1945 it was costing £28 a ton and ten years later the price had doubled to £58. By 1977 it was to cost about £250 a ton and the present price in 1989 is over £400.

Over the same period, there was a decline in advertising revenue. During the years of austerity, the big stores were not willing to take big display advertisements; there was no point because they could sell almost anything they could lay their hands on without advertising. Also, freed from the problems caused by very strict newspaper rationing, and with a choice of media at their disposal, those who had goods to advertise were able to keep the rates down.

Television, which had made its debut briefly in 1936 without making any great impact – the screens were tiny, the pictures poor in quality, the programmes puerile – resumed its activities in 1946. Very soon the BBC began to compete with the newspapers very effectively, in the sense that television was able to show pictures, even if at first they were only stills, of news events hours before the morning newspapers would arrive on the doorstep, though as yet television was not absorbing any of the advertising revenue.

By now, however, the press had another very strong competitor in the highly objective BBC radio news. Under Sir John Reith, the BBC had become a national institution, rather like *The Times* except that it enjoyed a far wider audience. More important still, perhaps, it offered an alternative to the 'it must be true because I saw it in the paper' argument. When the BBC began to broadcast authoritative news reports that made what had appeared in the newspapers seem exaggerated or distorted or unfair or even downright inaccurate, it was usually the BBC which tended to be believed.

The *Daily Mirror* responded to the threat of television by indulging in a kind of sensational journalism that TV had not yet thought of utilising. The *Express*, the *Mail* and the *Chronicle* still relied on putting the latest news and pictures on the nation's breakfast tables. They were very slow to realise that television had already done this the night before.

Long before TV had become a serious competitor, back in the thirties in fact, Cecil King and Bart had realised that their readers would almost certainly have been listening to the BBC news bulletins. 'One point we clearly had in view,' Cecil King wrote in 1969 in *Strictly Personal*, 'was that the paper had to be edited on the assumption that our readers listened to the BBC news every morning and that . . . any attempt to get news scoops was a waste of effort, though broadcasting had then been in existence for over ten years and the [other] papers were in the main edited as if the BBC did not exist.'

Hugh Cudlipp returned to edit the *Mirror*'s stable-companion the *Sunday Pictorial* after the war; the chairman John Cowley had died in 1944 and Bart was now chairman of both newspapers. Stuart Campbell (known in the street as Sam Campbell when he later became famous as editor of the *People*) had been in charge of the *Pictorial* in Cudlipp's absence.

By the end of 1949 the *Sunday Pictorial* was poised to hit the 5,000,000 circulation mark and squeeze past its immediate rival the *People* (the *News of the World* was then selling around 7,000,000). At this point Cudlipp was sacked by Bart for spiking a report from Cecil King, then touring West Africa in pursuit of the *Mirror* Group's interests there. Cudlipp spent a year with Beaverbrook's group as managing editor of the *Sunday Express*, and in 1952 when King had succeeded in achieving the *coup d'état* which resulted in Bart's abrupt dismissal from the group, Cudlipp returned to edit the *Sunday Pictorial* for the third time. But within a year he had been appointed editorial director of the *Mirror* and the *Pictorial*.

At this time the *Daily Express* still had the largest daily readership (4,200,000 by 1950); but by June 1954 the *Mirror* had passed the 5,000,000 mark and could boast that it was the newspaper with the biggest daily sale in the world. Cecil King was now rapidly becoming top baron of Fleet Street; in 1951 he had been appointed chairman of the *Mirror* group. He was at the height of his power after the purchase of what he referred to as his uncle's old business in Farringdon Road, Amalgamated Press Ltd, and the subsequent take-over of Odham's Press which will be dealt with more fully later. By this stage Cecil King controlled a total of twelve UK newspapers, eleven overseas newspapers, seventy-five consumer periodicals, 132 trade technical and specialised periodicals and the twenty printing works which together comprised his International Publishing Corporation.

He also had interests in Australia. In 1949 Bart had bought a controlling interest in the *Melbourne Argus* at a time when the big Australian success was the *Sun Pictorial* group. The latter was then run by Sir Keith Murdoch, father of a young man called Rupert, then at Oxford, who had his father slightly concerned over his extreme left-wing views. Sir Keith need not have lost any sleep; it did not take Rupert Murdoch long to revert to High Tory capitalism.

Sir Keith Murdoch had won fame as a war correspondent at Gallipoli during the First World War and ironically it was Lord Northcliffe who helped to get him started as a newspaper proprietor. In 1952, on his return to the *Mirror* Group, Hugh Cudlipp was sent to Australia to wind up operations there, which were now losing a million a year. This he did by leaking entirely fictitious plans for a new tabloid evening newspaper in direct competition with the *Melbourne Herald*, Murdoch's companion publication to the *Sun Pictorial*. This enabled the *Mirror*'s Australian chairman to sell the *Argus* – plus the non-existent new evening – to the *Melbourne Herald* at a profit of £80,000. The exultant Cudlipp, by yet another of the constant ironies of Fleet Street, could never have guessed then that Sir Keith's son Rupert would eventually beat him on his own home ground, Fleet Street, EC4, in his own particular chosen game, tabloid journalism. All this was to take place with a newspaper Cudlipp had himself created, 'a paper born of the age we live in', a phrase used by Cudlipp to launch it, the *Sun*.

But Cudlipp was as surprised as everybody else in Fleet Street at the success of Murdoch's Soar-away *Sun*.

During the late fifties, at the end of the period of post-war austerity, the newspapers which had found the going tough during the circulation battles of the thirties began to feel the pinch again. As consumer products became more plentiful and commercial television arrived to offer an alternative outlet for display advertising, those newspapers which could boast of high circulations but could not demonstrate that their readers were in the big spending league started to be squeezed out. Also after the war, when the papers started getting bigger and bigger, people stopped buying more than one: more people read fewer, bigger newspapers.

Revenue from advertising in the popular dailies dropped in this period from almost one half of the total number of column inches to just over a quarter, at the very time when the newspapers were getting bigger. This was also when the Fleet Street printing unions were starting to use all their considerable muscle to resist the many new labour-saving technologies that were beginning to appear on the horizon, and to maintain manning at an artificially high rate. The market for labour in Fleet Street had for years been a seller's one, because of restrictive practices which ensured that skilled workers would always be in short supply and that their normal hours of work would be so arranged that most of the useful work that they

ever did for the newspapers was on overtime. Since the arrival
of the linotype machine and the hot metal technology, printers
had been the aristocrats of labour, the highest-paid workers in
Britain. They were so highly paid and taxed, by the late fifties
and early sixties, that their average working week fell from six
to five, then to four and even three days. Many of them spent
their leisure time working for other newspaper groups, under
assumed names, in the black economy.

It was a bad time to be a proprietor of an ailing paper. In the
years between 1947 and 1974 three Royal Commissions were
appointed to try to find out what had gone wrong with the
press. They did not succeed in coming up with a clear-cut
answer.

The *News Chronicle* had been steadily falling back, though it
was still running in fourth place when the war broke out in
1939; the Cadbury family regarded it, if rather vaguely, as
being held in trust for the Liberal cause. During the mid-fifties
it was limping badly with George Cadbury's son Laurence
(who was also running the family's highly successful chocolate
business) in the saddle.

By 1960, the *News Chronicle* and its stable-mate, the *Star*, had
been losing money steadily for four years. Sales were falling by
about 15 per cent per year and talks had taken place with Lord
Beaverbrook and with the Odham's group. There had been
some talk about a *Daily Observer*, and the first of the new
generation of Fleet Street barons, the Canadian Roy Thomson,
had even been approached. He refused to help the *Chronicle* out
because it would have cost him £3,000,000 for a middle-of-the-
road newspaper; he had his sights adjusted higher. In the end,
Cadbury sold the papers to the second Viscount Rothermere of
Associated Newspapers who bought them to close them down
and so reduce some of the competition his own *Daily Mail* and
Evening News were experiencing, and for the price of the *News
Chronicle*'s debts.

When the *News Chronicle* was suddenly killed off in 1960, with
a circulation of 1,200,000 a day, although its great rival for the
middle-ground readership, the *Daily Herald*, may have briefly

rejoiced, the shock waves reverberated through Fleet Street. That a Liberal newspaper like the *Chronicle* should have been sacrificed to a right-wing outfit like Associated Newspapers seemed outrageous on the face of it. Yet Fleet Street said (because it was what they desperately wanted to believe) that the *Chronicle* had failed because it had a bad proprietor, Laurence Cadbury, and a bad editor, Norman Kersley, and because, despite a number of brilliant contributors like A J Cummings, Robert Lynd, Ian Mackay and the cartoonist Vicky, it was basically, in the last analysis, a bad newspaper.

However, the *Chronicle* and the *Star* were not the only papers in peril. In 1960 and 1961 the *Sunday Graphic*, the *Sunday Dispatch* and the *Sunday Empire News* all folded. This was a difficult period for many other papers, among them the ancient and venerable *Guardian*. The *Manchester Guardian* had for years enjoyed the status and a good deal of the influence of a national newspaper, despite the fact that it was still printed only in Manchester. It now began to suffer badly from the fact that display advertising was hard to come by in post-war, austere Britain, and also that as a provincial, it could charge only about one-fifth of the *Telegraph* or one-third of *The Times* rates. The figures were based on circulation or cost per thousand and were considerably lower for all provincial papers.

According to Alistair Hetherington's definitive book about the paper, *The Guardian Years*, loyal northerners believed that C. P. Scott would never have taken the paper to London. They were wrong; Scott had always wanted a London outlet and had talked about it as early as 1890. Furthermore, when the name of the paper was changed to the *Guardian* in 1959, as one of the preliminaries for the move down to London, Alistair Hetherington claims that the change in fact increased the newspaper's popularity in Manchester among what today would be called the yuppies there. They liked the *Guardian* but they did not like to be seen reading a local paper, and were very happy when it dropped the word 'Manchester'.

In view of the technological revolution which occurred nearly a quarter of a century later, it is interesting to look at the *Guardian*'s plans for the move to London. The company, working with the Muirhead Electrical company, had developed a prototype machine for facsimile transmission of entire pages by telephone or telegraph wire. In these days of portable home fax machines, this may not seem all that extraordinary but it was a complete innovation in the post-war period and today's ubiquitous fax machines almost certainly grew out of the *Guardian* invention.

In 1951, trials with this facsimile machine were carried out between Copenhagen and Manchester – the *Guardian* did not dare to try them out between two centres in Britain for fear of union repercussions – and proved a complete success. The cost of production using this method would have been a fraction of what it would have cost using the hot metal techniques at both centres, as many of the nationals had been doing for years. The *Daily Mail* had started printing in Manchester from 1900, the *Daily Express* from 1927, the *Daily Herald* from 1930, the *Daily Telegraph* from 1940 and the *Daily Mirror* and *Sunday Pictorial* from 1955.

Laurence Scott, grandson of C. P. and at this time managing director of the *Guardian*, approached the unions about this facsimile machine. Not surprisingly they were far from sympathetic, since it would need fewer men to operate than the old system. Scott had already opened negotiations to acquire a site in Southwark, near the South Bank, but when he heard that the unions were adamant that the system could not cope with large circulations, he let the site go.

Ironically in 1957 the Muirhead–Marwick prototype was sold to Asahi newspapers of Japan who used the system between Tokyo and Sapporo at a time when they were printing 6,000,000 copies a day of a joint morning/evening newspaper, and when the print order at Sapporo alone was more than anything the *Guardian* was ever likely to have required. Even more ironically, some bright Japanese industrial developers – they were never inventors or innovators – saw the possibilities of the fax machine for transmitting Japanese script, so complicated that it had so far defeated all efforts to adapt it for transmission by wire. The fax machine worked so brilliantly that they began to explore its more general applications, as a means, for example, of transmitting graphs, diagrams, blue-prints, sketches, even scribbled notes by telephone wire from one point to another – today's fax machine, in effect.

In the meantime, the firm which had invented this brilliant new system of printing newspapers by remote control, as it were, had to print their Manchester-edited newspapers by expensive conventional systems for another fifteen years until 1976. By that time the *Wall Street Journal* and the *New York Times* were both using facsimile machines to print their newspapers in the Middle West and California.

There was one respect, however, in which the *Guardian*'s London operation was not entirely conventional. Duplicated typesetting was already in use on a small scale by some of the provincial papers as well as by the *Scotsman* between London and Edinburgh and *The Times* between the House of Commons and Printing House Square. But until the *Guardian* began to print in London in 1961, it had never been used to print the bulk of a national newspaper.

In 1959, when the word 'Manchester' was dropped from the title of the paper, there was still one big question: where was it to be printed? The *Guardian*'s London office was a typical pokey little provincial newspaper office, in the same building as the Post Office in Fleet Street opposite the end of Chancery Lane; the Southwark site had been sold off. What they were ideally looking for was a newspaper plant with spare printing capacity during the week.

The answer came from a completely unexpected quarter.

'Uncle' Roy Thomson as he was known in Fleet Street, with his deceptively benign grin and his pebble spectacles, was the son of a poor barber from Toronto. He had peddled radio sets during the Depression, then went into the business of running small radio stations in Canada's mining camps. This latter activity led to an empire built on commercial radio stations and eventually to a chain of thirty Canadian newspapers. He came to Britain in 1953 and bought the *Scotsman* and an Edinburgh evening paper. Before long he had started to diversify. He created Thomson Travel, invested heavily and profitably in North Sea oil and when commercial television came to Britain, because he already possessed a newspaper, had a right to apply for the Scottish station and secured an 80 per cent slice of Scottish television. He is remembered in Fleet Street not so much for the things he did as for the things he said. Television soon made him a multi-millionaire and he very nearly queered the pitch for all the other television financiers by referring to commercial television as 'a licence to print your own money'. His most famous dictum on the subject of newspapers was: 'I buy newspapers to make money to buy more newspapers to make more money.' He was a widower of 59 when he first came to Britain and was 64 when he became interested in the fate of the Kemsley group.

By this time the aging Lord Kemsley, now 75, proprietor of the *Sunday Times* and twenty-three provincial newspapers, had begun to tire, like the Walter family had tired of running *The Times*, and the Levy-Lawsons had tired of running the *Daily Telegraph*. He was still conducting the affairs of his newspapers with the assistance of his four sons, all on the board, and all brought to the office every morning in chauffeur-driven Rolls Royce and Bentley cars. Roy Thomson bought the whole group for £5,500,000 and his first action was to strip the Berry family directors of their Rolls and Bentley cars and replace them with Rovers (without chauffeurs). He delighted in the prestige that ownership of the up-market *Sunday Times* bestowed on him, dining with Lord Beaverbrook, the Roseberys and Cecil King, appearing on television and travelling to Russia to meet Nikita Khrushchev and publicise his (and Fleet Street's) latest innovation, the colour magazine. The *Sunday Times* was the first to brandish this new weapon in the circulation war in 1962.

When Thomson took over the *Sunday Times* and wanted to expand it to forty-eight pages at the least, the *Daily Telegraph* presses were unable to cope, so Thomson had new presses installed at Gray's Inn Road. He was then presented with the problem of what to do with these highly expensive new presses during the week and an arrangement with the *Guardian* seemed the obvious answer. There was room – just about – for the *Guardian*'s London editorial and advertising staff and on 10 September 1961, the first issue of the *Guardian* to be printed in London was produced at Gray's Inn Road. The London edition was limited to twelve 'live' pages; the remainder of the paper, including the features pages, the small advertisements and even some of the news pages, had to be set in Manchester the previous day. Because of this, and because the readership became far more demanding once they knew that the *Guardian* was being printed in London – they did not see, for example, why reviews of London first nights should appear in the London-printed *Guardian* a day after they had appeared in all the other nationals – the circulation sagged a bit. It was not until 1971 that the *Guardian* overtook *The Times* and remained ahead with a figure around 350,000. In May 1989 it was selling 440,000 a day against *The Times*'s 431,000.

For a time, however, shortly after it began printing in London, all its activities were overshadowed by a new threat: the possibility of amalgamation with *The Times*. Laurence Scott proposed the idea to the editor, Alistair Hetherington, on the grounds that both papers were at that period experiencing considerable problems. Before printing in London, the *Guardian* had been losing between £200,000 and £450,000 a year, although the *Manchester Evening News* was still making a profit of about £1,000,000 a year.

The Times, on the other hand, had no asset like the *Manchester Evening News* and was barely paying its way. Gavin Astor was not prepared to put any more money into it, nor was his brother Hugh. Sir William Haley, who had recently been appointed chief executive as well as editor, was strongly in favour of the merger and could see the *Times–Guardian* as one of the world's great papers. The idea was that Haley would edit the combined paper for about five years and then Alistair Hetherington would take over. Gavin Astor would be president of the company and Laurence Scott chairman.

Hetherington was against the proposal for a very good reason: if the merger took place, right-of-centre readers of the new paper would still have the alternatives of the *Daily Telegraph* and the *Financial Times*, while left-of-centre *Guardian* readers would have nowhere to go other than the tabloid *Mirror*, the failing *Daily Herald* (or indeed the *Morning Sun*, formerly the *Daily Worker*, the official organ of the British Communist Party). This would mean in effect that the combined *Times–Guardian* would always be under heavy pressure not to offend too many of its Conservative readers. After endless meetings, at one of which it was suggested that as a compromise the amalgamated newspaper might be edited by some neutral figurehead such as Jo Grimond, the Liberal leader, the talks fell through and the idea was dropped.

Despite the difficulties of *The Times*, the *Guardian* and the *Observer*, the other heavies, the *Financial Times*, the *Daily Telegraph* and the *Sunday Times* were now doing well.

The arrival of television and its rapid spread throughout all the homes in the country had tended to drive the popular press, with the possible exception of the *Mirror*, down-market, a direction in which they were heading anyway. It seems quite likely that as the popular papers' reports grew ever shorter and less reliable, at a time when people where beginning to turn to their newspapers for background information on topics in which their interest had been stimulated by the very lively TV news bulletins and documentary programmes, many readers lost patience with the tabloids and turned to the heavies. Television news simply did not have enough time to give background material in the bulletins and this was something that the heavies could do superbly well.

Thomson was very quick to realise that a Sunday colour

magazine could provide much of the background material that television news had to leave to the occasional documentaries. A photogravure magazine could provide better, clearer pictures than television and in colour too, at a time when colour television was still something of a novelty. There was also the point that the quality Sundays were read by people with disposable incomes and the colour supplement was designed to offer another outlet for colourful display advertisements produced initially for the successful women's magazines. Although it cost a lot of money to get started, the colour supplement was here to stay.

The *Daily Telegraph*, now being run by the second Viscount Camrose (the first viscount, William Berry, had died in 1954) was also doing well and in 1961 produced the *Sunday Telegraph* which after a shaky start finally found its niche. In 1964, the newspaper produced a *Weekend Telegraph*, a colour magazine similar to the *Sunday Times* one, except that initially it appeared on Fridays and now appears on Saturday. The *Sunday Telegraph* now has a colour supplement entirely produced by web-offset.

It was the middle-ground papers which really were worst hit when television began to spread into every home in the land. The *Daily Express*, the *Daily Mail* (even with the addition of the *Chronicle* readers) and the *Daily Herald* all were finding the competition with each other and with television increasingly difficult. Their continuing emphasis on topical news and the arresting use of pictures placed them in direct competition with a medium which could give the viewers tomorrow's news before they went to bed, and by that time with moving pictures, too. Their nation-wide circulations were unable to provide advertisers with the regional variations which the new commercial TV companies could offer, and, by their very nature, they were not able to accommodate anything like the number of classified advertisements that *The Times* and the *Daily Telegraph* could run. Also, saturation point, so far as the public attention span was concerned, had been reached, and, when television came in, people who had been in the habit of buying two or more newspapers dropped at least one of them. In 1948,

60 per cent of Fleet Street's circulation was represented by this middle-ground readership band; by 1965, the proportion had dropped to 47 per cent and it has continued to drop ever since. For the first time since the Northcliffe revolution, fewer people were buying fewer papers.

The New Wave
of Fleet Street Overlords

The days of automatic, dramatic increases in overall newspaper circulation were over. After the war the total readership of the daily newspapers, despite the cover price increases, the circulation battles and money prizes that rivalled those offered by the Football Pools, settled down around the fifteen million mark. The overall circulation of the Sundays has tended to fall from a peak of around twenty-one million in the early sixties to about the same overall figure as the dailies, fifteen million.

After the disappearance of the *Chronicle*, its major rival for the progressive middle-ground, the *Daily Herald*, still financed partly by the TUC and partly by Odham's, found itself in the early sixties at the centre of a long-drawn-out and complicated take-over battle. The remarkable Julius Salter Elias (Lord Southwood) had died in 1946 though by some accounts he was still issuing instructions from the Other Side through his spiritualist successor, A. C. Duncan.

Odham's had acquired control of their old magazine rival George Newnes in 1939 – which by that time also included Pearson's very successful chain of magazines – and two years later found themselves being pursued by two very rapacious predators, Cecil King and Roy Thomson. King, as mentioned above, had already taken over his uncle Harold's Amalgamated Press, which he renamed Fleetway Magazines. In order to secure a viable monopoly of the magazine market, he now needed to get his hands on the two very successful women's magazines, *Woman* and *Woman's Own*. Both of these were part of the Odham's group which also included two Fleet Street papers, the *People* and the *Daily Herald*. Roy Thomson was equally anxious to gain control of Odham's to expand his empire and also because Odham's had made a very promising investment in Lord Grade's ATV, which offered him a foothold in television in England.

It was ostensibly over the future of the *Daily Herald* that the take-over battle was fought. Having lost the *News Chronicle*, there was panic among the politicians and communicators of the Left that any take-over might endanger the survival of the one broadsheet paper they could still count on to oppose the Tories.

Thomson withdrew from the fray when King topped his final offer with an undertaking to keep the *Daily Herald* going for seven years. The *People* (later the *Sunday People*), with a circulation of over five million and a readership of its own, and not in direct competition with King's *Sunday Pictorial* (now the *Sunday Mirror*), presented no problems. However, the *Daily Herald*, its circulation down to 1,400,000 – dangerously close to that of the *Chronicle* when it had folded – was a real headache for the chairman and soon became known within the *Mirror* group as 'King's Cross'.

King and Cudlipp gave the *Herald* an extensive face-lift and relaunched it yet again in September 1964, as the *Sun*, redesigned by Cudlipp as 'a newspaper born of the age we live in', aimed at a younger, wealthier, more dynamic market, and intended to appeal to women readers – a broadsheet for the Swinging Sixties. It was a total flop. Despite all Cudlipp's efforts, it still seemed to appeal mainly to the declining middle-aged, middle-ground market that had proved so infertile for the *Daily Chronicle* and the *Daily Herald*, and before long it was losing £175,000 a year. What was to be done? For Cudlipp to have turned it into a snappy tabloid in direct competition with the *Mirror* (which is what eventually happened) would have been pointless since both papers were in the same group and in any event the *Sun* presses were unsuitable for printing a true tabloid. A merger with the *Mirror* would have caused trouble politically and might have been referred to the Monopolies Commission. In any event the gain to the *Mirror* circulation would have been comparatively small and of a type not very helpful to the *Mirror* image – mostly elderly, mainly men. To have closed it down altogether – which they could have done technically since it was no longer the *Daily Herald* – would have meant about 2,000 redundancies at a time when a great many newspapermen were already out of work. King and Cudlipp decided to soldier on at any rate until the end of the guarantee period.

While Cudlipp was agonising over what he should do with the *Sun* that refused to rise and shine, King was flexing his muscles as the chairman of the new International Publishing Corporation, the biggest publishing group in the world. Beginning to develop the first symptoms of the malaise that had affected his uncle, Lord Northcliffe, he found that two more papers were getting into difficulties, which they did not seem to be able to solve through their own efforts.

The Astors had been sustaining the British quality press for nearly half a century since J. J. Astor (Lord Astor of Hever) had taken *The Times* under his protection some years after his father, William Waldorf Astor, had bought the *Observer* and left it to his son, the second Viscount Astor, to run. As early as 1946 a trust had been formed to maintain the independence of the *Observer*, and the Astor millions had provided the two titles with financial security.

However, by the early 1960s Lord Astor of Hever, the protector of *The Times*, had departed for the southern shores of France, mainly for tax reasons, and his son Gavin was facing a crisis as the family fortunes began to peter out. *The Times*'s sales had been stagnant for many years against the rising sales of its rivals, the *Guardian*, the *Daily Telegraph* and the *Financial Times*. All attempts at editorial reform were resisted by Astor, who, according to Francis Williams, the informal historian of Fleet Street, 'treated the paper as an ancient great house into which they had been allowed by the National Trust on condition that they did not alter it.'

By now, however, alterations were inevitable. *The Times*'s accountants Cooper Brothers had advised a higher circulation with news on the front page and a more aggressive editorial and commercial policy as one remedy for its ailments. A new advertising campaign – TOP PEOPLE TAKE THE TIMES – accompanied by generous student discount rates and a less stuffy editorial approach inched the circulation up to 250,000 in the mid-sixties, under Sir William Haley, former director-general of the BBC, as editor. A costly rebuilding of Walter's old premises in Printing House Square was completed in 1965, and a year later came 'Operation Breakthrough', yet another plan to save *The Times*.

News appeared for the first time on the front page instead of classified advertisements in May 1966 – the *Daily Telegraph* had gone over to front page news as early as 1939 – and although this did bring an increase in circulation, at sixpence a copy the cover price was only recouping a fraction of the production costs. The advertising rates could not be increased until the higher circulation had been maintained and audited. After the already mentioned talks with the *Guardian*, other talks were held with the *Guardian* and the *Financial Times*, which came to nothing. Then, quite suddenly, it seemed, Gavin Astor sold *The Times* to Roy Thomson, though not without first laying down certain conditions for its protection. These conditions were largely the work of Denis Hamilton, later editor-in-chief and chairman.

The package to which Roy Thomson agreed in order to attain the prestige which the proprietorship of *The Times* would bestow upon him included a guarantee to subsidise any losses on *The Times* from his recently acquired *Sunday Times*, by forming one company to run the two papers. If his profits from the *Sunday Times* were not sufficient to cover his losses on *The Times*, he agreed to use his personal family resources for that purpose rather than encroach upon the shareholders' dividends. He also gave a complicated series of undertakings to the Monopolies Commission to ensure that *The Times* newspapers would be able to continue publishing papers of quality in the national interest. This even included binding his son Kenneth to remain in England and see that these arrangements remained in force for twenty-one years, an undertaking that seemed – and indeed proved to be – beyond his power to control. Under the arrangement, *The Times* vacated its old premises in Printing House Square and joined the *Sunday Times* in a new building in Gray's Inn Road; the *Observer* remained in Printing House Square, with the old *Times* premises leased out as offices.

Roy Thomson was now printing his own two principal rivals; the *Guardian* in Gray's Inn Road and the *Observer* in Printing House Square.

At this juncture, two new members of the post-war wave of Fleet Street overlords appeared on the scene. Robert Maxwell, born Jan Ludwig Hoch, a Jewish Czech entrepreneur who fought with the Czech Resistance during the war, had built up a highly successful publishing company based in England. His Pergamon Press specialised mainly in academic works, many of them translations which had been out of print since before the war. Although his leanings were socialist, his methods were capitalist and he became a multi-millionaire and owner of the highly profitable communications conglomerate, the British Printing and Communications Corporation (BPCC). In the late sixties he was prowling around looking for a national newspaper to adorn his other achievements, though it was not until 1984 that he was able to attain this objective by buying the Mirror Group.

Rupert Murdoch came to Fleet Street initially to follow up his Oxford career with a stint on the subs' desk at the *Daily Express*. He then returned to Australia and made a fortune as proprietor of the *Adelaide News* at 21, establishing a chain of his own provincial newspapers right across Australia a few years later, and that continent's first national, *The Australian*. Young Murdoch arrived back in Fleet Street looking for a British newspaper to add to his empire, and, as it happened, there was one up for grabs.

In Bouverie Street, the Carr family were finding their heritage, the *News of the World*, a bit of a handful. After enjoying for more than a century the highest Sunday circulation of any newspaper in Britain, it had fallen slightly from its peak of over

8,000,000 in the late fifties, but more worrying still, the Carr family no longer held a controlling interest in the company, and it was ripe for a take-over bid. In 1968 Derek Jackson, one of the twin sons of a former chairman, Charles Jackson, had put his shares on the market. He had held slightly less than one-third of the total, and the Carrs were holding slightly more than one-third; the remaining shares were all in the hands of a very large number of small shareholders who might prove highly vulnerable to a generous offer.

Bill Carr just didn't have the kind of money to bid for the Jackson shares straight away, and when he heard that Robert Maxwell had put in a bid of more than £26,000,000 for the paper, he knew he would have to look for help elsewhere. The shares, held by about 3,500 private individuals, began to climb in value from 37s 6d to 48s 6d and then to 49s 6d. Maxwell increased his bid to £34,000,000. At this stage, Rupert Murdoch became involved in the proceedings. On 24 October 1968, the Stock Exchange suspended dealings in *News of the World* shares to give shareholders a chance to make up their minds on Maxwell's latest offer. On the same day the shares went up to 50s 6d.

Murdoch was in Australia, on his way to keep an appointment in Melbourne, when he heard that Maxwell was about to increase his offer again. He got straight back into the plane, flew back to Sydney and took the next plane to London. At a meeting of the shareholders in the Connaught Rooms in London on 2 January 1969, Murdoch proposed a link-up between the *News of the World* organisation and his own News Ltd of Australia, by creating a further 5,100,000 ordinary shares of 5s each, to be allotted as fully paid-up to News Ltd. Maxwell grumbled that the law of the jungle had prevailed, but the voting was 4,500,000 for Murdoch's proposal to 3,240,000 against it. Murdoch was now the new boss of the *News of the World*. When at that point somebody asked him whether he intended to change the character of the paper, and he replied: 'Only after I've had a long, hard look', journalists realised what they might be in for.

Murdoch now had a foothold in Fleet Street, control of a very popular down-market Sunday, which still had the highest circulation (over 6,000,000) in Britain, and he was looking for another newspaper to utilise the spare, weekday printing capacity of his *News of the World* presses in Bouverie Street. Again, he didn't have very long to wait.

By this time King and Cudlipp were in bad trouble. The *Sun* was down below the million mark and by the spring of 1969 the combined losses on the *Daily Herald* and the *Sun* had totalled £2,702,000. Advertising revenue was still declining, the cost of newsprint was due to rise again by another £2 a ton and the future looked bleak. King had been hoping that either the *Mail* or the *Express* might have folded in the meantime but it hadn't happened and there just was not room in the market for another text-size popular paper like the *Sun*. The International Publishing Corporation decided to put it on the market.

At the last moment, Maxwell, still smarting from his failure to secure the *News of the World*, put in an extraordinary offer. He proposed to continue to run the newspaper free, as a committed Labour daily, published only in London with a smaller staff, printed at night on the *Evening Standard* presses and supervised by a trust. He offered the editorship in turn to Bob Edwards, then with the *People*, Geoffrey Pinnington of the *Mirror*, Mike Randall of the *Sunday Times* and William Davis of *Punch*. They all turned him down.

Rupert Murdoch then bought the *Sun*, printed it on the *News of the World* presses and went into direct competition with the *Daily Mirror*. He took the paper further down-market and with his editor Larry Lamb introduced an entirely new element in Fleet Street journalism: a daily, almost full-page, almost nude model on page three. Many of the famous Page Three girls were clearly completely nude, but carefully posed to avoid anything approaching the *Playboy* style of full frontal shots. The *Mirror* initially tried to fight back with its own near-nudes, but they did it with a coy, half-hearted sort of prudery that was bound to fail against Murdoch's cheerfully brash approach. The *Mirror* claimed that it would only show nipples when they were justified by the circumstances; in other words, when the picture was a still from a film in which the girl had appeared topless. For a time the nipple count of the two newspapers was closely watched in Fleet Street and bets were laid as to which of them would be the first to feature pubic hair. Long before it came to that, however, the *Mirror* sheered off on another line, reverting to what it had always done superbly: turning out an entertaining but basically serious tabloid capable of presenting the weightiest affairs of the day in terms that its readership could easily grasp.

However, for a variety of reasons there was now in England a near-illiterate readership, if that's not a contradiction in terms, which much preferred the Page Three girls to anything the *Mirror* had to offer in the way of erudition. Murdoch's new *Sun* with its vigorous style of reporting scandal, true or false, its near-nude girls and its racy approach to sport had an instant success of a sort that harked back to Northcliffe's early days or Cudlipp's *Sunday Pictorial*. Within four years sales had gone from under a million to over four, and now it was the *Mirror* that was fighting to save its place. It has since lost; sales in mid-summer 1988 were 4,146,000 for the *Sun* as against the *Mirror*'s 3,122,000. Even before the move to Wapping and the introduction of the highly economical new technology, Murdoch's *Sun* was earning £26,000,000 a year.

For a period after he took over *The Times*, Roy Thomson, by now Lord Thomson of Fleet, poured millions into it to try to keep his part of the bargain. Under William Rees-Mogg, who became editor in 1967, and Denis (later Sir Denis) Hamilton, brought over from the *Sunday Times* to bring it up to the magic half million, the circulation soared by some 70 per cent, but costs rose by 100 per cent. The paper, which had been losing £250,000 a year in 1965, was losing over a million a year by 1970.

Crisis followed crisis – particularly during the recession of 1975–6 – and the paper was dogged by labour troubles, which will be dealt with more fully in the next chapter. To add to *The Times*'s problems, Roy Thomson died in 1976. Realising only too well that the new computerised technology which they had been resisting for years would eventually lead to large-scale redundancies, the print and production unions became engaged in a series of strikes and go-slows which lost the paper tens of thousands of copies just at the precise moment when *The Times* needed the extra circulation to consolidate its position. Newspapers, unlike other mass-produced commodities, do not keep: if they miss the train, they have to be pulped.

People wanted to buy *The Times* by now, but they could not always get it. In the mid-seventies 200 newsagents and 30,000 other shopkeepers who stocked newspapers marched on Fleet Street in a protest against *The Times*'s failure to deliver copies regularly. *The Times* couldn't do anything about it and circulation fell from 450,000 in the sixties to 284,000 by 1978, when losses reached £2,000,000 a year. The Thomson organisation forced a show-down with the workers towards the end of 1978 giving them until 30 November to allow the introduction of the new technology; otherwise they would shut down the entire plant. The unions refused to negotiate under management threats of closure and despite a last-minute attempt in the House of Commons to avert the stoppage, Lord Kenneth Thomson closed down the paper and neither *The Times* nor the *Sunday Times* appeared for nearly a year.

For most of the century, the British public had enjoyed a far wider choice of independent newspapers than any other major nation. This wide choice now appeared to be about to become rather more restricted. *The Times* and the *Sunday Times* unthinkably remained shut down week after week. The *Observer* and *Daily Express* had both seemed as much a part of the English scene as roast beef and Yorkshire pudding or the Oxford and Cambridge boat race – the *Observer*, after all, had been there since 1791 and the *Daily Express* had been consistently successful since before the First World War. Yet by the end of the 1970s they too were both in bad trouble.

The first to find itself beset by difficulties was the *Observer*. Its sales had been hit both by the new *Sunday Telegraph* – first published in 1961 and still losing money but not nearly as much as the *Daily Telegraph* was making – and by Thomson's new *Sunday Times* with its colour magazine of 1962. In 1945 the Astor family had relinquished direct ownership of the *Observer* and had set up a Trust to run it, the profits of which were to go to charities connected with newspapers and journalism. In 1975, the *Observer* was losing nearly £750,000 a year and was in bad need of some charitable assistance itself.

David Astor, William Waldorf's grandson, and the paper's editor and effective proprietor, launched a ruthless programme to cut costs which involved cuts of up to one-third in the staff. For once the unions seemed to accept that the newspaper's difficulties were genuine and that some cuts would have to be made; after a long series of consultations, which included, inevitably, a strike and several go-slows, cuts of 25 per cent were made. They didn't work and within months, David Astor was looking for a buyer for his paper; the Astor millions had all gone. Astor resigned and found another American proprietor to take over the Trust. He was the Texas oil millionaire Robert Anderson, backed by his Atlantic Richfield Corporation; unbelievably, by 1976, the *Observer* was being run by an American oil company with its headquarters in Los Angeles.

Even after the sale of the *Observer*, nobody expected that the *Daily Express*, which had gone from strength to strength through the two wars and had continued to prosper after World War II, even when the *Daily Mirror* had briefly topped its circulation in the sixties and early seventies, would ever fall upon hard times. The firm was commercially sound; according to *Newspapers: The Power and The Money* by Simon Jenkins, £100 invested in Beaverbrook Newspapers in 1930 would have been worth £983 in 1960, compared with £171 if invested in Rothermere's Associated Newspapers Ltd, and this was before inflation had really started to bite into the pound. Unlike many of the other newspaper barons, Beaverbrook's prime interest had always been in his newspapers, the *Express* particularly, rather than money, or even power for its own sake. 'We are in the business of making newspapers,' he once said.

Accordingly, he had refused to diversify or protect the long-term future of his group in a rapidly changing world. He believed that too much diversification would damage his newspapers. On the other hand, his printing plant was antiquated by the sixties and over the years, investment had been minimal with profits generously distributed and put into family trusts. When he died in June 1964, aged 85, he had run the *Express* newspapers for fifty years; his son, Sir Max Aitken, who succeeded him, refused to take the title. 'There will only be one Lord Beaverbrook,' he said as he renounced the peerage. Up to that time he had not shown any great enthusiasm for newspapers; he was more interested in sailing, flying and enjoying himself generally, though he had a brilliant war record.

After his father's death he concentrated on the circulation of the *Express* which was still making money, though the *Evening Standard* – another of London's older papers which had been going since 1827 – was just as rapidly losing it. Aitken managed to get the *Express* circulation back to what it had been in the forties and fifties, but that was no longer enough. In 1971 Max Aitken, then 61, met the 72-year-old second Lord Rothermere (Harold's son Esmond) at his house in St James's to discuss merging the two groups and turning the *Daily Express, Evening Standard, Daily Mail, Daily Sketch* and *Evening News* – by now all losing money – into one morning and one evening newspaper. The idea might have been a good one from the point of view of the two companies concerned, but if it had happened at that time there would have been terrible redundancies among journalists and printers; however, in the event, their discussions came to nothing. Rothermere retired soon after the meeting and handed affairs over to his son Vere Harmsworth, born in 1925. The third Viscount Rothermere took over complete control of Associated Newspapers in 1971 and today, at 63, is the sole survivor of the first wave of Fleet Street barons.

Vere Harmsworth now proceeded to carry out his own rationalisation programme. He closed the company's ailing tabloid, the *Daily Sketch* – also badly hit by the *Sun* and unlike the *Mirror* unable to sustain the blow – which had been bought from Kemsley in 1953 and for a time, before the Murdoch take-over, was printed on the *News of the World* presses in Bouverie Street. By the 1960s its Tory working-class politics had brought its circulation down to 900,000, and the appearance of the *Sun* sealed its fate. Vere Harmsworth merged it with Northcliffe's *Daily Mail* and turned it into the new tabloid *Daily Mail* under David (now Sir David) English.

English succeeded in closing the gap between the *Mail* and the *Express* by appealing to a new readership, mainly middle-class, mainly Conservative, mainly young and female, and, by very skilful use of type-faces and layout, turned out a newspaper that looked far more like a miniature, easily manageable text paper than a true tabloid. At the same time Associated Newspapers were busy diversifying into North Sea oil, property, wood pulp, even restaurants, all of which managed to achieve a much higher ratio of profit to turnover than the newspapers had ever done. Before long the tabloid *Daily Mail* had a Sunday edition, the *Mail on Sunday* complete with colour magazine.

Beaverbrook newspapers were not so lucky. Long before the failure of the 1971 merger talks with Rothermere, Max Aitken had begun to show signs of something approaching panic which exhibited itself in the choice of a succession of different editors of the *Express* with totally different briefs. Derek Marks had been appointed editor in the late sixties to go after the *Telegraph* circulation; then in 1970 Ian McColl was brought in and instructed to go down-market and chase the *Mail* readership. John Coote, managing director, was replaced by Jocelyn Stevens, who had earlier been employed to brighten up the *Evening Standard*, and was now appointed chief executive. He closed the *Scottish Daily Express* which had been losing a great deal of money and raised £14,000,000 mainly in America, to buy new printing equipment. McColl in turn was replaced by Alistair (now Sir Alistair) Burnett, former editor of *The Economist* and subsequently a popular ITN television journalist, with instructions to go up-market again. Within a year dogged throughout with labour problems, he was replaced by Roy Wright who was instructed to lower the market profile once more.

Plans to turn the *Express* into a tabloid had to be postponed until 1977 because of what in these days is known as a negative cash flow (or at least an insufficiently positive one) and when Sir Max Aitken was ill, recovering from a stroke, Stevens went to Associated Newspapers and offered to sell them the *Evening Standard* for £10,000,000. The idea was that it was to be merged with the *Evening News* and the sale was intended to provide the cash needed to bail the *Daily Express* out of its financial difficulties. There was also talk of printing both the *Daily Express* and the *Daily Mail* on new plant the Beaverbrook company had bought to launch its tabloid version.

In the spring of 1977, plans for the merger of the *Evening News* and *Evening Standard* leaked out and Stevens found himself confronting Charles (now Sir Charles) Wintour, former editor and by then chairman of the *Standard*. At this stage Sir James Goldsmith, a 35 per cent holder in Beaverbrook shares, intervened, and there was a good deal of confusion which involved among others Lord Goodman, Rupert Murdoch, Rothschilds the bankers, and Tiny Rowland of LONRHO, a conglomeration of mining, transport and trading interests.

Rothschilds, it seems, had approached Nigel Broakes of Trafalgar House, the property amalgam which included the Cunard Steamship company and the Ritz Hotel; and Sir Max Aitken had gone to Rupert Murdoch looking for backing for his flagging papers. Murdoch made an offer of £10,000,000 in cash, but Jocelyn Stevens went back to Vere Harmsworth of Associated Newspapers who offered him an undertaking to keep the *Evening Standard* in existence plus a corporate merger and the added attraction of an amalgamated printing plant. Trafalgar House then raised the bid to £13,700,000 and gave an undertaking to retain the existing management. That clinched the matter. The Beaverbrook empire passed into the hands of Nigel Broakes and his partner, Victor Matthews (subsequently ennobled by Mrs Thatcher). Matthews was the man who had been manager of the building firm Trollop and

Colls when they had constructed the Beaver's black palace for him forty-five years earlier.

Right beside the *Express* building stands the staid and sober headquarters of the *Daily Telegraph*. Here, aloof from all this wheeling and dealing, Lord Camrose's second son, Michael Berry, was running, as editor-in-chief and chairman, the extremely prosperous *Telegraph* group, which included the *Sunday Telegraph* launched in 1961 and a couple of colour magazines. In 1968 Michael Berry was made a life peer by the Labour Government and became Lord Hartwell. The *Daily Telegraph* was a private company and therefore never published detailed accounts but it was common knowledge that it was the success of the daily which kept the whole group going.

William Deedes, now Lord Deedes, its editor from 1974 to 1986, and still an editorial executive and contributing to its columns regularly, makes no secret of having been part at least of the inspiration for the character of William Boot in Evelyn Waugh's novel *Scoop*. He was then a foreign correspondent for the *Morning Post*, which was amalgamated with the *Telegraph* in 1937. He has since been lobby correspondent for the *Telegraph*, he spent years on the back benches of the House of Commons as Conservative MP for Ashford, Kent, he did a stint as Minister without portfolio, and, as editor of the *Daily Telegraph*, he gave the newspaper's ever-growing readership (160,000 in 1930; 1,250,000 in 1960; 1,400,000 in 1970) exactly what was wanted.

As the inevitable show-down with the unions appeared to be looming – for the *Telegraph*, as it was for the remainder of the papers in the street – the *Telegraph* seemed in many ways the best-equipped of all the national newspapers to cope with it. It was outselling the rest of the quality market by a huge margin and it carried more classified and display advertising than any of them. It had perhaps one weakness: alone in Fleet Street it was not part of any great conglomerate and didn't even possess one single paper mill.

The other papers which seemed equally sure of their identity when the closure of *The Times* newspapers for almost a full year brought the whole of Fleet Street to its senses, included the *Sunday Times*, now a 'quasi-quality' paper offering the well-heeled, high-spending middle-brows a mix, as Simon Jenkins puts it, of 'a preoccupation with consumer durables and sensational investigative reporting'. The success of the *Sun* had been very simple; it just did, under Murdoch and its editor at this period Larry (now Sir Larry) Lamb, what the old *News of the World* had been doing, but it did it every day, and rather more slickly. It was successful in finding a new market far further down-market than anybody had ever suspected a market to exist. Perhaps it hadn't existed before that period.

The *Guardian*, for years largely subsidised by its very successful stable-mate, the *Manchester Evening News*, was well protected from all predators by the Scott Trust. This was a self-elected body of what might well be described as typical *Guardian* readers – usually including several senior ex-members of the editorial staff – who constituted the real proprietorship of the paper and ensured its continuation 'on the same lines and in the same spirit as heretofore', a phrase from the will of the son of the founder, John Edward Taylor.

In the late fifties and throughout the sixties, and notably after the move down to London, the *Guardian* found a new market in the booming education industry and became the prime advertising medium for the schools, universities and Further Education colleges. Consequently it was favourite reading matter both of the growing number of men and women who made teaching their career, and of those determined that their offspring should get the best possible education. Its sales climbed steadily from 160,000 in 1956 to 350,000 in 1973, as against *The Times*'s 340,000. Throughout the entire period it maintained a very high standard of journalism.

In the meantime, the two London financial papers, the *Financial News* and the *Financial Times*, started to shape their own future. Immediately after World War Two, in October 1945, they merged to form a new six-page *Financial Times*, retaining the eye-catching pink newsprint adopted by the *Financial Times* in 1893 but incorporating a great many of the ideas of the bright young journalists on the *Financial News* about widening the appeal of the paper by including industrial and even general news, including the arts and the theatre. The merger had been the inspiration of Brendan Bracken, after whom the *Financial Times*'s headquarters, right beside St Paul's Cathedral, were subsequently named. Bracken, an Australian of Irish origin, had been Churchill's Minister of Propaganda in the War Cabinet.

Throughout the fifties and sixties, the paper's layout and make-up changed dramatically and its size increased to forty-eight pages per issue. Editorial coverage now embraced general, political and economic news as well as news about the arts and it was rapidly becoming a formidable competitor for the *Guardian* and *The Times*.

The ownership changed in 1957 when the Pearson group – an amalgam whose publishing interests at that time included the Westminster Press, Longman and Penguin Books, and despite the name had nothing to do with the old Arthur Pearson empire – bought the *Financial Times* from Lord Camrose. Under Lord Cowdray, head of the Pearson group, the *Financial Times* rode the crest of the booming economic wave and achieved record advertising and circulation figures. During 1986, circulation passed the 250,000 mark, with a quarter of the sales coming from overseas. Today, printing in New York as well as London and Frankfurt, it has become a genuinely worldwide paper. It was among the first of the Fleet Street newspapers to announce a radical change in its printing techniques in 1986, which included a £70,000,000 investment in new plant in London's Docklands.

While the proprietors of the newspapers which had been battling for survival throughout the seventies were busy with mergers and takeovers and rationalisations – not to speak of ever-increasing trouble with the print unions – the editors and journalists, managers and circulation and promotion men were equally busy trying to sell yet more papers for their bosses.

One method which they used has come to be known as cheque-book journalism, the practice of buying up the exclusive rights to anybody who happens to be in the news; in effect they were usually what were quaintly called 'vice girls' – typified in the public mind by Christine Keeler and Mandy Rice Davis – international spies, moles, spy-catchers, double-agents and criminals of all kinds. The decent British public, if consulted about it, would probably claim to deplore this practice of paying out vast sums of money to people whose only claim to fame is that they broke the law by stealing or murdering, pimping or whoring, dealing in drugs, or worse, but it worked. It sold newspapers because even the people who most fervently disapproved of cheque-book journalism in principle were avid readers of the revelations that resulted from it.

On a higher plane, the investigative journalism of the quality papers achieved more or less the same goal via a different route; it often provided sensational revelations about people in high places. A lot of investigative journalism was solid and sincere and performed an extremely useful public service – the investigations of the *Sunday Times* team under Harold Evans into thalidomide and other medical matters and many of the Insight inquests, for example – but a great deal of it boiled down to just another form of invasion of privacy for the sake of selling newspapers, and it too worked.

The increasingly important part played by women in the conduct of the world's affairs generally was echoed, if not indeed pre-empted, in Fleet Street. What had always been a predominantly, almost monastically, male world – apart from a few agony aunts and the writers on fashion and household matters – was increasingly invaded at all levels by women in all the roles formerly reserved for men. Women began to appear in the newspaper columns as motoring correspondents, wine experts, financial advisors, aviation authorities, even war correspondents. They began to infiltrate the editorial floors in such capacities as sub-editors, features editors, art editors and ultimately as editors. It is true that when the *Daily Mirror* first appeared in 1903 it was edited by a woman; but that experiment was not repeated again until more than three-quarters of a century later when in 1987 Wendy Henry became editor of the *News of the World*. In the same year, another woman journalist, Eve Pollard, was appointed editor of the *Sunday Mirror*; by 1989 there were three female editors of traditional newspapers.

Another way by which the ailing newspapers sought to increase circulation was by offering big cash prizes in competitions. Most of the competitions were run on an accumulative basis; if there was no winner for several weeks, the prize money got bigger and bigger, until it had reached an impressive total when it was usually won by someone quite unaccustomed to handling vast sums of money who promptly went berserk. These competitions certainly boosted circulation, but not on any permanent basis. People who buy a newspaper to win £10,000 in a lottery are very quick to switch to another as soon as the big prize has gone, because they know that the newspaper which has just paid out will take time to recover. This method of selling newspapers reached its climax in the Bingo war of the early eighties, which I shall deal with later.

Most of these devices to increase newspaper sales were publicised by yet another means: expensive campaigns on the commercial television and radio networks which also produced surges in circulation which did not stick. People intrigued by the publicity for the Christine Keeler story in the *News of the World* might buy it for a couple of weeks while the story was running, but they would then go back to the paper they had always taken on a Sunday. On the other hand, because of union problems, the Sundays were not always available.

The Ten Years War
for the New Technology

The root cause of all the difficulties experienced by the
newspapers in the late sixties, throughout the seventies and in
the early eighties was the cost of production by the continued
use of nineteenth century hot metal printing practices, or
expensive compromises between the old and the new technology, combined with the loss of countless millions of copies of the
papers through constant labour disputes.

Anybody who has ever worked in a newspaper office in the
old hot metal days could give a hundred examples of the sort of
wasteful restrictive practices that were costing the newspaper
proprietors so much money and aggravation at this period.
Basically they were all variants on the same theme: the unions
had no objection at all to the introduction of new, labour-
saving techniques provided that precisely the same number of
men (or more) were employed at the same (or higher) wages
for doing (or not doing) the job involved. Thus when
newspapers started to use a punched tape system which
produced a signal which could be sent along a wire to duplicate
linotype setting in two or more centres, the unions raised no
objections provided that a fully qualified linotype operator sat
at each machine that was being worked automatically by
remote control. The operator might then read a novel or do
whatever he chose to do to pass the time while the machine was
doing all the work, provided, of course, that he was paid at
exactly the same rate as if he had been doing all the work
himself.

That is basically what it was all about and if anybody says it
should have been stopped long before it reached the stage at
which Thomson had to close down *The Times* newspapers
indefinitely, or before Murdoch was forced into plotting the
retreat to Fortress Wapping, the answer is that these practices

started when Northcliffe and Rothermere and Beaverbrook were making millions out of their newspapers. If their managers had come to them and urged them to take a stand against the unions before it was too late they wouldn't have agreed. This was for two reasons: they felt that they couldn't really complain if the workers on the floor wanted a slice of the prosperity they were so obviously enjoying, and they also wanted the production of their newspapers to continue at all costs, for fear of losing out to their competitors.

Until Roy Thomson and Rupert Murdoch appeared on the scene, none of the press barons was in the game of newspaper production purely for the money. Some of them, like Beaverbrook, were rich already; others like Northcliffe and Rothermere became very rich but their prime interest was always in the newspapers, and in the power and prestige those newspapers conferred on them. They wanted their papers out there selling in the streets and over the years they always preferred to pay up if there was a union dispute, rather than face a show-down and a stoppage, or a strike. Once the unions came up against men like Matthews, Thomson and Murdoch, who were in the newspaper business mainly to make a profit out of it, they found that the rules of the game had been very drastically changed.

The newspaper industry was the last mass-production industry conducted right in the very heart of London, and everybody concerned with it should have realised, long before they did, that it would have to move out, like all the other industries over the past century to greener pastures, far outside the city centre where land was cheaper and more plentiful, where parking was feasible and the arrival and departure of dispatch lorries less of a headache.

From the early 1970s a form of computer technology was available and in use in many provincial papers as well as in the States and elsewhere. Operators used a keyboard with a monitor screen which produced type on paper which could be cut and pasted down to form a page. Each page was then photographed and transferred to a polymer printing plate, which could be used on the old Hoe rotaries. This meant that journalists and advertising staff could type their copy straight into the computers and sub-editors and lay-out men could assemble the paper in the form of paste-ups. This threatened the members of the National Graphical Association (NGA), an amalgamation since 1964 of the skilled and semi-skilled societies which had stemmed from some of the old printing crafts and guilds. Each of them had its own 'chapel' and its own Father of Chapel (FOC) demarcating and jealously guarding the various skills involved in the early printing processes and designed to ensure limited entry, a lengthy apprenticeship and a permanent shortage of staff. Now the NGA sought to retain control by insisting that access to computers was the preserve of its members, and that everything that appeared in a newspaper produced by a computer would have to have been fed in by an NGA member.

This came before a whole host of problems caused by the arrival of earlier automated processes had been resolved. To take just one small example, when the new bailing and stacking machines were introduced, they stood unused in their packing cases for years, while men continued to count the copies of the newspapers by hand – ignoring the fact that this was already being done automatically by the printing presses – wrapped them up in brown paper parcels, tied with string, and finally stuck on to each parcel a label indicating its destination, using a paste pot and brush.

The principal unions involved, apart from the NGA, and the journalists' union, the NUJ, were NATSOPA (the National Society of Operative Printers and Assistants), SOGAT (the Society of Graphic and Allied Trades) and SLADE (the Society of Lithographic Artists, Designers and Engravers). These unions have amalgamated, split and re-amalgamated, NATSOPA and SOGAT emerging in 1982 as SOGAT 82 under Brenda Dean as general secretary; these days the FOC frequently turns out to be an MOC (Mother of Chapel).

SOGAT 82 covered distribution, packing and loading, messengers, copy boys, copy takers, librarians, telephonists, cleaners and tea ladies. There were a few more esoteric unions, for example RIRMA, the Revisers, Ink- and Roller-Makers and Auxiliaries. The jealously guarded customs and practices of some of the unions went back a long time; some of the NGA customs to 1785 when the first ever trade union agreement was struck between the master printers and the compositors' union setting out a scale of piece-work charges. The use of the terms Chapel and Father of Chapel probably hark back to the days when the production of manuscripts was very largely confined to the monasteries.

The pre-entry closed shop was a tradition in the industry long before the Northcliffe revolution. A printer would enter the trade somewhere other than in Fleet Street, which had no apprenticeship scheme. When a vacancy occurred in Fleet Street, it was notified by the chapel concerned, not to the newspaper's management, but to the London branch of the relevant union. The vacancy was either filled by the chapel itself from among a pool of friends and relatives or was not filled and the money would simply be shared out among existing chapel members who theoretically would thereafter work that much harder.

Casuals, both on the printing and journalistic sides of the business, have always been a feature of the Fleet Street scene; also many staff workers had a second job, doubling as a casual, often under an assumed name. A printer in pre-Wapping days never retired; in some of the papers as many as two-thirds of the 'regular casuals' were over 65. Over the years the print unions had built up the most elaborate system of pricing their work to guarantee them their place among the richest members of the working-classes: so much per thousand 'ems' (the space taken up by the letter 'm'); a bit extra for larger or smaller type, a third extra for manuscript or 'bad' copy; a quarter extra for lists of names, racing cards or football results; a half extra for copy in any language other than English; and at the rate of one line for every word in Greek. Charges were even made for work that was never done, because of a stoppage somewhere else in the plant, for example, or for advertisement copy set not in the newspaper office itself but in some advertising agency. Also there was an arrangement by which operators were paid for leaving blank spaces between the lines of type under which a man who had set fifty lines of type and had been instructed to space them out widely, could charge for having set 100, 200, or even 250 lines.

Then there was the system by which compositors working on papers like the *Sun*, which ran short stories, were paid at a far higher rate than comps working on papers like *The Times* which used a lot of words. These systems had resulted by the early 1980s in some *Sun* printers breaking the £1,000 a week barrier, while linotype operators on high-setting papers like the *Telegraph* were averaging £400 a week for a four-day week, usually compressed into three nights.

There were also the cuts and the blows. Introduced to give printers a fair deal, they were soon incorporated into all agreements. If an edition went to press ahead of time, the printers were allowed to take a cut; then a one-hour cut became the standard, and if an edition required the men to work a full shift in order to get the paper away on time, the operators had to be paid an hour's overtime, or other men had to be taken on to cover the extra hour. Conversely, after a very heavy news story, which might entail a particularly arduous job of production, the print unions were traditionally allowed to take a blow, a short rest period; then blows were written in to all agreements. By carefully manipulating cuts and blows, men could sign on at one paper, then walk around the corner and sign on for a later shift at another paper; this was known as 'double-banking'.

Ghost shifts were built into a negotiated manning level on the assumption of a much higher level of production than that genuinely anticipated by the union. If these extra shifts were for any reason required, the chapel instructed its members to work harder or, more frequently, demanded more staff. At the *Telegraph*, in the late 1960s, the manning level in the machine room for a 28-page paper was 306 shifts; in practice only about 250 men ever turned up for work. The remainder were 'ghosts' whose wage packets were shared out among the 250 who reported. In order to make it look as if the agreed number of men were being employed, the men who turned up often signed more than once, using false names; and an indication of their arrogant attitude to the whole business was the fact that no attempt was ever made to invent credible pseudonyms. Mickey Mouse or Charles Chaplin were good enough.

Throughout the sixties there had been various attempts to negotiate comprehensive house agreements, but the unions always found ways of getting around them and things got worse instead of better. In the 1970s the union leaders and the newspaper proprietors formed a joint standing committee to consider all the implications of the new technology. In 1976 this committee produced its 'Programme for Action' which proposed flexibility on staff reductions on the union side in return for new pensions and redundancy arrangements. The union leaders recommended acceptance but the programme was thrown out by the NGA chapels by a majority of 80 per cent.

There were also attempts by individual proprietors to make their own compromises with the unions. In 1975, the *Financial Times*, now a quality general newspaper with a circulation approaching that of *The Times* (190,000), announced a plan for conversion to the new technology with generous safeguards and redundancy payments in return for an end to all demarcation disputes and allowing a measure of direct access to the computers by non-NGA staff. Negotiations dragged on for two years, the *Financial Times* expanded its sales with a European edition published in Frankfurt and when the paper went over to partial computer typesetting in 1981, it was on the basis of normal demarcation with computer access reserved for NGA members.

When Cecil King was sacked from the *Daily Mirror* in 1968 by his fellow directors for endangering the group's future by his interference in national affairs – unlike the other press barons, King was a salaried employee of the Group and held only about 5 per cent of the shares – the *Daily Mirror* passed through a difficult period. Murdoch's *Sun* had ended its role as the most popular working-class paper and in 1970 a merger took place with the Reed Group to form Reed International. The *Mirror* group – which as King's International Publishing Corporation had been the lion wagging a tail that included, among others, the Reed subsidiary, producing newsprint in its own mills – now found that Reed International had become the lion and controlled the IPC. Hugh Cudlipp, who had succeeded Cecil King as chairman of the IPC empire, found himself in charge only of the editorial division of the empire as deputy chairman (editorial) of Reed International. Cudlipp retired, as he had always said he would, in 1972 when he reached the age of sixty and in 1973–4, for the first time since World War II, the *Mirror* started to lose money.

Alex (now Sir Alex) Jarratt, who took over as chairman of Reed International in 1975, produced the *Mirror*'s white paper for introducing the new technology under the title 'Programme for Survival'. Negotiations went on for two years, an agreement was finally signed in 1977, and by 1979 whole pages of the *Daily Mirror* were being computer-set, but as a result of last-ditch interventions by the chapels, at an astronomical additional cost (Fleet Street estimates put the price of achieving the change-over as high as £3,000,000). The NGA had proved a point: if their industrial muscle could not prevent the proprietors from installing the new technology, it could still make the operation disastrously expensive.

At the *Observer*, where the unions had earlier agreed to a reduction in manning to help out in Astor's time, the Atlantic Richfield Corporation (ARCO) had spent over $2,000,000 in just four years, mainly to pay for the higher circulation which had resulted from the closing down of *The Times* newspapers in 1978, when the sale of the *Observer* had almost doubled from 670,000 to over 1,120,000. The NGA machine-minders now decided to increase the number of shifts to the level at which they had been in Astor's time, threatened strike action and finally accepted the management's final offer which amounted to about £100 for a single night's work. ARCO headquarters in

Los Angeles decided that they could no longer conduct an industrial war of these proportions from 5,000 miles away and, in February 1981, a secret deal was made under which the paper went to Tiny Rowland and LONRHO's Scottish publishing subsidiary, Outrams. On the *Observer*, the chapels had achieved a sell-out before the question of the new technology had even been mentioned.

Within a few months of taking over the *Express* newspapers, Victor Matthews of the Trafalgar House group was in his turn running into trouble with the unions. In September 1977, the skilled maintenance engineers in the *Daily Express* went on strike for parity with the highest paid workers in the plant. Matthews claimed that they had sacked themselves when production stopped and he refused to take those responsible back on to the payroll. After arbitration, the union agreed to end a variety of restrictive practices and Matthews was forced to reinstate them.

He then turned his attention to the editorial content of the paper. He took Derek Jameson from the *Daily Mirror* to replace Roy Wright as editor and instructed him to go after the *Mirror* readership. The *Daily Express* was relaunched as a tabloid with plenty of pretty girls and a down-market image. The circulation picked up a bit, at a cost to Trafalgar House of £5,000,000 a year in promotion, but then started to slide again and by 1979 was down to 2,400,000, a quarter of a million less than it had been selling when Trafalgar House acquired it.

The next ploy was the production of the *Daily Star*, a tabloid printed in Manchester, to compete initially with Murdoch's *Sun* in the north of England, but eventually to have nation-wide distribution. The Manchester option looked for a time as if it might provide the answer to the proprietors' problems; management–union relationships were much better in Manchester and printers' earnings were way below the Fleet Street level. The unions on the *Daily Star* retaliated by insisting on full London manning levels and rates of pay and were largely successful. The paper was not a commercial success and soon fell from its initial sale of about a million to half that and its losses continued to add to the burdens on Trafalgar House, though the *Express* newspapers share of the market did increase from 17 per cent to 22 per cent.

In 1982 Trafalgar House floated the *Express* group away into a separate public company, Fleet Holdings. Jameson was replaced by Christopher Ward, also from the *Mirror*. He was sacked in turn and replaced by the *Sun*'s Larry Lamb. The *Express* circulation continued to drop, dipping below two million in 1983, before it was rescued by the very costly Bingo operation, referred to earlier and on page 103.

With Rothermere, Matthews had already formed, in 1980, a subsidiary to merge the former's loss-making *Evening News* and his own *Evening Standard* into a new paper. To be printed by the *Express* group with Rothermere's editor, Louis Kirby, in charge, it was eventually to be called the *London Evening Standard*. This transaction turned the losses on the old Beaverbrook *Evening Standard* into a very valuable piece of real estate property in Shoe Lane which could now be sold off, not to mention a £4,000,000 a year contract for printing the new merged evening paper on his Fleet Street presses. But so far Matthews had not attempted to introduce the full new computer technology.

When Lord Thomson died in 1976, his son Kenneth Thomson fully accepted his father's commitment to *The Times* and the *Sunday Times*. Although he was living in Toronto, where the holding company of his International Thomson Organisation was based, he was fully prepared to honour it until the journalists went on strike in August 1980.

Roy Thomson had always said that as long as he had the support of the journalists he would continue to fund *The Times* and Kenneth Thomson thought that by striking for a twenty-one per cent increase after they had been paid in full during the year long shut-down was a betrayal that released him from his commitment to finance *The Times* out of his own resources.

Accordingly, after a series of meetings in the weeks following the journalists' strike, the board of Thomson British Holdings put the two papers, *The Times* and the *Sunday Times*, up for sale. The Thomson Organisation had already put more than seventy million pounds into the papers; in the current year a pre-tax loss of some fifteen million pounds was expected, with further borrowings of about twenty-two million from Thomson British Holdings. According to *The Story of The Times* by Oliver Wood and James Bishop, Lord Kenneth Thomson commented, 'My father and I have repeatedly made it clear that our continued support for *The Times* newspaper was conditional on the overall co-operation of the newspaper employees.'

The Times group's plans for introducing the new technology had been introduced in 1976 under the title '*Opportunity for Success*'. This plan involved giving journalists direct access to the computers as well as manning cuts in all departments. Installation of the new machinery was to begin in 1977. The Thomson Organisation agreed not to take any profits out of *The Times* newspapers for five years to enable the plan to be implemented.

When a series of industrial disputes began seriously to affect the production of *The Times* and the *Sunday Times*, *The Times* management, alone in Fleet Street, dug in their heels and decided to enforce their pay policy. They knew that there was no point in expecting any help from the other proprietors; Murdoch had tried to achieve a united front against the unions' demands back in 1973 but Sir Max Aitken could not bring himself to shut down the *Daily Express* for the sake of the *Sun*.

In April 1978 the board of the Thomson Organisation agreed to support *The Times* management, led by Gordon Brunton and 'Duke' Hussey – Brunton was an ex-Odham's man and Hussey was from Associated Newspapers – in a stand against the unions. Taking a leaf from the book of the *New York Times* which in 1974 had managed to survive a long shut-down in order to wring an agreement from the unions on the new technology, *The Times* management insisted on agreements from about 60 chapels on the 'Opportunity for Success' package or a complete close-down. The *Washington Post* had also survived a show-down with the print unions; the machine men sabotaged the presses but the *Post* lost only one edition during the 139-day strike. About 300 amateurs, using the new technology, did all the print work which had formerly been done by 1,220 craft workers.

The Times's ultimatum ran out in November 1978, by which time only 19 of the chapels involved had voted on the issues involved. Both titles were back on the streets in just under a year's time, but in the 17 weeks after the end of shut-down the *Sunday Times* only completed its full run ten times. Production delays were blamed for the low circulation of *The Times* which dipped to 300,000. By August 1980, *The Times* newspapers were down by £40,000,000, largely as a result of the stoppage, which had not helped the rest of Fleet Street either. In the short term, the *Guardian* and the *Observer* both lost money through *The Times* shut-down since their sudden expansion and subsequent contraction led to financial and industrial difficulties.

The Thomson Organisation had had enough. They put the papers on the market and threatened that if no buyer had come forward by March 1981 the papers would be closed down. The interested parties included Rupert Murdoch, Robert Maxwell, Lord Rothermere, Tiny Rowland of LONRHO, Sir James Goldsmith, Lord Matthews, Lord Barnetson (of the provincial chain, United Newspapers, who was soon to be succeeded by David Stevens), the American shipping magnate James Sherwood, the Aga Khan, the Australian entrepreneur Robert Holmes a' Court, and even the Atlantic Richfield Company, despite the difficulties they had already encountered in Fleet Street over the *Observer*. *The Times* management favoured Murdoch and so did the journalists in the group, as well as the unions.

Murdoch was thus able to add *The Times* and the *Sunday Times* to his stable.

By 1981 it was becoming abundantly clear to everyone, apart from some union leaders, that a final solution would have to be found to the impasse and that that final solution must lie in a total break with traditional union practices and in the introduction of all the new technology.

There was, however, one big snag. Legislation introduced by the Thatcher Conservative Government had made it a great deal easier to force a show-down with the unions by penalising them financially for the secondary picketing, which had caused so much trouble in Fleet Street whenever a father of chapel or a shop steward took exception to some editorial comment on the miners, or an anti-Labour cartoon, or a news story about the strike at the Grunwick photographic laboratories. Nevertheless, the installation of the new computerised machinery involved a vast outlay of capital, to say nothing of the amount of money involved in compensation for the thousands of workers who would be made redundant by the operation. Many of Fleet Street's proprietors just did not have that kind of money.

Then, just at exactly the right moment, a genie appeared from the wings in the form of Reuters news agency. In 1983, at the very height of the Fleet Street crisis, Reuters declared its first profit in 41 years and distributed over £1,900,000 to its shareholders, most of them national or provincial newspaper proprietors. This fact would not in itself have meant very much, nor would the amount of money distributed. What was important lay behind this sudden ability on the part of Reuters to pay a dividend on shares which for years had been regarded as hardly worth any more than the paper upon which they were printed. What had happened behind the scenes was that Reuters had been developing a sophisticated electronic successor to the old ticker-tape which used to flash stock prices around the world. Ticker-tape was slow and tended to fall behind in times of crisis when absolutely up-to-the-minute information was required. Also, physically, it was messy; you had to rummage around among miles of tape to find the bit you needed, and there was no easy way of displaying it so that prices could be compared at a glance.

These disadvantages were a mere inconvenience when the world's stock exchanges were primarily concerned with stocks and shares in the public companies, normally a fairly slow-moving business. But the speed and flexibility of the new electronic system became vital when in December 1971 the old Bretton Woods Agreement collapsed. This agreement had had the effect of keeping the major world currencies virtually frozen in relation to one another. It was replaced by the Smithsonian Agreement by which the major world currencies could fluctuate according to supply and demand. This meant that it suddenly became extremely profitable for the world's top financiers to start dealing, not in stocks and shares, but in money. Slight fluctuations in the value of the pound as against the dollar, occasioned, say, by a rise in the interest rate in England, could mean a fortune if you knew about it early enough and could buy and sell instantaneously.

There was, however, no equivalent to Wall Street, or the stock exchanges of London, Hong Kong and Tokyo where such instant deals could be made, so Reuters supplied one: an electronic money market-place, known as Reuters Monitor Service. It took off with the acceleration of a space rocket. By the end of 1981, when rising inflation everywhere and the spiralling price of oil had aggravated the uncertainties of uncontrolled currencies, subscribers to the Monitor Service in New York and London, Moscow and Tokyo were able to do their deals in under four seconds, eleven seconds faster than they could by telephone, always assuming that they could get through instantly. By this time Reuters' new financial services were contributing more than 90 per cent of the agency's total income, and revenue had shot up from £13,800,000 to £180,000,000 in less than ten years.

In 1983, Reuters – still run by a Trust whose chairman now was Sir Denis Hamilton, former editor of the *Sunday Times* and editor-in-chief of *The Times* newspapers – needed money for research and development to keep ahead of its rivals in this new and highly expensive field of information technology. Many of the shareholders, supported by Sir Denis himself, felt that their obligation to the Trust, which had been formed in 1941 to protect the news agency from predators, carried far more

weight than the company's executives' arguments that the only
way they could get their hands on the money they so badly
needed for development was by going public. But other
shareholders – notably Matthews of the *Express* group –
favoured going public because shares which had been almost
worthless for years could now be cashed in to provide the
money they needed to buy new plant and equipment and pay
off redundant workers. Murdoch, a big shareholder in Reuters
by virtue of his ownership of *The Times*, the *Sunday Times*, the *Sun*
and the *News of the World* – to say nothing of his provincial
newspapers – was strongly in favour of floating the company,
and this was reported in the financial pages of *The Times* though
it was denied by Sir Denis Hamilton, still chairman of *The
Times* Newspapers.

There was a great deal of confusion over many issues. Over
shares which had been transferred from one newspaper group
to another, for example, following the collapse of a paper like
the *News Chronicle*. Over the fact that the *Financial Times* had
signed the initial agreement on the same terms as a Sunday
newspaper and was now a flourishing daily, challenging *The
Times*. Over the situation of the racing guide, *Sporting Life*,
which held a bigger interest in Reuters than the *Sunday Times*.

There was much wrangling behind closed doors in the
Newspaper Publishers' Association, and considerable opposition from Lord Hartwell, proprietor of the *Telegraph*, who was
implacably opposed to any move which might undermine the
agency's independence and integrity as a news agency.
However, the Reed Paper Group started the ball rolling by
floating the *Mirror* newspaper group on the stock market in
1984, on the back of the *Mirror*'s stake in Reuters, now said to
be worth £78,000,000. Sir Alex Jarratt, Reed's chairman, may
have thought that the *Mirror* group could remain independent
as a public company, but within a year, it was snapped up by
Maxwell for £113,000,000, including the Reuters shares. A
scheme for flotation was drawn up containing what were
meant to be safeguards for the agency's independence, along
with an updating of the Trust and a re-assertation of its

authority and duty to supply unbiased news. Reuters went public on 5 June 1983 on the London and New York stock exchanges.

The flotation of Reuters with an initial valuation of over £800,000,000, a figure which was subsequently trebled, gave the newspapers, which owned the bulk of the shares, a much-needed injection of capital at just the right time. Fleet Holdings, whose *Express* newspapers were not doing at all well, was suddenly worth an extra £56,000,000. Matthews immediately diversified into other media, something Beaverbrook had always been reluctant to do, buying a 31 per cent share in TV-am. Associated Newspapers, whose *Daily Mail* had been losing money heavily, found itself richer by about the same amount. The *Guardian* picked up £28,000,000, the *Daily Telegraph* £26,000,000.

This windfall gave the publishers a chance to escape from Fleet Street to the wide open spaces, where land would be a lot cheaper and a once-and-for-all chance of standing up to the printing union chapels also seemed to be on offer. A new tax haven, the developing Docklands, beckoned invitingly, and there was the added temptation of the value of their Fleet Street premises as real estate. This had been very sharply brought home to them when the City of London School for Boys, off Tudor Street, was sold to Morgan Guaranty Company for £96 million.

Murdoch was the first to make a move. He had already realised that a new plant would be needed to accommodate his enormous new empire and was building one on a 13-acre site in the old London docks at Wapping. Not far away, on the Isle of Dogs, printing plants were soon being built for the *Guardian* and the *Daily Telegraph*. The *Daily Mail* had booked a site in Surrey Docks. It was well known at the time that the *Mirror* group and the *Financial Times* had also booked space in the docklands. Initially they were intended as printing plants with all the typesetting continuing, for the time being anyway, in London and the facsimile, pasted-up pages being transmitted electronically to the docks.

Murdoch's plant was ready by 1984 but his negotiators resolutely refused to accept chapel demands which would have made printing at Wapping just as expensive as it had ever been in Bouverie Street. Murdoch could afford to wait, but the *Daily Telegraph* could not. It now had £60,000,000 worth of machinery due to be ready for use in 1986 on the Isle of Dogs and in Manchester. Lord Hartwell badly needed the £20,000,000 a year that he hoped the new plant would save him. After repeated attempts to reach agreement with the unions which resulted only in a deal on the basis of already existing demarcations, he tried to raise the £60,000,000 the machinery had cost, plus another £3,000,000, which he would need for redundancy payments, by offering up to half of the equity to new shareholders. When 14 per cent of the shares, worth about £10,000,000, were not taken up, a bid was made in June 1985 by the Canadian businessman, Conrad Black. By December of that year, bidding against the Al Fayed brothers – who had not long earlier bought Harrods department store – David Stephens of the United Newspapers provincial group, and the Australian Fairfax group, Black managed to secure 51 per cent of the shares for another £30,000,000 cash. He installed the editor of *The Economist*, Andrew Knight, to run the newspaper and Lord Hartwell remained, but only as titular chairman. His second son, Adrian Berry, stayed as the *Telegraph*'s science correspondent. For all practical purposes, the Berrys were now out of the business, though the family still retains 11 per cent of the shares.

The Reuters windfall also had the effect of making Fleet Holdings, the *Daily Express* newspaper group, more attractive to investors. In 1985, David Stevens of the provincial United Newspapers group won control of the old Beaverbrook empire with a bid of £317,000,000, £70,000,000 more than the market value of his own company. Matthews withdrew from the scene after only a very brief spell as a press baron, later retiring as chairman of the *Standard* company, still jointly owned by Rothermere and the Trafalgar House group. Rothermere, the only survivor of the original Fleet Street dynasties, bought out the Trafalgar House half-share and was able to enjoy the luxury of a London evening newspaper monopoly, as well as his very successful *Daily Mail*. The *Daily Express* went tabloid in January 1977.

It was beginning to look as if the war to introduce the new technology was over, and that the Fleet Street unions had been the victors. While the *News of the World* and the *Sun* were still being printed on antiquated presses – two of them nicknamed the *Flying Scotsman* and the *African Queen* after railway locomotives because of record runs they had made in the thirties – the new plants at Wapping and the Isle of Dogs built by Murdoch and the *Daily Telegraph* were lying idle and nobody knew precisely how many other Fleet Street newspapers had invested in a costly move that now did not look as if it was ever going to take place. After the failure of the 'Programme for Action' at *The Times*, it seemed as if any joint effort across the industry would fail, though *The Times* senior management consoled themselves with the thought that someone would have to take on the unions, sooner or later. Murdoch, the only proprietor with enough fire-power to hold out against the unions, had backed down, or so it appeared. The *Express* and the *Mirror* had both seriously considered the possibility of printing in Manchester or elsewhere; and *The Times* had contemplated printing in Nottingham or even Frankfurt.

Almost all the Fleet Street newspapers were still being set by turn-of-the-century linotype machines whose operators were averaging around £400 a week. The machines they used set type about as fast as a moderately competent secretary, say about 60–70 words a minute or the equivalent in newspaper terms of approximately 12–14 column lines per minute. By now Murdoch and the *Telegraph* had photosetting machines capable of turning signals from computer inputs into the equivalent of type – the so-called cold type – at the rate of 4,000 column lines per minute.

As one of the tabloids might have put it, the familiar rattle of the linotype machines turned out to be Fleet Street's death rattle.

The Retreat
to Fortress Wapping

For a time it looked as if the Wapping option had disappeared down the tubes along with the Manchester option, as the newspapers continued to be produced in the same old way on the same old machines with all the same old demarcation disputes and demands for extra men cropping up all the time to halt production and lose the proprietors tens of thousands of copies of the paper and tens of thousands of pounds. Among the newspaper executives frustrated beyond endurance by the disputes and stoppages, feelings ran very high; in at least one office the phrase 'the new technology' was banned on the grounds that it had already been in general use for over a decade elsewhere, including the Third World. The reporters and features writers were less tense; they were happy enough to stay on in Fleet Street, close to their sources of information and the journalists on other newspapers, to say nothing of their favourite watering holes. The printers were grudgingly confident; it was beginning to look as if they had won the war.

In 1983 the *Financial Times*, owned by the Pearson group now under Lord Cowdray, was off the streets for nine weeks during the election campaign, a stoppage which cost the company about £10,000,000. The NGA machine-minders, who must have realised by this time that there was no place for them in the new technology, struck again in 1984 and 1985 when the *Financial Times* company took an injunction against them with some slight effect.

Murdoch's delight at acquiring *The Times* was rather soured by the fact that, week after week, for one reason or another dreamed up by the union chapels, the *Sunday Times* never seemed to complete its production run. Shortly after he took over *The Times*, Murdoch had completed the move to photocomposition; in Thomson's day, only the Stock Exchange prices were produced using any of the new technology. Also, by moving Harold Evans – unquestionably one of the most brilliant editors of recent years – over from the *Sunday Times* to revamp *The Times* completely, he now had a product with considerable popular appeal; all he lacked was a means to ensure that he could print enough copies to get it out to all the people who were now prepared to buy it.

Before the sale of the *Mirror* group by Reed International to Robert Maxwell, just prior to the Reuters flotation, Maxwell had promised that he would maintain the editorial influence of the newspapers and offer shares to the employees 'as soon as practicable'. Maxwell promised too that all his papers would back Britain. He also promised to overtake the *Sun* in circulation, to support the Labour Party and to make a profit of £15,000,000 a year. Fortified by the exhilarating sight of his own familiar features in the *Daily Mirror* day after day, Maxwell tackled the paper's union problems with a persistence rare among Fleet Street proprietors, old or new. By January 1986 he managed to get union agreement to the redundancy of 2,100 of his 7,000 staff.

On the *Express*, David Stevens of United Newspapers hired a new chief executive, Roger Bowes, who succeeded in forcing an even more drastic reduced-manning package on the unions. The number of staff decreased by 2,500, from a total of 6,000. Over in the *Daily Telegraph*, the new Canadian proprietor, Conrad Black, was about to follow suit when another newcomer appeared in the wings, and once again completely changed the name of the game.

The first scene in the drama that not only changed the whole face of Fleet Street but completely obliterated it as the centre of national newspaper production, took place not in London but in Warrington, in Cheshire. Eddy Shah, the son of a cousin of the Aga Khan, had an English mother, was educated at Gordonstoun School and worked for a time in television in Manchester. His first experience in newspapers was in the business of free through-the-letterbox newspapers, a notion imported into Britain from the States in the late sixties and thriving by 1985. By this time 785 free daily or weekly papers were bringing in about £262 million a year in advertising revenue and were being distributed to more than 85 per cent of British households.

Shah systematically set about introducing non-union labour into his various plants and was very careful to separate his operations into different companies as a protection against secondary picketing. When a strike at his Stockport, Lancashire, headquarters was followed by secondary picketing at Warrington (now illegal under the 1980 and 1982 employment laws introduced by the Thatcher Government as part of its legislation to curb the power of the unions) Shah sued the NGA for damages and the union was the first to find its funds sequestered under the new laws. Shah's action did not go unnoticed in Fleet Street, either by the newspaper proprietors or by the unions.

The dispute spread south. There was a short lock-out when the NGA decided to call out its Fleet Street members spontaneously to avert a charge of collusion, but a joint attempt by the Stevens, Maxwell and Murdoch managements to achieve solidarity against secondary picketing collapsed yet again.

Flying pickets turned up outside Shah's Warrington works where the striking printers were supplemented by dockers, miners and other assorted activists, and the police had to intervene. The first much-publicised pitched battle in this new phase of the war occurred on 29 November 1983, and the new laws prevented the TUC from supporting what had now become an illegal action. Without the TUC's support the NGA had to call off its pickets, having lost according to some Fleet Street estimates as much as two million pounds in fines and legal fees.

Shah, openly encouraged by Andrew Neil, editor of the *Sunday Times*, now began to contemplate a new national daily paper, entirely produced by non-union labour. With a staff of 500 and a circulation of 700,000 (half that of the *Daily Mail*, its nearest market rival), the new daily along with its Sunday counterpart should make, he reckoned, about thirteen million

pounds a year on a turnover of fifty million. So low would the
running costs be that he estimated he could break even with a
circulation of 600,000 on the cover price alone; any advertising
at all would represent a profit margin.

He decided to print on four extremely advanced colour
presses, one based at Heathrow and the other three in the
provinces. Pages would be faxed to them by Mercury cables
from the newspaper's head offices on Vauxhall Bridge Road in
London.

Shah's astonishing figures were studied not only in Fleet
Street – where every daily national newspaper still employed at
least 2,000, not counting all the 'ghosts' – but also by the union
leaders. In 1985 Shah was approached by Eric Hammond of
the Electrical, Electronic Telecommunications and Plumbing
Union (EETPU), who offered him a deal which swept aside all
the customs and practices of a century and a half. Hammond's
one union would supply the men to do all the printing work at
Shah's plant with no closed shop, with equal status for all staff
whether they were union members or not, and a joint board to
decide all terms and conditions of employment which would
represent staff and management on a fifty-fifty basis. Hammond
regarded the new technology as electrical/electronic rather
than mechanical (which indeed it was) and considered
therefore that his union was the appropriate one to control the
operation of the new machines.

This offer enabled Shah to launch his new national, *Today*, in
March 1986, but by then it had been eclipsed by a much bigger
event, triggered off by Shah's victory over the unions. Long
before the first issue of *Today* had appeared in the streets,
Murdoch had launched his final assault on the power of the
unions. Eddy Shah's *Today*, dogged by printing problems and
uncertain management, never fulfilled any of the promises
Shah made for it, and is now, with Murdoch owning 90 per
cent of the stock and a circulation of 408,000, on a par with the
Guardian and *The Times* but without any of their prestige.
Shah's initial impact on Fleet Street however had been
decisive; and his conviction that newspapers could now be

produced without the connivance of the unions and their various chapels spread rapidly among the Fleet Street proprietors.

Rupert Murdoch's new printing works at Wapping and in Glasgow had been more or less ready since 1983. Both had originally been intended, eventually, to print the *Sun* and the *News of the World*, though neither had been regarded initially as non-union works. Murdoch had planned to continue all editorial and type-setting work in Bouverie Street and merely transfer the facsimile pages to Wapping and Glasgow. Fearing that this move might challenge Manchester's importance, Brenda Dean of SOGAT 82 told Murdoch that the unions would not let him proceed as planned. Murdoch then gave the unions a three-month deadline to reach agreement to print a new evening *London Post* at Wapping. The unions were still pressing for a guarantee of jobs for life with no redundancies. Murdoch was quite happy that the high Bouverie Street earnings should continue to apply at Wapping but he wanted a much lower manning level and written guarantees that there would be no more stoppages. During a breakdown in one of the innumerable inter-union and management talks, an EETPU official approached Murdoch's chief executive Bruce Matthews and indicated that if Murdoch wanted to transfer the *Sun* and the *News of the World* to Wapping, his union might be able to help. Although this offer was made *before* Hammond made much the same offer to Eddy Shah, there is little doubt that it was Shah's victory over the unions in Warrington that had started the whole landslide.

Matthews put this proposal to Murdoch who immediately realised that if he did attempt to transfer the *Sun* and the *News of the World* to Wapping and Glasgow on what amounted to a non-union basis, he might well be forced to move the *Sunday Times* and *The Times* out of Gray's Inn Road and produce them in these other two centres as well, also using non-union labour.

Then came another crisis, precipitated by the Bingo war. It was started in the early eighties by the *Star*; the *Daily Express* immediately followed suit and very soon the *Sun*, the *Daily Mirror* and the *Daily Mail* were all running their own versions of the game. Finally, after he had *The Times* safely under his belt, Murdoch joined the fray as well with a more up-market version of the game. It was known in the corridors of *The Times* building as Dingo, and it was based on the number of points gained or lost on the Stock Exchange by carefully selected portfolios of shares which took the form of numbered cards, in no way different from the ordinary Bingo cards used by the popular papers. The whole thing got a bit out of hand when Maxwell took over the *Mirror* and turned it into a game he rechristened 'Who Dares a Million?'

The use of computers and a small number of potential 'winning' cards was designed to ensure that the tempting prize money would not have to be divided up among tens of thousands of competitors, each receiving derisory sums of a few quid, but could be carefully controlled to give an outright winner, or a very large sum shared by not more than two or three people, at regular and convenient intervals. When the computers went wrong, as they sometimes did, to the great embarrassment of the newspapers concerned, large queues formed outside the offices to collect tiny dividends worth nothing at all in terms of publicity value. Like the free gift war in the thirties, the Bingo war of the eighties did increase circulation, but it was not necessarily sustained and did not lead to any kind of brand loyalty, as the admen put it, and it cost the newspapers a lot of money. It cost Rupert Murdoch more money than any of the others, though in the end he was the outright winner of the game. He took up Maxwell's challenge and was the first proprietor to part with £1,000,000, announcing in a headline in the *Sun*: WE SAID WE'D DO IT – BY GOD WE'VE DONE IT.

The introduction of the up-market Portfolio Bingo in June 1984 had *The Times* running neck-and-neck with the *Guardian* by December 1985. *The Times* desperately needed to print more copies but the machine room chapel now suddenly demanded seventy more jobs at an extra cost of £1,000,000 a year. By now

Murdoch controlled about one-third of Fleet Street's total newspaper production. As a result of his pressure, *The Times* had become the first national newspaper to be entirely set by photo-composition in May 1982. Now his *News of the World* staff were refusing to print any more copies of that paper in Bouverie Street; the union chapels in the *Sunday Times* were preventing any further expansion of that newspaper at Gray's Inn Road, at a time when Murdoch felt that the market was ready for Sunday papers of 104 pages or more, and were causing disruptions which lost thousands of copies every weekend; and now *The Times* machine room men were looking for another £1,000,000 to print the extra copies he needed to put *The Times* ahead of the *Guardian*. It was the last straw. Murdoch accepted Matthews' proposal that he should accept the EETPU offer and began to plan the move to Wapping.

In the process of preparing for a new evening paper, the *London Post*, which was to be expanded into a round-the-clock, 24-hour newspaper with national distribution and direct computer input by journalists, new terminals and equipment – far more than could ever be required by one newspaper – were installed at Wapping in total secrecy. The fact that all the plant and equipment could be used to protect his existing four national newspapers was initially regarded (or represented) as being merely a contingency plan in case of a complete break-down in relations with the unions. The equipment he was installing was the most advanced in the world, Atex computers from Boston and Antologic APS-5 photosetters. Every termin-al in the plant was connected to two computers, one on line and the other 'listening' and making an exact copy of everything fed in, as a safeguard. Each disc drive had a memory capacity of 300,000,000 characters or commands, and half a dozen photosetters, no bigger than juke boxes, could set a newspaper quicker than 100 linotype machines and without any noise, mess or fuss.

A row of London dock warehouses was converted into offices for the editorial staffs of *The Times* and the *Sunday Times*; the staffs of the *Sun* and the *News of the World* could be comfortably accommodated in what might have become the *London Post* editorial department, if things had worked out differently.

Matthews then made an informal agreement with the EETPU, whose Southampton office agreed to supply men with all the specific skills which Murdoch required on short term contracts. The men had to be free of any hint of union militancy and they had to be men who could be trusted not to talk about what was happening. Buses would collect them in Southampton and drive them straight to the plant at Wapping. The pay was good, up to £500 a week, and the men were to be put on a six-month contract, later extended to one year.

Murdoch's lawyers took the same precautions as Eddy Shah's had done, putting the Wapping and Glasgow plants under a separate company from his Fleet Street operations, so that any union action against them would be secondary and therefore illegal. The workers who could clearly be seen pouring into Wapping every day were dismissed by Murdoch's spokesmen as temporary workers, preparing the site for ultimate newspaper production, pending agreement with the unions on manning the plant. Arrangements were made with an Australian transport firm, Thomas Nationwide Transport (TNT), to buy 800 unmarked lorries and employ 2,000 men to distribute the newspapers to nearly 40,000 retailers in the United Kingdom when the time came. TNT, in which Murdoch had a small stake which he now increased considerably, had established a British subsidiary which had been delivering parcels from its Lancashire headquarters since 1978.

London Post's launch was postponed and postponed again and in September 1985 the Wapping machines were tested with an initial run of a dummy newspaper; Southampton EETPU electricians were at the controls. By this time there were fifty-nine staff in the press room and more were expected from Australia and America. Ten Australian girls had been employed for editorial/advertising input at the terminals. The plant was fully equipped with newsprint and ink and this test-run was only the first of several. News of the test-runs reached the unions and should have alerted them to what was happening, but the NGA was still insisting on machine-minders at Wapping, SOGAT 82 was still demanding unrealistic manning levels in the publishing room, and none of the unions would give a guarantee that there would be no more stoppages.

In October Murdoch presented the unions with a document which he knew they would never accept. It demanded from them the flexibility he was already getting from the EETPU: total freedom for management over allocation of staff; an end to the closed shop; a legally binding no strike clause allowing the management to adopt the new technology at any time with any consequent reductions in manning levels; and agreement by Christmas 1985. The alternative, as was now becoming very clear to everyone, was a non-union operation at Wapping. By Christmas no agreement had been reached.

The first indication that the Wapping plant was going to be used for newspapers other than the projected *London Post* came after Christmas in the form of a statement from Murdoch, printed in *The Times*. It said that as the talks with the print unions had broken down, he was bringing Tower Hamlets and Kinning Park (Glasgow) into a state of readiness both for the launch of the *Post* and 'to enable the company to meet the urgent requirements of the other group newspapers'.

The *Sunday Times* of 12 January carried a panel on the front page announcing that a section of the newspaper would be printed at Wapping next week, and, on 19 January 1986, Murdoch produced the biggest newspaper ever printed in Britain – 104 pages – which had been made possible by the commissioning of the new plant at Wapping. It contained a 12-page supplement about the new plant and an interview with Murdoch in which he explained why a legally binding no strike clause was so important to him: 'Newspapers are under great threat all over the world from electronic competition and in many countries there is a decline in readership. The greatest asset newspapers have is the habit factor. We cannot afford to go on interrupting that.'

On Wednesday 22 January the unions announced the result of their strike ballots. SOGAT 82's national executive had recommended a Yes vote but 82 per cent of the SOGAT members voted for a strike.

Four kilometres of coiled razor wire were imported from Germany and set up around Fortress Wapping like the barbed wire barricades of World War I. To delay the storming pickets until the riot police arrived, extra security guards were taken on and there were detailed discussions with the local police. At the last minute the unions made a final offer, described by TUC general secretary Norman Willis as 'the best deal ever offered by any union to any national newspaper'. But it failed to include the total discretion demanded by Murdoch and, in any event, Murdoch was no longer interested in any deals with the print unions.

The print unions later claimed that Murdoch had trapped them into a strike in order to deprive them of their redundancy money but at that time, they too had an option, and they chose strike action. They were confident that mass picketing and the disruption of Murdoch's new distribution system would force him back to the negotiating table, but they were wrong.

At the last minute, the NUJ, the journalists' union, decided that Wapping should be 'blacked'. The journalists generally had mixed feelings about the issue. Many of them believed that the time had come for a show-down with Murdoch – he had, they felt, been interfering in matters of editorial prerogative. Murdoch had ousted Harold Evans – the new wizard of Fleet Street, who had edited the *Sunday Times* very successfully for fourteen years – in less than one year, in 1982, and had made a number of what the journalists considered were arbitrary and unnecessary staff changes. On the other hand, they had no great sympathy with the print unions either as they had all suffered in one way or another from the restrictive practices and the strikes and stoppages.

On Friday 24 January, Murdoch's journalists were given a

choice: they could move to Wapping, with a bonus of £2,000 to recompense them for learning how to use visual display units (VDUs), plus additional health benefits, or they could refuse to go and be deemed to have sacked themselves by going on strike. Journalists on the *Sun* and the *News of the World* voted overwhelmingly (by more than three to one) to go; journalists on *The Times* and the *Sunday Times* were split about half and half (68 in favour of the move, 60 against) but enough of them agreed to the move to enable Murdoch to ensure the continuity of all four titles. When the last printers and journalists left *The Times* office in Gray's Inn Road that Friday night, they saw that cars had been moved from the adjoining streets and the area was surrounded by police.

On the night of 25 January, TNT's unmarked lorries began to poke their bonnets uneasily out of Fortress Wapping and thread their way through the barbed wire barricades to be greeted with a storm of sticks and stones and shouts of 'scab'. The copies of the *Sun* they were delivering carried the headline: A NEW SUN IS RISING – TODAY WE BEAT THE STRIKE THUGS.

The total print order was not met for several weeks and the picketing, violent at times, continued well into the autumn. Murdoch's newsprint warehouse was burnt down, several members of his staff were physically assaulted, many of the lorries were vandalised.

But these were mere skirmishes: the war was over.

The following week the *Guardian* announced that it was changing over to computer type-setting and within a year all the national newspapers had either moved or had announced plans to move out of Fleet Street. Another newcomer, the *Independent*, appeared on 7 October 1986; it was produced, using the new technology, in an old building in City Road. It was followed by yet more: the *Sunday Sport*, with a semi-nude in colour on almost every page; its stable-mate on Wednesdays, known simply as the *Sport*; and in November 1988 Eddy Shah had a second go at producing a popular tabloid the *Post* edited from Warrington, which folded in a matter of weeks. His *Today*, which by mid-summer 1988 had passed the 500,000 mark, was now for all practical purposes part of the Murdoch empire.

But this book is about the legendary Fleet Street of the great press barons and their successors over two generations; not about what the future may hold for the new national newspapers or whether, and if so how, the economies effected by using the new technology will enable newspapers to thrive without warring for circulation and advertising.

By the time this book is published, the last of the great national dailies will almost certainly have moved out of Fleet Street for ever. The great black glass frontage of the *Daily Express* building – London's first 'curtain' wall – will be preserved as a national monument, as will the formidable frontage of its near next-door neighbour, the *Daily Telegraph* building; but there will be ordinary city offices behind the facades. The Bouverie Street buildings – until recently shared by the *Sun* and the *News of the World*, and which once housed the *Daily Mirror* – are being knocked down to be replaced by a development of offices and shops for the Japanese firm of Kumagai Gumi Ltd. The area around Northcliffe House, home of Rothermere's Associated Newspapers ever since Alfred Harmsworth first started the *Daily Mail* in a rented shed there in 1896, are to be redeveloped and will be dominated by the Morgan Bank of America. The old headquarters of the *Financial Times*, called Bracken House after Brendan Bracken, Churchill's wartime propaganda minister – a bit further up Queen Victoria Street from Printing House Square – has been acquired by the Japanese firm of Ohbayashi UK Ltd.

Presumably the people who will work in these new office blocks will meet for a drink at lunchtime in El Vino or the King and Keys or The Clachan or one of the many other pubs and wine bars in the street which still survive. But I doubt very much if the crack will be as good as it was in the days when this was the centre of the British communications world. And whatever they will be doing in the spaces vacated by the news and foreign desks, the back benches and subs' tables, the linotype halls and the case rooms of the departed dailies, it will not be nearly as exciting nor, as is abundantly clear from the recollections which follow, nearly as much fun as it was, making newspapers in Fleet Street.

Part Two:
THE
FLEET STREET
EXPERIENCE

An Anthology
of Memories

Introduction

First, a word about the interviews. I started out with about twenty-five approaches, some by letter, some on the telephone, and as I began to work my way through the first batch of interviews, I sent out more letters and made more telephone calls, trying to keep the interviews far enough apart, so that I could stand back a bit and look at them dispassionately, to see how the book was developing.

Initially I began with people whom I had known personally in Fleet Street, and people to whom I had a line, so to speak, through mutual friends, but there were exceptions: there were quite a number of highly important Fleet Street people whom I had never met and to whom there were no short cuts available to me. I'm thinking about people like Lord Deedes, Sir John Junor and Harry Chapman Pincher. In such cases, and in many others, I simply wrote a letter out of the blue, asking for their co-operation. A few of the people I approached in this way, or through mutual friends, were either too busy with other commitments, like Lord Rees-Mogg and Michael Foot, or were writing books of their own, like Sir Larry Lamb and Derek Jameson, and felt, wrongly in my opinion, that their own sales would be damaged if they contributed to this book. And a very small minority did not even bother to reply.

Most of the people I approached were extremely generous of their time and their patience, and I am extremely grateful to them.

As soon as I started assembling the memories into an anthology, another problem presented itself. In what order should the recollections be printed? Alphabetical? Nonsense. In terms of seniority in Fleet Street? Possibly, but of age or position? How do you rate one ex-editor against another: Sir John Junor against Lord Deedes? And, if you decide to put them in the order of their popularity with the public, how do you rate Nigel Dempster against Jak, or Marje Proops against

Jean Rook? And there's the further point that many of the people with the most interesting stories to tell were never known to the public at all; I am thinking about people like Leon Pilpel who was chief home sub-editor of *The Times* for over twelve years and has been editing *The Times* letters since the year-long shut-down of 1978–9.

So I decided that the order in which I would run these memories would have to be completely arbitrary, chosen to follow almost a conversational pattern, with a few words of my own in between, to link them together. In other words, an anthology as personal and perverse as any other anthology . . .

William Neil Connor (Cassandra)

If my old friend Bill Connor (Cassandra of the *Daily Mirror*) happened to be around still, there is no doubt whatever that he would have been the very first person I would have approached in connection with this anthology. However, since he isn't, it seems appropriate to open with what, to my mind, is the very best piece ever written about the perils of Fleet Street.

Bill Connor joined the *Daily Mirror* in 1935. He had an Irish father and a Scottish mother and he went to the *Daily Mirror* from the J. Walter Thompson advertising agency where he had been using his prodigious power with words to advertise, among other things, Harpic. He took his pen-name from the Greek lady prophet who always foretold the truth and was never believed. He wrote the most scintillating, incandescent, coruscating column Fleet Street has ever known. He died in 1967.

I have been on Fleet Street for thirty years and I have never laughed so much. There is no other job like it, so preposterous, so wildly improbable. The task which we impudently assume is to chronicle the whole pageant of life, to record the passing show and then, with unforgivable brazenness, to draw conclusions, to give a verdict and to point the moral. Damn and bless our bloody eyes.

I would never advise anybody to come to Fleet Street. Learning this trade is like learning high diving – minus the water. But I wouldn't have missed it for all the treasures of Araby. The man who when he was asked what it was like to be in the First World War said: 'Oh, the noise, AND OH, THE PEOPLE!' You can say the same thing about Fleet Street – 'Oh, the noise, AND OH, THE PEOPLE!'

You can get used to the noise but I've never got used to the people. The lovely nuts. The gorgeous crackpots. And all those wonderful, generous, self-derisive folk who spend their lives making dirty great black marks on miles and miles of white paper. Newspaper people are the greatest company in the world. They know but they will never learn. Fleet Street is a pavement where the manhole covers are missing. The aspirants who walk down it are warned by notices which say: CAUTION – MEN WORKING. They stride on and in a trice are below ground. I know. I've done it.

Fleet Street is snakes and ladders. Fleet Street is the greasy pole with the old duck pond waiting scummily below if you fall off. I know. I've done it. Fleet Street is the slippery slide with the banana skin laid there for all to see. And the saints and sinners go marching on until bingo we all fall down. I know. I've done it.

The way to get on in Fleet Street is never let it be known what you want to do. Hide Ambition's dark face. Never ascend the heights.

The newspaper business, especially in Fleet Street, is over-shadowed by an angry towering mountain with the summit lost in the eternal hostile snows. Way down in the warm valleys below the foothills, life in the print business can be serene and relaxed. The place is stuffed with bee-loud glades where the idle, as well as the able, the incompetent as well as the efficient can relax. The vegetation is thick and the great warm fronds provide shade for those who wish to lie down in the noonday sun. Reporters, sub-editors, feature men and sports writers can all have a relatively pleasant time and, if they wish, can make love to the secretary birds under the kindly foliage.

A little farther up the mountain, the foothills begin and the humming birds are no longer seen. The flowers are still bright, but there is a freshness in the air that old journalists suspect and young ones too often relish. Above the foothills you can see the sky between the trees.

Still farther up, the foliage begins to diminish. There is a nip in the air and old hands shake their heads. The conifers grow shorter and more stunted. The undergrowth thins out. Bushes take the place of trees, and there is little cover under which to hide. But the eager beavers press on. Like young wild pigs they grunt and bolt around, sniffing the freshening wind.

Far below in the valley there were flowers and berries and fruits to be found. Here there is little. Nor is the bark of the trees edible. But still rooting and snorting, the ambitious porkers press on. It is the charge of the Gadarene Swine in reverse – upwards instead of downwards – to disaster.

Above the bushes comes the scree. Above the scree come the boulders. Above the boulders, the snow line. The ambitious journalists have thinned out now. Some are exhausted. Others are killed by their fellows. But here and there a burly brute with a red gleam in a beady angry eye that indicates the fevered image of the Editor's Chair, still scrambles and scrabbles upwards.

I call them to come back. But it is too late, and as I stumble down the mountain to the softer climes below, I see the last of the Go-Getters, the I-Believe-In-Me mob, struggling ever upwards. Little black dots slowly ascending the North Col.

Ultimately, one of them makes it. O the Power! O the Glory! But they have still reckoned without the Abominable Snowman – the mysterious yeti, nine foot tall, covered in silky ginger fur with great gorilla-like feet leaving imprints in the dazzling snow. Sooner or later they meet him face to face, and another familiar mountaineer has the millstone of Editorship around his neck and dies the death. And the faithful Sherpas who always knew that one glance from the Abominable Snowman meant disaster were right.

Editors! I seen 'em come. And I seen 'em go. But way up on the mountain overshadowing Fleet Street the Abominable Snowman goes on for ever.

So, young stranger, my advice is don't come near us. Don't come in 'for the water's warm'. It's not, it's hot. It's also freezing cold and it's rough too. But it is the best, the finest, the most furious, the most exciting bath of life that anybody could ever take.

But, for Gawd's sake, mind the plug 'ole.

Hugh (Lord) Cudlipp

There is only one possible way to follow a piece by Bill Connor, and that is with a piece by his mate, Hugh Cudlipp. I had hoped to have a chat with Hugh over a tape recorder, as I have done with most of my old Fleet Street colleagues, but he decided instead to send me a written memoir plus some notes on his own career which I might like to include in any c.v. I was printing; and as soon as I read them, I realised how right he was, as he has been, most of the time, over the years.

Hugh Cudlipp began his career as an eager reporter aged fourteen on the *Penarth News* in Glamorgan. His weekly wage was 2/6 (12.5p) plus his railway season ticket from Cardiff. At twenty-four, he was editor of the *Sunday Pictorial*, the youngest editor in Fleet Street at that time. He was one of three journalist brothers from Wales, all of whom edited national newspapers; Percy, the *Daily Herald* and Reginald, the *News of the World*. Hugh Cudlipp became editorial director of the *Daily Mirror*, then joint managing director, then chairman, and succeeded Cecil Harmsworth King as chairman of the IPC before retiring from the jungle, as he puts it, in 1973. As sole surviving editor of the pre-war years, his memory of the street sardonically recalls one aspect of the lighter side of life in the editor's chair.

23 November 1988

What the hell, somebody had to do it, and it was I who did it.

Nowadays in the soar-away eighties, you have to be lucky to pick up a tabloid newspaper that doesn't specialise in a Monday to Saturday mammary exhibition; I understand that six to a page is the record, though heaven knows, I may have missed a souvenir issue of the *Sun* when there were sixty-six.

Lord Rees-Mogg does not mention it often now that he's gone up-market as chairman of the Broadcasting Standards Council; nonetheless he is entitled to claim his niche in Fleet Street history for publishing the first and only nude woman to appear in *The Times*. The indecent exposure was in a full-page advertisement.

To resolve any misapprehensions, it was I who published

the first topless lady in the editorial pages of a British newspaper, not Mr Rupert Murdoch or Sir Larry Lamb, as they would no doubt wish you to believe. Mind you, it was not the sort of topless lady who adorns Page Three in this decadent decade, selected, one suspects, because they are flaunting the biggest bust or the most protruding nipples the art editor on duty that night has ever seen. And the event occurred long before Miss Samantha Fox was a twinkle, albeit a prominent twinkle, in her father's eye. I would say from memory that my lady was a modest 34″, or possibly 36″.

I had just been appointed editor of the ailing *Sunday Pictorial* at the age of twenty-four, which may partly explain the whole affair. The other explanation is that it was springtime. The readers were deserting in their hundreds of thousands and I was anxious to indicate that the newspaper was under new management. Springtime, apple blossom time was the appropriate moment to make my mark, or mark my exit.

I briefed the photographer meticulously. I didn't want gambolling lambs. I didn't want a tortoise – awakened early from his hibernation by popping him for a short time in a low oven – clawing a path through the daffodils in Regent's Park. I didn't want crocuses in St James's Park, or any other park, and I didn't want bloody ducklings popping out of chocolate Easter eggs, courtesy of Lyon's or Fortnum and Mason's. I told him what I did want and it arrived on my desk on Saturday morning, a tasteful study at an orchard in Kent of a comely, smiling model reaching her arms towards the sky through the branches of an apple tree in full blossom. The top half of the lady was also in full blossom; young, burgeoning womanhood, innocent but topless.

The nearest the *Sunday Pictorial* before my time had ever edged towards nudism was a cartoon of Pip, Squeak and Wilfred on holiday in Torquay wearing one-piece bathing costumes. To avoid an outbreak of mass heart attacks among the board of directors, I decided to give a sneak preview of the picture to Cecil Harmsworth King, my immediate boss, then editorial director. King was a shy, lofty, self-embarrassing

Wykehamist, honed in Christ Church, Oxford, where he wooed and subsequently wed a daughter of the Dean. A student of constitutional history was not a natural ally in the dubious cause I was espousing. 'Cudlipp,' he said, 'I'm afraid you can't publish that picture without showing it beforehand to the chairman, and if you do show it to the chairman, you won't be publishing it.' Furthermore, he warned me that although it was a Saturday afternoon, John Cowley, the chairman, was in.

Cowley was a family man of oppressive moral probity this side of the English channel with a mistress in Villefranche. 'I'll try,' I said as King and I set off along the corridors to Cowley's austere, oak-panelled chambers. The only publications on his desk were the *Financial Times* and the *ABC Railway Guide*. He kept pigs, so after we had listened patiently to a dollop of porcine patter and his useless views on life in general, I steered the conversation towards the fertile weald of Kent he farmed. I casually mentioned trees in blossom. 'Ah yes,' he said, 'they are now at their best, a sight to see, especially the apple blossom.' 'Sir,' I said, avoiding the eye of the Wykehamist, 'I am sure you will agree that it is imperative that the new *Pictorial* is accurate in everything it prints, particularly pictures portraying the countryside where so many of our readers live.'

'Perhaps I can help you,' said the countryman. I mentioned that I had with me a charming study illustrating the arrival of spring but I was concerned to be assured that the apple blossom in the background was truly at that particular stage at this very moment. Cowley studied the picture for longer than was strictly necessary to settle the horticultural query and then pronounced: 'You need have no fear, Cudlipp, of the accuracy of this picture. My apple trees are exactly in that condition now. Full bloom. The picture might have been taken in my own garden yesterday.'

On our return journey along the corridors, Cecil King paused, the whole six feet of him, planted his right hand against the wall and laughed hysterically, until there were tears in his eyes. I thought he was going to be sick. I had never heard him laugh like that before, and certainly never since.

The photograph of the comely, smiling lady in an orchard in Kent occupied a half-page in the new, new *Sunday Pictorial* the next day. Topless.

Tell them that in Wapping and on the Isle of Dogs.

Sir John Junor

If Hugh Cudlipp holds a minor Fleet Street record as the sole survivor of the pre-war editors, Sir John Junor holds another as the longest reigning post-war editor of a popular newspaper, the *Sunday Express*: he was editor of the paper for thirty-two years and still writes a popular weekly column for it at the age of 70.

Born in 1919, John Junor stood as a Liberal candidate for several seats in Scotland in the period immediately after the war. When he failed as a politician, he joined the *Daily Express* in 1951 as assistant editor, becoming editor of the *Evening Standard* in 1953. He was editor of the *Sunday Express* from 1954 until 1986 and has been chairman of the paper since 1968.

23 November 1988

I became a Sunday newspaper editor because Beaverbrook asked me to edit the *Sunday Express* and I can think of no newspaper that I would more gladly have edited.

I think there is one essential difference between editing a daily newspaper and a Sunday. The editor of a daily newspaper has to edit looking backwards; he can't possibly be responsible for everything that appears in his newspaper, he simply hasn't got the time. He has to devolve responsibility and Christiansen, perhaps the greatest of all the daily newspaper editors, did this by means of his daily bulletin, in which he distributed praise and blame and it was done so brilliantly that he was actually creating standards for the next day's issue, and indicating what he liked and what he didn't like. And of course at the same time, his physical presence was there directing the section of the newspaper which he could personally direct.

Whereas the editor of a Sunday newspaper, on the other hand, having a whole week to prepare, can be responsible for everything that appears in his paper. A small part of it is the ability to stand back and look at it as a whole, but it's really far more being able to know precisely what is going on. There's many a feature that appears in a daily newspaper which cannot, in the nature of the job, be read by the editor until after it has actually appeared in the paper.

Towards the end of the war I'd been in the Fleet Air Arm and I'd actually spent the last year of the war in the Admiralty, editing a Fleet Air Arm magazine, and during that same year, because I finished work at six o'clock in the Admiralty and was living in London, and because they were so desperately short of subs I was able to moonlight on an Australian organisation called the Australian Associated Press, which was a wire agency, filing copy to Australia. And, because I'd worked for them for a year, when the time for my demobilisation came round, I'd got to know a few people in the Press Association building, and in some Australian newspapers, including the *Sydney Sun*.

So, when I came out of the forces, I had an offer to join the staff of the *Sydney Sun* and I worked there until Christmas 1947 when I was sacked, though through no fault of my own. What had happened was that I had been writing a column for the *Sydney Sun* called Gordon Gilmour's London Diary. Gilmour was London editor of the paper. But for a variety of reasons I did the column on his behalf, and when they found out about it in Australia they fired him on the grounds that he wasn't writing his own column, and they fired me too, because I had been doing it for him. They wanted someone who could write his own column.

I applied to the *Daily Express* for a job and although the paper was down to four pages at that period, and there weren't too many jobs flying around, Chris took me on as a reporter. I'd had no family background in journalism, and no experience in provincial newspapers, but that didn't bother me. If you don't know what the man at the end of Rhyl Pier is thinking, whether you've ever worked in a provincial newspaper or not, then you shouldn't be in journalism.

I really wanted to be a politician and it was only because I had failed as a politician that I became a journalist. I was a committed Liberal – no family background in Liberalism, or even politics for that matter – but I joined the Liberal Party as it was then, a half-way house believing in free enterprise and social justice.

In 1945 I came within 612 votes of winning Kincardie in West Aberdeen. I then fought a by-election in East Edinburgh and finally in 1951 I fought Dundee and got 33,000 votes, but that still wasn't enough to win the seat. If I'd succeeded, I'd have stayed in politics, I wouldn't even have looked at journalism.

But, as it happened, I became a journalist. It was still wartime and I remember the wonderful camaraderie of the old Press Club, the way it embraced people from the provinces, total strangers; it was the only place in London where you could get warm food and sustaining comfort. I remember the Fleet Street pubs. The Punch was a great haunt in those days, and The Codgers, near St Bride's, which was an Australian pub with a barmaid called Eve; all the Australians from the RAAF used to go there.

I ran the *Sunday Express* from 1954 to 1986. Is it the same newspaper? Of course it's not. But you don't constantly or consciously change a newspaper, it's the readers who change it for you. You don't consciously change yourself, do you? You look in the mirror in the morning and you're looking at the same face that you've been looking at for forty-five years or whatever it is. You're changing, though you don't notice it. And the readership of your paper is changing. Readers don't fade away, they're simply replaced by their children.

A newspaper is every bit as much a living thing as your own reflection in the shaving mirror and it's constantly changing because the news is constantly changing. It's life that's changing, not an editor sitting there like a computer, working things out. Why did I never change the *Sunday Express* to a tabloid? For a very simple reason. Why do you think that the *Sunday Telegraph*, the *Observer* and the *Sunday Times* are still text newspapers, still broadsheets? Because it's impossible to deploy an argument in a tabloid. Tabloids are small papers for people with small minds.

The *Sunday Express* has been consistently successful under various managements because the management has always been the same, really. The difference was in the proprietors, the publishers. Beaverbrook was a genius of a journalist, the best journalist this century. Murdoch is a financier. You can say that he's a newspaperman, but it's newspaper finance that he understands. He's not a great journalist; he doesn't come out with great journalistic ideas, as Beaverbrook did.

I think it's a tragedy that the community of newspapers is being split up by the moves out to Wapping and the Isle of Dogs and elsewhere. There was once a political correspondent called Wilfred Sendall and Wilfred Sendall, at a ripe old age in his fifties, quit the *Daily Telegraph*, where he was firmly established, to come to the *Sunday Express*, but he made good here and then to my consternation, at the age of – I guess about sixty-one – he said: 'I'm going to the *News of the World*.' I replied: 'You're crazy, Wilf, you can't.' But he just smiled at me and said: 'Oh, John, this is just a village. It's not like leaving home. I'm just moving to the other side of the street.' And, by God, he did just that with great success and finally came back to the *Daily Express* and ended his career on the *Express*.

I think papers are certainly going to change as a result of all this upset. I'm not sure whether it's for good or not, I just don't know. But the situation at the moment is that I've got a portable computer, I've got a fax machine and I can sit at home and type out my column because I've got access to all the news through the newspapers, from my television screen, through Oracle and Ceefax and all I've got to do is plug into a telephone and press a button and that's it.

I think if I had it to do all over again, I wouldn't bother about politics, I'd just head straight for newspapers, because I got to know a lot of Cabinet ministers, and I realised how terrible it was for them to cope with the change when they lost office, when a government was defeated. From being lords of all they surveyed, they suddenly became impoverished, miserable little chaps standing on the street waiting for a bus or looking for the tube station. All their power had disappeared and they were completely deflated.

And I think out-of-work politicians are far more pathetic than out-of-work journalists. Apart from the fact that an out-of-work journalist automatically becomes a free-lance journalist, he hasn't ever known the potentials before that, he hasn't had the trappings of power. An out-of-work Cabinet minister who suddenly has no car, no driver, no influence, he's a very pathetic figure, he no longer counts.

The point really is that journalists, even editors don't have any real power: perhaps the power to influence slightly, but that's all. The guy that's really got the power is the executive, the prime minister. Journalism is a great life, it's been fabulous fun.

Eve Pollard

When Sir John Junor became editor of the *Sunday Express* in 1954, the very idea that there would ever be a female editor of a national newspaper was totally unthinkable. It had been tried out once, very briefly and with disastrous results, when the *Daily Mirror* was first launched in 1903, and was then firmly pushed under the carpet. Yet by 1987 there were two woman editors in Fleet Street; and Eve Pollard was one of them. There are now three. Eve is married to Nick Lloyd, editor of the *Daily Express*. She has worked for the *Mirror* group, the *Observer*, TV-AM, Murdoch's *News of the World*, Rothermere's *Mail on Sunday*, and she now works for Robert Maxwell as editor of the *Sunday Mirror*.

Eve Pollard started in journalism as fashion editor of *Honey*, then the youngest, brightest IPC publication. She was fashion editor of the *Daily Mirror* magazine from 1969 to 1970; she joined the *Daily Mirror* in 1970, and was woman's editor of the *Observer* magazine from 1970–1; woman's editor of the *Sunday Mirror*, 1971–81; assistant editor, *Sunday People*, 1981–3; features editor and presenter of TV-AM, 1983–5; editor of the American edition of *Elle*, 1985–6; editor of the *News of the World* Sunday magazine, 1986; editor of *You*, the magazine of the *Mail on Sunday*, 1986–7; and she has been editor of the *Sunday Mirror* and *Sunday Mirror* magazine since 1988.

3 December 1988

I don't think being a woman has posed any special problems for me as an editor. I wouldn't say that I have any more problems dealing with the men on my staff than I have in dealing with the women journalists. There are difficult men and difficult women in all walks of life, and if you're running anything, you'll find that there are some people who have to be handled more carefully than others, but that's nothing to do with sex really, that's just personalities.

On the other hand, if there are any special advantages in being a woman when it comes to editing a national newspaper, I can only say that I've yet to find them. It was different in the old days, when I was assistant editor on the *People*. When I made my farewell speech at a lunch in the Café Royal, I remember saying that I particularly wanted to thank a man to whom I had been far nicer than I had ever been to either of my two husbands, and everybody wanted to know who that was going to be, and of course, it was the head printer.

In those days I was the only female assistant editor in Fleet Street and so I was the one who always had to go down to the stone and say, please, I know it's getting near edition time, but could you ever manage to make this change in page one? I had to try to charm him into making the change. At that period it was a definite advantage to be a woman. But it's all changed now, it's a different world. And in a sense, we are pioneers, we women who have managed to get to the top in Fleet Street, and we can't afford to show any sign of weakness now.

But I don't believe in so-called tough editorial conferences. I think the best editorial conferences are those when you are encouraging people to put forward their ideas, and there's a genuine exchange of views; it's much more intelligent to use editorial conferences in this way, rather than use them to harangue people for things that have happened.

My first job in journalism was as fashion editor of *Honey*. I worked for Audrey Slaughter who taught me a lot. As a child, I'd always wanted to be a writer, and I read everything I could lay my hands on, all the newspapers when I came home from school, Keats and Shelley, poetry, everything.

I wanted to go into journalism because I thought it was one way of becoming a writer. I never had the slightest notion of becoming an executive and it certainly didn't occur to me that I would ever become editor of a national newspaper. I don't think it would have occurred as a serious possibility to any girl in those days. Fleet Street was still very much a man's world when I came to the *Mirror* in 1969. Women subs, or lady subs as they used to call them in those days, were still pretty thin on the ground. I think the worst of the prejudice against women executives in journalism had died down by then, but you still had to fight your corner.

There's a joke on the *Daily Mirror* that I was appointed by mistake. I was interviewed jointly by Mike Molloy and Dennis Hackett for the *Daily Mirror* magazine, and apparently they'd made up a series of signals to one another to indicate whether I was to be hired or not, and the story goes that one of them got the signals mixed up and gave the wrong one and that's how I got the job. It's a good story, but I like to think that it's only a story like so many Fleet Street tales.

How did I feel when the offer of editorship of the *Sunday Mirror* came up? By this time things had changed so much in Fleet Street that I wasn't really surprised that the *Sunday Mirror* was considering a woman as editor. In fact I imagine that there will be many more women editors of national newspapers in the future, but I was surprised that they asked me, because it must be always a surprise to be asked to edit a national newspaper. What happened was that Mike Molloy telephoned me and asked me if I'd like to come in and see the Captain, which I did, and that was it. Anyhow, I have never planned my career. Anything that has ever happened to me has been the result of someone phoning me up with an offer. I don't think journalists are planners by instinct, I don't think we can be.

I've always thought that women journalists worked harder than men, and I've always thought that they were every bit as good as men, not only as reporters and feature writers but as executives. I think I am a good deal more approachable than many editors but it's only fair to add that on a Sunday newspaper there's that much more time to encourage people to drop in and have a chat about things.

I'd quite like the challenge of editing a national daily but I can't say that it's a burning ambition. The last ultimate ambition I ever had was when I was a child and wanted to grow up and be a great poet and that failed and since then I haven't had any ultimate ambition.

Being an editor today is a very different business from what it used to be. It's not enough these days to run the paper, and have a flair for picking the sort of stories that will appeal to your readers. You also have to know about the business side of it, plus marketing and advertising; my television production experience has been extremely useful there. I think it's essential that editors should be involved in all the decisions about their newspapers, like whether they should be advertised on television, the price of newsprint, the printing side of the business, everything that could affect the circulation, which after all, is the bottom line, the thing by which your perform-ance as editor is going to be judged.

All these matters are vital components, not as vital as the editorial content perhaps, but it is important that the editor should be involved.

I've always been very interested in politics. I went through a left-wing period in my teenage years and I'm still fascinated by politics. Captain Bob likes to see the leaders, but he's always open to discussion, and otherwise, he's too busy with all his other interests to get deeply involved in detail. When we launched the *Sunday Mirror* magazine last year he did intervene; he insisted on making the magazine larger, against the advice of all the accountants, who said it would cost a fortune, but he was proved right. The extra size gave us a much larger canvas to work on, and it's been a great success. The circulation has gone up by 300,000 since we launched it.

I think it's probably true that people don't believe what they read in the newspapers any more, but that's because some of the newspapers make up stories. I don't see the point of that. Why make up stories when there are so many fascinating true stories around? What's the point of making up stories about someone like Koo Stark and then paying out a quarter of a million pounds in damages? It would be far smarter to spend that quarter of a million on a television promotion campaign, or on sending a journalist to America or Russia or somewhere to get a real story.

Of course I'll miss Fleet Street when the papers have all gone. I love the place and I love the people. But the job will still be the same. Editing a newspaper is very exciting and I find it most enjoyable. Where else could you get a job where you could be so nosy and curious and be fed with an endless supply of constantly new information? In what other job could you have a life in which no day is ever like any other?

Lord Rothermere

Although the *Mirror* and *Express* newspapers dominated the scene in the forties and fifties, the first of the popular daily newspapers was, of course, the *Daily Mail*, launched by Alfred Harmsworth (Lord Northcliffe) in 1896. So I naturally wanted to meet Lord Rothermere, proprietor of Associated Newspapers Ltd, and the only surviving member of the original dynasty of Fleet Street barons. I talked to him in what used be the dining room of Associated Newspapers Ltd, a room on the fifth floor of New Carmelite House, with a stupendous view over the Thames.

Vere Harmsworth, third Viscount Rothermere, joined Associated Newspapers Ltd in 1951, when he was aged 26. He has been chairman of Associated Newspapers since 1971, when he launched the new tabloid *Daily Mail*, and he has been chairman of the *Daily Mail* and General Trust since 1978.

9 December 1988

I don't remember Lord Northcliffe for the simple reason that he died before I was born, but I was always conscious of his personality; he was a legend in the family from the time I first sat up and started to take notice of things. Consequently, when I was a boy, I always wanted to be a newspaperman, not an engine driver, nor an airline pilot. I think maybe the first thing I ever wanted to be was a newspaperman and a politician, but I soon found that I was far more interested in newspapers.

I accepted from a very early age that whatever else I did in life, ultimately I would become responsible for running a newspaper empire. I regarded this as a very exciting prospect; the burden side of it didn't bother me very much. I also regarded it as a trust, something with which I had to keep faith.

I regard myself primarily as a newspaper proprietor rather than a publisher or a journalist, though I do occasionally throw out journalistic ideas, as Beaverbrook did. Being a newspaper proprietor is a state; either you own a newspaper or you don't. Becoming a publisher is a craft which you can learn, or fail to learn.

I think I read all or most of the material written in my newspapers. I know most of the well-known people who write in my newspapers personally, people like Lynda Lee Potter, John Edwards, Nigel Dempster, Ian Wooldridge. But I don't get in touch with them as often as Beaverbrook used to get in touch with his journalists. I do it through the editors.

I was, however, very closely involved in the planning of the new *Daily Mail* and the *Mail on Sunday*. It was my decision to go tabloid. First of all, I thought that the size was a great advantage in every possible way; in a motor car, for example, in a crowded commuter train, you can read a tabloid paper so much more easily, wherever you are.

But there's another point: the material above the fold in a broadsheet is always far better read than the material below the fold, and that goes for advertising as well. It's the top half of a broadsheet above the fold which is the dramatic area, whereas with the bottom half there's always a problem to make it look attractive. With a tabloid on the other hand, the whole page can be given a tremendous impact, and you get twice the number of pages for the same total of newsprint.

That's the first reason. The second reason was strategic. If we could successfully produce and sell the idea of a middle-market, tabloid-sized paper, then we could leapfrog the *Express* so that they wouldn't be able to compete with us directly. We would be standing at an angle to them and they wouldn't be able to get at us. And we would be exploiting a different market, a young people's market particularly, because young people like that size of newspaper, and they were not addicted to the broadsheet which retained the image of the sort of paper that Dad had always liked. Dads were by habit addicted to the broadsheet and habit is a hard thing to break, whereas the young people like new things and women, particularly, found the tabloid far more convenient.

So it opened up a new possibility for us, which was to angle the new *Daily Mail* towards women's readership. The *Daily Mirror*'s success was built on the realisation that the working classes had suddenly emerged as a readership group with political and spending power. We realised when we were re-launching the *Daily Mail* that women were the last emergent group with spending power, and the ability to influence spending.

If you ask whether the next emergent group might include the ethnic minorities, the blacks, for example, I would answer that the blacks in general do not read newspapers. At least, that's what they've found in New York, and presumably it applies here also, but that's another issue, really.

When we decided to make the new *Daily Mail* a tabloid, it was also decided that it should look more like a miniature broadsheet than a true tabloid because our readership was middle-class, and the paper had to have the style of a middle-class paper which up until then had been always a broadsheet. This meant that it had to have a serious look, a serious approach to lay-out, which David English brilliantly accomplished. The publisher basically chooses the market in which he wants his paper to go. And having decided to remain in the traditional middle-class market, it then became a matter of devising a format which would appeal to people within that market. Our middle-class readers certainly didn't want to buy a conventional tabloid in any circumstances, and one of our problems, in going tabloid, was to convince our readers that we were not in any sense becoming a popular tabloid, that we weren't necessarily going down-market.

The *Express*, on the other hand, assumed that because we had gone tabloid in size, we would go tabloid in nature. They therefore plunged down-market to pursue us and left us with a free field.

I was also very closely involved in the launch of the *Mail on Sunday*. I went through all the dummies with them and, figuratively speaking, I took off my coat and got down to it like any of the other members of the team.

I don't have any problems about people coming into Fleet Street from anywhere in the world and I don't regard Canadians or Australians as colonials. I never have. Maxwell is a naturalised British citizen.

It doesn't bother me a bit that so many British newspapers are now controlled by people who are not British; for example, Murdoch produces newspapers which the public wants to read and if the public wants to read them, then that's that . . . I certainly don't think, as some people do, that the Government should have done something to keep the control of British newspapers in British hands; I think, on the contrary, it's a question of whether the British can produce people any more who are capable of running successful newspapers.

It doesn't appear at the moment as if the British are capable of running newspapers successfully, apart from the Pearson family, who have done a good job on the *Financial Times*. Brendan Bracken, of course, who was really responsible for the success of the *Financial Times*, wasn't English at all. The family came from Ireland originally, but his family emigrated to Australia, I think, and he returned from there. So if the British have any objections to non-British people running their newspapers, neither Brendan Bracken nor Lord Beaverbrook would ever have made it here.

I don't share the apparently generally held view that there's been a noticeable deterioration in the British press over the past ten or fifteen years. As regards accuracy, truthfulness, honesty, no. Invasion of privacy, yes. I think there has been a far greater invasion of privacy than there ever was before.

On the whole question of the invasion of privacy, apart from revelations into Major Ferguson's private life, that sort of thing, or stealing the Queen's private photographs, these are the sort of invasions of privacy which have a high profile now. Intrusions into private grief have largely disappeared, largely thanks to the efforts of the Press Council; it's one of the areas where the Press Council has had a bit of success. As for television, that's another medium. It's not directly connected with the press but it has affected the press because I'm afraid television perpetrates all the sins of the newspapers and commits even more sins than the newspapers ever committed. Television is very much given to intrusions into private grief, using foot-in-the-door methods of all kinds. And it tends to divert criticism towards the press, while committing exactly the same sort of sins itself. They do everything that the press ever did, and then blame the press for doing it.

As far as cheque-book journalism is concerned, it covers so big an area that you have to be very specific. If we are talking about paying convicted criminals for their stories, to me that is cheque-book journalism, and it doesn't happen all that often now. As for paying people who are not criminals for their stories, then I think every single case is unique, really.

I think Wapping was inevitable. It's been on the cards for years. Ever since the NPA in conjunction with the trades unions produced the excellent scheme called 'The Way Ahead' or 'The Plan For Progress' or something like that, a good twenty years ago now, in 1969 I think it was, and since the membership of the unions went against their own leaders in rejecting it, Wapping was inevitable. Because if Wapping hadn't occurred, there would have been bankruptcies, there would have been closures, and in the end, Wapping would have happened anyway.

What the move to Wapping and everything that followed has meant is that it has enabled management to get on with managing, which they couldn't do before. And this of course has made life a lot more positive and consequently easier than the negative, depressing activity which went on during the years when management was forced to spend all its time negotiating with the unions.

It's very sad that we have to leave Fleet Street. I shall certainly miss it. I'll miss the view over the Thames from this room. But everybody's left by now and we'd have to reconstruct all the buildings; we can't stay in them, they're completely obsolete. The problems of access by lorry or by truck is one of the objections to the place; the narrow streets, the traffic jams, the difficulties we would have in putting in the new machines. All the arithmetic indicates that it is better to go to a green-field site and start all over again. It wouldn't make any sense to pull these old buildings down and try to adapt them for modern machinery.

Looking back on it, I'm delighted that I happened to be born into a newspaper dynasty, if you like to put it that way, into a family that produced newspapermen rather than writers like the Pakenhams, or bankers like the Rothschilds. It's been enormous fun being a newspaper baron, more rewarding probably than anything else. In the end, more rewarding even than politics could ever have been.

Bill (Lord) Deedes

Long before the appearance of the *Daily Mail*, the *Daily Mirror* and the *Daily Express*, the *Daily Telegraph* was the best-selling newspaper in Britain. And nobody knows more about the *Daily Telegraph* – or indeed about Fleet Street – than Bill Deedes, who is widely believed to have been the inspiration for Evelyn Waugh's character Boot in his Fleet Street novel, *Scoop*.

W. F. Deedes (Lord Deedes) was editor of the *Daily Telegraph* from 1974 to 1986. He still writes for the newspaper at least once a week. He was with the *Morning Post* from 1931 to 1937; has been a Conservative back-bencher for Ashford, Kent, for twenty-four years; was Parliamentary Secretary to the Minister of Housing and Local Government in 1954–5; Parliamentary Under-Secretary to the Home Department 1955–7 and Minister without portfolio 1962–4.

25 October 1988

I think that the thing to grasp is that the Fleet Street that everybody's just packed out of was a shambles. It wasn't at all the Fleet Street that we'd known before the war, or indeed for a time after the war.

The Fleet Street I remember in the thirties, and this is curious, is that it was not so much connected with the national newspapers as with the provincial ones. Every window in Fleet Street carried the insignia of some provincial newspaper; even the weekly ones had offices there. This gave the whole place a homogenous appearance, and I dare say, a *raison d'être*. I suppose what happened was that rents got too high. I don't think I've noticed a provincial newspaper in Fleet Street for a long time. There may be a few there still.

Before the war industrial relations were pretty good and during the war we had small papers, four or six pages only, so that when newsprint became plentiful again, after the war, there weren't all that many complaints from people who felt that they were overworked. But gradually, through the sixties and seventies, the print unions obtained the mastery, if that's the right word, of Fleet Street and could virtually demand whatever they chose to demand. At the end of it all, some people were being paid a thousand pounds for a fifteen-hour week. The unions will deny this, of course. Naturally, it led to chaos. Not only were the newspapers grossly over-manned, but management seemed to have lost all control. *The Times* tried going out of business for a whole year but it did no good at all.

The decisive things were Eddy Shah standing firm at Warrington and the Thatcher legislation which fined the unions for disobeying the courts over practices like secondary picketing. Shah's victory at Warrington was just one step along the right road, but it paved the way for Wapping and Murdoch. That was the real revolution. I dwell on this because a lot of people think that some of us are sorry about Fleet Street and feel sentimental about leaving it. I don't believe any journalist has the smallest regret about leaving the conditions we had arrived at in Fleet Street just before we moved out.

Of course it's possible to look back nostalgically on the Fleet Street of the pre-war days, or even of the immediate post-war days, but the Fleet Street we left in 1987 had become a nightmare. I was editor of the *Telegraph* from 1974 to 1986 and I don't think we had a trouble-free night in our lives. We may have had mildly less trouble than some of the other papers, but we certainly lost millions of copies, which infuriated our readers, as indeed did all the dirty, badly printed newspapers we were forced to produce.

I'm a writer now, not an executive. But I used to travel a lot and there wasn't a country in the world that wasn't away ahead of Fleet Street in terms of modern print technology: America, South Africa, Australia, all of Europe, even the Third World countries had started moving into the future long before Fleet Street got round to it. Because of the sheer power of the unions.

I often wonder whether it was ever a good idea to have all the national newspapers printed in the capital. Sometimes I think the American system is far better, the system by which great newspapers like the *Los Angeles Times* and the *Chicago Tribune* come out of provincial capitals. What having all the national titles produced from London has meant, particularly with people like Murdoch and Maxwell around, is intense competition, and no particular regret if anybody falls by the wayside.

I was a pretty rare visitor to the Newspaper Publishers' Association but I knew what went on there; they would all sit around looking at each other, never prepared to take a united stand over anything because secretly they were half-hoping that if there was a crisis, somebody else would go under, and there would therefore be one competitor less. That was broadly the philosophy that obtained, and it really began with Beaverbrook. Both he and Rothermere ran extravagant ships, and the devil take the hindmost. In this way the philosophy of the Fleet Street proprietors became very atavistic, very much the law of the jungle. And of course this played right into the hands of the unions, because they were very well aware that the proprietors were never going to unite against them, and so they could leap-frog over one another and over the newspapers.

There was also the point that packed there, all together, in that tiny area that was Fleet Street, everybody drank in the same pubs and if you dared to raise anybody's wages by fourpence, the whole street would know about it in an hour. This meant that if the NGA, one of the print unions, scored a victory, SOGAT, another of them, would immediately hear all about it and insist on having the differential wiped out. To be perfectly fair to the printers, I think you can demoralise people very quickly if you allow them to behave as they wish. And that is exactly what happened, towards the end, the printers were totally demoralised. The money was easy, restrictive practices were totally out of hand, but don't forget, these were craft unions, they could claim a continuity going back to the time when Caxton set up his first press in Westminster. But there was a big difference between what had been an ancient practice and what became a racket.

Before the war Beaverbrook, and to a lesser extent Rothermere, ran their newspapers for what they wanted to say. The Berry family, which produced Lord Camrose and launched the *Sunday Telegraph*, were perfectly satisfied if at the end of the year they broke even. All they really wanted was to produce a newspaper that was a credit to them. But the time came when you couldn't keep newspapers on a tick-over, when you found, as we did with the *Telegraph*, that what with escalating costs, new plant, new requirements of all sorts, and in the meantime endless haemorrhaging, there's no other word for it, to the print unions, you just couldn't run the thing in a happy family way any longer.

Inevitably, people like Murdoch came in and I'm not denigrating his standards. He is a very efficient operator and has taken over more sick newspapers and made them work than anyone else alive, and for that reason we all have to be grateful to him, whatever one thinks about his methods. Still, with somebody like Murdoch around, newspapers have changed their whole style. They're no longer information sheets, they're there as commercial entities and if they're not profitable, someone's going to take them over and make a profit out of them.

So, for better or for worse, we have now become far more commercial. But I think as newspapers have become more efficient, with larger circulations, far better to look at, and with far better marketing, they have become less influential. I'm convinced that the editorial influence of newspapers today is lower than it was at any period of my life. I don't think the public takes the newspapers very seriously any more; their commercial success has virtually invalidated any message they had to deliver. I'm going back to a time when *The Times* had an editorial about Czechoslovakia which convulsed Europe; it had said that if only the Czechs would yield a little bit, there'd be no more trouble. That is something *The Times* would be ashamed of today, but it also indicates a time when editorials really mattered. I don't think they matter any longer.

Even after all these years, people still ask me about *Scoop* and Ethiopia. I was out there with Evelyn Waugh and we shared the same *pension* and he was a very experienced traveller. We took out about a quarter of a ton of luggage because we thought we might be holed up there for quite a time. I took out a full riding kit and God knows what else, but it was all great fun and I enjoyed every minute of it. We would have done a lot better if we'd known that we were going up to an altitude of 10,000 feet, so all the clothes we brought with us were entirely wrong. And there's no doubt that Waugh did make a mockery of the luggage; mine was in the next room to his and was strewn all over the floor. I had exactly eleven pieces, supplied not by Harrods but by Austin Reed, because they were the only people who could do it fast enough. I still have a lot of the stuff, tropical suits and so on; I keep them because it had been my first tropical assignment.

I didn't go to university. I passed my matriculation and spent six months learning shorthand and typing and then, through an uncle, I got a job on the *Morning Post* in 1931. When it closed in 1937 – it was taken over by Camrose – those of us who were young enough joined the *Daily Telegraph* staff, and I've been on the *Telegraph* ever since.

I don't remember what my first job was, but one of the first was accompanying the Duke and Duchess of Kent on their honeymoon? Can you imagine it today, accompanying a Royal Couple on their honeymoon? The idea was to report all the cheering crowds on the way.

I also worked on the Abdication crisis. It was the Bishop of Bradford who broke the story with his sermon, which was carried by the *Yorkshire Post*. The Fleet Street newspapers didn't comment on the affair until after the crisis broke. Today they would have been rattling away from the word Go. I was reading Harold Macmillan's memoirs the other day and I discovered that his wife had been carrying on with Lord Boothby. Now that's a secret that hardly anybody knew until after the war. Today it would have all been in the tabloids from the very start. The main difference – and it's a very big difference – is that it wasn't reported at the time. I like to think that might have been because we lived in an age that respected privacy more. All the same, I've got to admit, there was never a time when I wished I'd chosen another occupation.

It was great fun, indeed it still is, though it's all been depersonalised to a great extent and you've got to remember that ironically people consort far less in open-plan offices than they used to do in the old cells. In those days, you'd gather in each other's rooms for a cup of tea or whatever. You can't gather for a cup of tea or a natter over a VDU, a computer terminal.

The effect of television on newspapers has only been superficial. Television can't really handle news. Television has got to have pictures and its priorities will always be pictures. If there's a bank crash and a train crash on the same day, the train crash will always dominate the television news, even if only three people are involved, because they happen to have good pictures of the smashed train. A bank collapse may affect a million people, but how do you illustrate it, apart from talking heads? Basically I don't think television makes anything like as good a fist of news as the old newspapers did, and some still do. So, if the newspapers would only stick to their last and continue to produce news as opposed to entertainment, they couldn't possibly fail.

I'm past the age of feeling ashamed at recent invasions of privacy, but I think they've been enormously damaging because they give the Government a pretext for acting against the newspapers and no great hullabaloo will go up when they do. The Government can now do really what it likes with the newspapers. How many people would march on Trafalgar Square next Sunday if the Government were to do something really rough with the newspapers? Not a solitary soul, because nobody holds the press in high regard any more. When you see the methods employed by certain newspapers – bullying the Royal Family, bullying people who can't defend themselves, the raising of scandals for scandal's sake, and above all, the hypocrisy that it's all being done in the public interest – it would make you despair.

But the answer lies in the public's own hands. There's a deep-seated reason behind all this, and I don't think it's often discussed. We have far more illiteracy in this country than we've had for a very long time. We have got some millions of semi-literates for whom the tabloids have an immense appeal. There's not much doubt that the tabloids today are catering for people who can barely read. Given less illiteracy, and that implies more taste, a great many of these newspapers would be phased out by public taste, public choice. But you have to be realistic about the public, and at the moment, the public taste for these tabloids is outstanding, unfortunately in my view for the profession of journalism. But so long as these tabloids flourish, there is nothing much any of us can do about it.

Michael (Lord) Killanin

Another journalist who covered the Abdication crisis is Michael Killanin whom I've known ever since I joined the *Irish Times* in 1940. He was a regular member of editor R. M. Smyllie's select circle in Ireland's El Vino, the Pearl Bar in Dublin's Fleet Street, almost opposite the *Irish Times*.

Lord Killanin joined the *Daily Express* as a reporter in 1935, straight from Cambridge. He then moved to the *Daily Mail* and in 1937 was sent out to cover the Sino-Japanese war. On returning to London, he became political and diplomatic correspondent of the *Daily Mail* and wrote a political column for the *Sunday Dispatch*. Since the war he has been a film producer – he was associated with John Ford on the production of *The Quiet Man* – a businessman, and a director of some 120 companies. He has been associated with the Olympic Games since 1950 and Honorary Life President since 1980.

23 November 1988

I'll tell you what my first impression of Fleet Street was; it was of everybody whispering. Tom Driberg had just been acquitted at the Old Bailey on a buggery charge. You can date my arrival in Fleet Street from that, one day in July 1935, when I was still twenty. I'd just come down from Cambridge where I'd got my degree before I was twenty-one. It was a very bad degree, but I'd got the job on the *Express* because I'd edited *Varsity Weekly* and because I'd been president of the Footlights.

My family wanted me to join the *Morning Post* where Bill Deedes worked. He was the youngest political correspondent in Fleet Street and I knew him very well. I thought the shortest cut would be through Lord Castlerosse who'd been taken prisoner on the day my father was killed during the First World War. As it happened he was in bed with flu or something at Claridges, so I went round to see him there and he rang Beaverbrook who rang Christiansen and told him to give me a trial.

I was a probationer and a member of the NUJ and at the end of the first week I remember the Father of the Chapel coming and looking over my shoulder as I did my expenses.

'What's this?' he demanded suddenly. 'One penny. What's that supposed to be for?' I told him that I had done a little story in Waterloo and that the bus fare had been one penny.

'Well, young man,' he said, 'you may travel by bus if it pleases you to do so, but kindly remember that the minimum fare from the *Daily Express* to Waterloo is the cab fare, which is ninepence plus a penny tip for the taxi driver.'

Beaverbrook sent for me shortly after I joined the paper. Chris was the editor but Beaverbrook knew every reporter who worked on his papers and kept an eye on everything we wrote. I remember that there was a list pinned up, I believe it was known as the White List; it was a list of people who could never in any circumstances be mentioned in the *Daily Express*. There was also a list of words that could never be used.

I was just an ordinary reporter. I did whatever stories came up and eventually I got sacked. I had been told to check on a story but I thought that would have been too boring and I knew the story was okay anyway so I just took a chance on it and got sacked for not checking.

But in those days that was no problem. If you worked for the *Express* and managed to get yourself sacked, you would immediately be employed by the *Daily Mail*. They assumed that you must know all the innermost secrets of the *Daily Express*. This was absolute nonsense, because nobody knew anything apart from Christiansen and Harold Keeble perhaps and maybe the features editor, John Raynor. But it was very useful, and it worked the other way round too; anyone sacked from the *Mail* was certain of a job on the *Express*.

The *Daily Mail* sent me out to China to cover the war with Japan. I flew out as far as Marseilles and took a boat the rest of the way. I suppose the whole journey took a little over three weeks and when I got to Hong Kong I met O'Dowd Gallagher and Pembroke Stephens who'd flown the whole way out, in short, easy stages and were waiting there for a boat to take

them up to Kwan Tung. Eventually we all left together on a
boat for Shanghai and the extraordinary thing was that there
were no male passengers on this boat apart from us; they were
all women, which seemed very strange to me. A very nice
American lady came up to us and asked us whether she could
sit at our table; she told us that she'd lived in the Far East for a
number of years.

Anyhow, we arrived in Shanghai and went from there to
Nan King and came back to have a night on the town in Short
Time Maggie's in Soochow Creek and it turned out that this
nice American lady who'd shared our table with us on the boat
was Short Time Maggie herself and all the women we'd seen on
the ship were her staff, her whores . . . They'd had to leave
Hong Kong because they couldn't possibly compete with the
wives of the British officers there.

We had no contact at all with Red China and couldn't get to
Peking. I was accredited to both sides, to Chiang Kai-Shek on
the Chinese side, whom I didn't like much, and also to the
Japanese. So, in the morning, I'd go to a Chinese press
conference and get the story from their side and then have
lunch and in the afternoon I'd go to a Japanese press
conference and hear it all from their side. The Japanese always
got the best coverage because they always gave us a couple of
whiskies. When I came back from China I was a political
writer, pure and simple. I was in a unique position in that I
was a peer with a lobby ticket so that I could use both Houses.
One got all one's stories in those days by bribing MPs with
drink.

I covered the Abdication from Fort Belvedere. We had all
been taking it in turns, waiting for it to happen. We were
staying at the Wheatsheaf in Virginia Water and I was lucky
enough to be the one waiting at the gates when the King drove
out to make his last broadcast from Windsor Castle. And I had
the *Daily Mail* motoring correspondent, Stuart McKenzie,
with me. The idea was that he was supposed to be able to get
me down to the coast faster than anybody else. But the King
easily beat us to it, down to Portsmouth. By the time we arrived

at the gates of the naval dockyard, he was already on a destroyer, on his way to France.

Throughout my entire life, I've always found that the best possible training I ever had was as a general news reporter. It even held good when I became a businessman, and I'm a director now of about a hundred and twenty companies. Because even as a businessman, basically what you have to do is find the story beneath the surface, and that applies as much to a company balance sheet as it does to anything else. When I became president of the International Olympic Games Committee, I don't think I approached the press any differently. On the contrary, I was always trying to ask myself: If I were down there as a reporter, what questions would I be asking? But I have to admit that I was often reported inaccurately.

On the other hand, even when I was a reporter myself, I don't think I ever wrote a story about which I could have said, when I'd read it afterwards, that it appeared in the paper as accurately and correctly as I had written it. That's thanks to the subs. They get a lot of credit for correcting mistakes made by reporters but I can honestly say they fucked up more stories of mine than anybody could ever imagine.

I got involved in quite a few libel cases as a result of the efforts of the subs. For example, one lady I interviewed told me that she was nearly broke. The sub couldn't manage to fit the word 'nearly' in and, as the story appeared, it looked as if she'd said that she was broke. Well, she wasn't ever broke after that, thanks to that sub. When you write a story and the subs get at it and you read it again in the paper, you often wonder if you'd ever been there, out on the story.

I can't possibly say, now that I'm seventy-five, what I would want to do if I were twenty again. But I think I'd still go back into newspapers. I did it originally to learn something about life. In those days I wanted to be a writer. I'd read English at Cambridge, and I'd been president of Footlights and I wanted to write novels but I realised that I knew nothing at all about the real world. So that's why I became a newspaperman in the first place: to learn about the world. And it was great fun, if one wasn't married. It was great to go into the office one morning and find out that you're on the way to cover a war in China. But you can't do that if you're a married man. And after the war I decided that what I wanted was to get married and go back to the land where I'd spent my childhood, around Spiddal, in Galway.

I'm not saying that I didn't return once or twice to Fleet Street to file another few stories. I returned for the Queen's coronation to write a couple of pieces for the *Daily Mail* and for a few American newspapers from inside the Abbey and when I'd done my stint, I went down to Fleet Street again in all my full regalia, to have a pint or two, and suddenly I found myself in the Poppinjay, the *Daily Express* pub, conducting the Red Flag with my ceremonial sword.

I suppose that the most exciting thing that ever happened to me in Fleet Street was reading my own by-line under a story I'd written. When I was elected a member of the Garrick Club long before the war, there were no journalists there. Well, there might have been one or two theatre critics, but that was about it. There were a lot of publishers, a race of people far higher up on the literary scale than newspaper reporters. I had been elected at the age of twenty-three, and one day soon after that someone asked me: 'What do you do?' When I told them I was a reporter on the *Daily Mail*, it cleared the bloody room in seconds.

The next day Gerald Duckworth, the publisher, came to me and said: 'The next time they ask you in the Garrick what you do, you'd better not tell them that you're a reporter. Why not tell them that you're a peer of the realm?'

These days the Garrick is full of journalists. You can even hire the place for PR functions.

Leon Pilpel

In view of Michael Killanin's slashing attack on subs in general, I felt that this was an appropriate place to ask a very special sub to speak out on behalf of his branch of the profession. I first met Leon Pilpel during the brief period he spent on the *Irish Times* in the late forties and was delighted to meet him again in the still slightly eerie atmosphere of Fortress Wapping.

Leon Pilpel left school at sixteen to work for *Advertising World*, the trade journal started by Michael Berry in 1901. He served in the army and then took a degree at Trinity College, Dublin, working as a sub-editor on the *Irish Times* at night. In 1950, he joined *The Times* as junior sub-editor and was chief sub-editor (home news) for twelve and a half years until 1978. Since 1979, he has edited the readers' letters.

10 November 1988

I have worked under six editors of *The Times*: Casey, Haley, Rees-Mogg, Harold Evans, Douglas-Home and the present editor, Charles Wilson. I'm one of the few members of the staff who come out half-way decent in Harold Evans's book. Perhaps I should start by explaining the difference between *The Times* as it was when I joined it in 1950, and as it has since become.

The old tradition was that you built up a good solid reputation in the provinces, and at the age of forty or thereabouts, you came to Fleet Street, and, if you had set your sights pretty high, you came to *The Times*, if they'd have you. You then finished up your career on *The Times*, the last twenty years. When I came here in my mid-twenties, I was very much an exception to that rule, and I was made to feel it; a very junior, junior sub-editor. But I'd had a great deal of experience. I'd gone straight from school at sixteen to work for *Advertising World*, a trade paper printed by Odham's. In effect, because of the war and the call-up, after a year in the job I was actually editing it and writing most of the copy, and making the paper up, and going over to Odhams to put it to bed. We had a succession of editors who would stay for a few months and then push off; I was the only one with any continuity and so I did the bulk of the entire job myself every week. I acquired all the journalistic skills it was possible to acquire because I was the only one who'd been around long enough to know what was going on.

I had no family background in journalism. It had never even crossed my mind to become a journalist. It was just a job that happened to come up at the right time. It certainly never occurred to me that I'd wind up editing the letters to *The Times*, though I did edit the letters to the editor of this little paper, and write a few myself as well, if they were a bit thin on the ground. That's something you could never do on *The Times*. Every letter is genuine and every letter is checked; and we get about sixty or seventy thousand a year, that's about thirteen hundred a week.

After my military service, I managed to get into Trinity College, Dublin and paid my way by working every night as a sub on the *Irish Times*. When I left, its famous editor, R. M. Smyllie, who was also Dublin correspondent of *The Times*, gave me a letter of recommendation, which did the trick.

Not very long after I joined *The Times*, Casey retired and Haley, who had been director-general of the BBC, was appointed editor. He was a rather difficult man of immense rectitude, and he had a very difficult job: to bring *The Times* into the very different post-war era with a very static or even a declining circulation and very limited resources. It was during this period that we started to think about putting news on the front page – though it didn't happen until 1966. Up to then we had been largely a subscription newspaper, and you couldn't compete on the bookstalls with a blank-looking front page, all small, pre-paid ads, with only a little ear-piece which we used to put up, a panel listing all the news of the day; it was pitiful when you looked at it against all the other screaming headlines. Even the *Daily Telegraph* had been printing news on its front page since 1939.

By this time *The Times* had been sold to Roy Thomson and we had all been assured that the whole thing was going to take off and become a mass-circulation paper to rival the *Financial Times*. It was going to sell a million in ten years and it was going to be bigger and brighter and more important and better informed but still remain a journal of record. It didn't quite work out like that.

I never met Thomson. He kept very much in the background and didn't interfere. It was said that he was more interested in reading balance sheets than newspapers, but he had a great respect for *The Times*. It had been his ultimate ambition to own *The Times*.

I never thought the link-up with the *Sunday Times* was a good idea because the two papers really had nothing in common apart from the word 'Times', but then in those days everything was called 'The Times' this or that, like The Times Furnishing Company, because the words really did stand for something a hundred and fifty years ago.

It was a very different kind of paper from the *Sunday Times* and there was a lot of rivalry between the staffs, and not much co-operation. We did try to use common foreign correspondents which worked up to a point, but in my view it was not a happy marriage and the disruption caused by the move from Printing House Square to Gray's Inn Road was very considerable indeed. After the move, things began changing very rapidly. When Thomson took over the race was on to get all the bright young journalists they could lay their hands on, especially city men. It started to become far more like the *Sunday Times*. Haley was very opposed to the 'Top People Take *The Times*' campaign, so they changed it to 'Those on the Way to the Top Take *The Times*' to meet his objection. He had also grasped the fact quite early on that *The Times* had more women readers than anybody else had imagined, and that's why they started a women's page.

Somebody described Rees-Mogg as kindly but not kind. He became editor in 1967 shortly after Thomson bought the paper. In my dealings with him I always found him kind as well as kindly, very much an eighteenth century, Lord Shaftesbury type figure. Under Rees-Mogg we took a sharp turn towards popularity and it just didn't work. It frightened off a lot of old readers without really winning any new ones. Although the circulation shot up under the impetus of all that hype, it didn't stay there.

Evans was a very live wire, a man in a hurry and a great starter of things but in my view he needed guidance and control of the kind he used to get on the *Sunday Times*, where he would just throw off ideas and others would carry them out. Anyway, I don't think he had enough time on *The Times*; you can't really do much with a paper like *The Times* in one year. Evans undoubtedly had many good ideas, a lot of which have been absorbed into the paper since. Murdoch comes into the office and wanders around in a pullover, looking at what you are doing, asking a question or two, just one of the boys.

But the man who had the most influence on me at *The Times* was Clifford Haigh who was chief home sub-editor when I joined the paper. I admired his careful approach, checking everything; that's something you don't see around much these days. Sub-editing suited my temperament, I'd far rather be a sub than anything else. I don't regard myself as being creative; I'm a craftsman and I take a great pride in my craft for its own sake. I like words, I enjoy language and it's enough for me if a piece of writing by somebody else has been tidied up and checked and made as clear as I can possibly make it.

I used to keep an image in my mind of a man in outer Siberia who knew nothing at all about what had been going on in the the world and so you had to make sure that he knew exactly what every story was about. Consequently, we never used initials without explaining what they stood for somewhere; well, we did allow the BBC but almost all other initials we explained.

I suppose the night that sticks out in my mind as the most exciting in my whole career – and mind you, you must remember I was chief home sub-editor, I was not concerned with what was going on abroad – was the attempt that was made to kidnap Princess Anne on her way back to the Palace. I sent this story out on the flashes we were getting from the Press

Association, one sentence at a time right until midnight. It's the nearest I ever got to that sort of evening newspaper journalism. We managed to get a full column into the first edition and it was a coherent story and read very smoothly despite the fact that it had been sent down sentence by sentence and I found that very satisfying.

The move to Wapping was sudden and startling – none of us knew anything about it in advance. The editor just called us in at about eight o'clock on the Friday night and told us to turn up at Wapping on the Sunday. There was no question of voting whether you'd go or not, we were just told either we'd go or we'd be sacked. I reported at Wapping on the Sunday and it was absolute chaos, as you can imagine. But as far as I'm concerned, it's just another newspaper office. In essence we're only doing what we've been doing for years, but with better typography, better pictures and aiming for a circulation and a news coverage which can be far greater now than it could ever have been before, because of the instant transmission the new technology has given us. Sub-editors are pretty desk-bound anyway, we don't have a great deal of time to socialise or meet other people.

I think I've been very fortunate and if I had it to do all over again, I don't think I'd want to do anything else. It's been great fun, I've enjoyed every minute of it, though it's been hellish hard work too, eleven, sometimes twelve hours a day. They used to say that Delane, one of the great editors of *The Times* in the last century, always maintained that there was not a single proof that ever went to press in his days on the newspaper without his handwriting on it somewhere. I don't know whether that's true or not but I do know that for the twelve and a half years I was chief home sub-editor on this newspaper, there was not a single home story that ever went to press without my handwriting on it somewhere.

Ken Smiley

The first Fleet Street character I got to know really well was Ken Smiley, who was chief sub-editor of the features department when I joined the *Daily Mirror* in 1959. If you think about it, the paper was still quite small in those days, and under Hugh Cudlipp, the editorial director, we had Jack Nener, the editor, Reg Payne (assistant editor, features), myself (features editor), Freddie Wills (deputy features editor) and Ken Smiley (chief sub-editor, features) before you really got down to anybody who was actually doing any work for the sheet. And my first recollection of Ken was that whenever I tried out a piece of copy on him, he would always ask: 'Would you like me to run an educated pencil over it for you?' and if I said yes, he would then immediately hand it to Roy Harris, who was next down the line, to deal with it. From Ken Smiley I think I learned what was wrong with Fleet Street; inadvertently, perhaps, he demonstrated to me that it was a glorious picnic that couldn't possibly go on for very much longer . . . .

Ken Smiley's first job in newspapers was as a reporter with the *Belfast Newsletter*. He then worked for a time as sub-editor on the *Belfast Telegraph* before coming to Fleet Street in 1953 as a sub-editor on the *Daily Mirror*. In 1955 he went to Africa for a year to work on the *Mirror* group's newspapers there and he returned as chief sub-editor, features in 1956. He worked in the New York office of the *Daily Mirror* for a couple of years in the early sixties and then moved to the circulation department of Odham's Press shortly after the *Mirror* take-over of Odham's Press. He is now freelancing.

26 October 1988

The first time I knew the *Mirror* would never be the same again was when Maxwell came in. Before that, the *Mirror* had always been something mystic that we worked for, and then suddenly somebody came in who owned the shares we had never felt were owned by any of the previous people who had run the *Mirror*, and who had never made us feel as if we were owned by anybody.

As far as Fleet Street itself is concerned, I've never been anywhere that I enjoyed better, because I like Fleet Street people better than anybody else. They never bore me. They annoy the hell out of me sometimes, but they've got something that sets them apart from other people. To be blatant about it, Fleet Street was the best in the world, and we could even say of some *Mirror* character, he was no bloody good on the *Mirror*, but anywhere else in Fleet Street, he'd be terrific. We all had the feeling that when you got here, you'd made it, and if you couldn't stay here, then you weren't good enough.

Once the meat market went to Smithfield, everything to do with meat was called Smithfield, and I think it was the same with Fleet Street. The whole of British journalism was centred there, all the stars of the provincial newspapers. However, having said that, I don't think the quality of the papers will be changed by the move to Wapping, or wherever. If you're sitting down in front of a VDU, it doesn't really matter where you're sitting. It's pleasant to meet other journalists, but you don't need to. I was in the bally place for thirty odd years and I hardly spoke to anyone from the *Daily Express* or from any of the other papers. Even when I was in New York for the *Mirror*, we never saw the *Mail* or the *Express* people. They never came near us and we never went near them. I've only been in the *Daily Mail* building twice in my lifetime and once was to meet one of the secretaries and once was to be interviewed by some fellow who wanted me to work for the *Evening News*.

The only paper other than the *Daily Mirror* I've ever done any work for was when I freelanced for a time for the Ladies Page of the *Daily Telegraph*. That must have been about 1980. It was a magnificent experience. I did one summer with them. They were absolutely delightful. If I changed a 'but' to an 'and', they'd come in the next morning and say: 'Dear Ken, I see you've changed my copy, you've rewritten my copy.' It was beautiful. They were doing a thing about English clothes, which at that time were being bought by working girls in Paris and I put up a headline: FRENCH WITHOUT FEARS. All their beads were jangling, and they said: 'Have you seen what Ken's written?' It was wonderful. But that was the only time I ever strayed outside the *Mirror* group.

My first impression of Fleet Street, when I got there, was that I was now sitting at the best subs' table in the world. At that time the *Mirror* was the best-produced newspaper in the world, and they very soon made you realise that. I thought the big problem would be over the front page headlines, but not at all, not at all. In those days, if you misplaced a comma, the entire roof would fall in. For the inside pages, you were given the headline type and you had to make it fit. Damn difficult it was sometimes, because you only had about five minutes, but you soon got it.

The most embarrassing thing that ever happened to me was the first night I was chief sub, features. There was an article by Keith Waterhouse, and he'd been in New York, and he'd done a piece on the high cost of living there, and this was the first story I'd handled as chief sub, features, and I thought it would be a good idea to run a photograph of a mocked-up expense sheet. Even Dick Dinsdale, the deputy editor, who was never known to be enthusiastic about anything, thought it was quite a good idea. And so, in it went. And when the paper was delivered to my flat the next morning, I was surveying it with great pride when it suddenly came to me that I'd added up the total wrong. I rang up the newsagent and said that I never wanted to see the *Daily Mirror* at home again, and I never have, ever since. I preferred to wait until I'd got into the office to discover what cock-ups I'd been responsible for.

Monty Fresco

But Fleet Street wasn't only about words. From around 1904 when the technique of printing half-tone plates on high-speed rotary presses was developed, pictures became every bit as important as words, in some ways more important. There had been an earlier generation of press photographers, of course, who had covered the Crimean and the Boer wars, but in the absence of any means of reproducing their pictures in the newspapers, they had to be copied by artists and published as engravings. Monty Fresco was one of the first generation of photographers whose work went straight into the paper from his own bromide prints.

Monty Fresco was born at Spitalfields in the East End of London in 1919, the youngest of fourteen children. He left school at 14 and became a messenger boy for a photo agency. His mother pawned her wedding ring to buy him his first camera, and he had his first picture published when he was 15. On leaving the army at the end of the war, he rejoined Topical Press and within two years was chief photographer. In 1959 he joined the *Daily Sketch*, and since 1970, has been with the *Daily Mail*.

2 November 1988

When I left school there was very little education and not a lot of employment around. I had a brother-in-law who worked as a machine-minder for the *Daily Mail*, and unlike most of the rest of them in the East End, he never seemed to be out of work. So with a sixpenny piece and a bag of sandwiches I come down to Fleet Street and get a job as a messenger boy for the Topical Press Agency.

In those days the newspapers mostly got their pictures from the agencies. They didn't have any staff photographers, or if they had one, then that was it. The idea was to beat all the boys from the other agencies at getting the pictures around to the newspaper offices, and I was pretty good at it. For every publication, that's every time a picture I delivered was published, I got a halfpenny or a penny. But that wasn't really the point. I always felt like I'd taken the photo myself and I got a thrill from that. I still get the same kind of thrill, even today, when a photo of mine is published in the paper.

Within six months I was in the darkroom, making up the chemicals, and inside a year I was a junior printer in the darkroom. I learned a lot that was extremely useful to me in those days, because when you became a photographer you developed and printed your own pictures. These days, it's all automatic. Once they take the film out, you've no control over anything. After that I became a cameraman.

Then the war came and I spent three years in the infantry and three in the Royal Engineers, the photographic section, and when I went back to Fleet Street it was as chief photographer for the Topical Press Agency. But by this time, all the newspapers had their own staff photographers and the agencies were going to the wall. So when Topical Press folded in 1952, I went free-lance for a bit, working for the *Daily Sketch* in the evenings.

By this time I'd developed a bit of a technique. If I saw a crowd of photographers congregated together, I'd always go off somewhere else on the grounds that there was no point in getting the same picture as all the rest of them were getting, if by any chance I could find something different. I can remember the picture that got me a staff job on the *Sketch*. I'd been sent to cover Prince Charles at Bertram Mills Circus, he was about five at the time. It was a rota job and all the rota boys were inside the big top. As a free-lance, I was on the outside, where they were having a sort of fun fair, and I was just wandering around, looking for something different, when suddenly I catch sight of one of the Royal detectives. Now, whenever you see a Royal detective, you know that one of the Royals has got to be about somewhere. What I didn't know was that Prince Charles had left the main arena of the circus and was taking a ride in the ghost train with this little girl about his own age. But I just kept close behind this Royal detective and he was standing right at the exit to the ghost train when Prince Charles comes shooting through the swing doors with this little girl beside him, both of them looking very scared, and *click!* I get my picture.

I've been doing the Royals all my life. I was the first photographer ever to be allowed into the quadrangle of Buckingham Palace, that's right inside it, to photograph the Queen returning from her Coronation, and I've been doing Royal assignments ever since.

My number one favourite subject is the Queen Mother. I must have photographed her thousands of times. But the thing with the Royals is you don't ever know for sure whether they recognise you or not. The Queen Mother, in the old days, was always a four-yard shot. If she stopped and turned round to face the photographers, you could always bet on it that she was exactly four yards away, and she'd always wait and make sure that all the flash bulbs had gone off before moving on. Once at a premiere, just before the King died, a little kid was giving her a bouquet and my bulb didn't go off, so she held on to the kid's hand until I'd had time to change the bulb and take my picture.

I reckon Prince Charles recognises me; he told me a couple of years back that I should have retired long ago. Charles is great, he's easy. But with the Queen, I was never sure. Normally she'd never give any indication that she recognised you. But once on a tour of India, I was called over by her private secretary who told me that she wanted to talk to me. All the other photographers got the dead needle about this, but she only wanted to talk about the old days. 'You haven't been on a Royal tour for ten years,' she said, and this surprised me. And then she added: 'Japan was the last tour you were on.' She hadn't had the time to do any homework or consult anyone. So I reckon she must have recognised me.

Thatcher is a good publicity woman, she's great. Funnily enough, most of the Conservatives are quite good, it's the Labour ones that can be a pain, apart from Denis Healey. Wilson was always very difficult.

Pope John Paul, of course, is marvellous. I was sent to Poland to cover his return to his homeland and after I'd been out there for a few days and had photographed him a few dozen times, he started to recognise me. Then we had to photograph him with a bunch of Cardinals and I wasn't too happy to see that the photographers once again were being kept about two hundreds yards away.

I was wondering how I could possibly get a bit closer when I spotted a cluster of about twenty Cardinals marching out towards a row of chairs set up about fifteen yards from where the Pope would be sitting. So I nipped past the guards, mingled in amongst the Cardinals, marched in with them, and sat down in the middle of them. There was so much excitement going on about the arrival of the Pope that nobody seemed to notice me there, or if they did, they decided that they didn't want to upset the whole proceedings by making a big fuss. But the Pope certainly noticed me. He couldn't really fail to have noticed me, since I was wearing one of those jazzy Hawaiian short-sleeved shirts and slacks as usual, and I must have stuck out like a sore thumb among all the Cardinals in their scarlet robes. But all the Pope did was to stare at me with a funny, quizzical look in his eyes, as if to say, 'What the hell are you doing there?' or, being the Pope, probably, 'What in heaven's name are you doing there?' and *click*. Again, I had my picture. One of the best I've ever taken.

I'm going to miss Fleet Street when we move away from here. I miss the old Fleet Street already, the ink and the hot metal and the noise of the machines and all the excitement. Above all I'm going to miss the people. There's hardly anybody left in the street any more. I remember the big race days, when the bookies used to come down here and set up for business in the Courtway around the side of Northcliffe House and you'd have queues of men, mostly printers, from the *Star* and the *News Chronicle* and the *Sunday Dispatch* and the *News of the World* and the *Daily Sketch* and the *Daily Mail*, thousands of them, all waiting to place their bets. And although this was all highly illegal in those days, the police would always come down to help regulate the queues and keep order. Occasional-ly, on a day when there were only a few little races on, they'd knock off the odd bookie, just for the record, but they'd never do it on Derby Day or during Ascot Week.

Generally speaking, journalists work for their wages these days, not for the paper any more, not for the sake of the job itself, for the fun of it. We had more fun when we were all on low wages and time meant nothing to us. When King George VI died, I was only a lad and I was at the cinema when I heard about it. But I didn't ring the office or anything, I just went straight back in there, and worked right through the night.

When I think about Fleet Street in the old days, what comes to mind is the smell. And when I think about smells, there are only two I'll always remember. One is the smell of a baby just out of the bath, with Johnson's baby powder all over it, and the other is the smell of a newspaper going to press, the ink and the oil and the burning flong and the paper and the foundry. It's all gone now.

I don't know anything about computers and so I can't say whether we've progressed since those old days, but I do know that we press photographers haven't progressed any as a result of modern technology. We used to be in a business where we could put our view of the story we were covering across to the public. Now all we're able to put across is the camera's view. Today's cameras are so highly developed technologically that you can't control them properly any more, they really control you. And to my mind, that's not what press photography used to be about.

Philip Wrack

Another man who shares Monty Fresco's attachment to the Fleet Street we all used to know is Phil Wrack of the *News of the World*. When I rang him at Fortress Wapping and asked him whether he would like to meet me to contribute a few memories to this anthology, he said, 'I don't get to Fleet Street much before one-fifteen these days.' In view of the sheer distance between Wapping and EC4, I said, 'You don't go to Fleet Street every day, do you?' 'Sure,' he said. 'I still live in Fleet Street. I only work here in Wapping.'

Philip Wrack started as a news-paper boy in Scunthorpe. He worked as a sub-editor in Grimsby and for the *Manchester Evening News* before coming to London as a sub on the *Evening News*. From the *Evening News* he moved to the *Sun* under Larry Lamb and has been deputy editor of the *News of the World* under ten editors.

24 November 1988

I started in newspapers by delivering them, in Scunthorpe, for ten shillings (50p) a week. That was in 1943. I very quickly realised that the most interesting part of a newspaper was the editorial department and I set my mind on getting in there.

In Scunthorpe the news editor used to sub all the local reporters' copy before sending it on to the head office in Grimsby. So I moved to Grimsby and got a job as a sub. I went from Grimsby to the *Manchester Evening News* in 1954 under the legendary Tom Henry and in 1955 moved down to Fleet Street to work for the *London Evening News*. I used to consider that my job, with nine editions a day, was the most highly pressurised in the world. The pressure on an evening paper chief sub is far greater than the pressure on anyone who works for a daily newspaper.

My great god in Fleet Street at that time was Arthur Christiansen because the *Daily Express* in those days was the greatest newspaper in the world. But I also greatly admired Cassandra of the *Daily Mirror* and still remember some of the columns he wrote. For example, the one about an atom bomb test which began: 'Today I watched a dress rehearsal for the end of the world.' I also read every word written by Vincent Mulchrone.

The Lewisham rail disaster sticks in my mind, because the train carrying me in to London had to slow down to a walking pace past the wreckage which we knew still had scores of bodies trapped in the tangled wreckage.

Everybody remembers the assassination of President Kennedy but for me it was curiously memorable in a totally negative way. By this time I was chief sub on the *Evening News*, and I had caught the 7.10 p.m. to Orpington not having heard about it, because it had happened after the last edition of the evening had gone to press. My wife met me at Orpington station and told me that I'd got to go straight back, because President Kennedy had been shot. She'd left my seven-year-old son in the house, and when we got back home to drop my wife off, so that I could take the car back to Fleet Street, he was on the doorstep and shouted: 'He's dead, Daddy, he's dead.' But when I got to the office I found that there was no way we could produce another edition of the *Evening News*; we would only be getting in the way of the production of the *Daily Mail* and the *Daily Sketch*. That was very frustrating.

Another big news story that sticks in my mind is the Aberfan disaster. It happened at about ten o'clock in the morning and the evening papers got all the initial coverage. There were two unforgettable pictures that day: one of the slurry sliding down the mountain, and another of a police officer carrying a child aged about seven in his arms. There was a lot of debate in the office that day about which picture should go on the front page, and I was very pleased that we managed to get both pictures – one of which was later judged the picture of the year – on to the front page.

Budget Day was always exciting on the *Evening News* and we used to pride ourselves that our Budget edition was every bit as good as the morning papers next day.

I remember the *Evening Standard* arriving at the office one evening with a lead story, FLEET STREET EDITOR SACKED. What had happened was that Derek Marks, on his way from the *Daily Express* to El Vino, had run into Stafford Somerfield who was also just going out for a drink and had asked him whether anything was happening. 'Yes,' Stafford replied, 'I've just been sacked.' So Derek immediately phoned the *Evening Standard*. We didn't have the story because there was no way we could have known about it. But it's a good example of how tight a society Fleet Street used to be.

I've worked under ten editors: Larry Lamb at the *Sun*, Tiny Lear, Bernald Shrimsley, Peter Stephens, Ken Donnelan, Barry Askew, Derek Jameson, Nick Lloyd, David Montgomery and Wendy Henry at the *News of the World*. They were all different. Tiny Lear was captain of his ship and he was happy to let his crew get on with it while he did the steering, but increasingly the recent editors have wanted to get more closely involved with things, which is clearly what Murdoch wants from his editors. It can be a bit demoralising for some members of the staffs and I'm not sure that it produces good newspapers.

I suppose I'm the first deputy editor of a Fleet Street paper to work under a woman editor since 1903. But working for Wendy Henry is just like working for any other talented editor; the only difference between her and any other editor I've ever worked for is her shape. She's always had an unerring instinct for spotting a story that will interest the *News of the World* readers. Frequently the *News of the World* runs stories which, if it were left to my judgement, we would not run. Which undoubtedly is one of the reasons why I've never been editor.

The newspapers are there to entertain as well as to inform and if there are times when the readers don't believe everything they read, it's not going to do them any harm if it's not hurtful. The papers have been very skilful in meeting the challenge of TV by running stories about the players in the TV soaps, by turning the whole TV thing into a sort of news, in fact. The death of Dirty Den would be read as a news story even though the readers knew perfectly well that the actor who plays the part was still happily drinking a pint in his local. The character is far more real than the actor who plays him but there is nothing new in this either. There are those of us old enough to remember the death of Grace Fairbrother in a blazing barn in *The Archers*, and that was something like forty years ago.

I rarely go down Fleet Street these days before one-fifteen. If I had been a doctor I would have wanted a practice in Harley Street, and if I'd gone into advertising I'd have wanted to be in Madison Avenue. For newspapermen, the place is Fleet Street, it's as simple as that. I don't suppose the term Fleet Street as a collective noun for the national newspapers came into use until around the Beaverbrook era, and I suppose it will drop out of use eventually, but not for a long time yet.

The new technology is superb; it's exciting, it's clean and it's quick and it's a great joy to be free from all the wrangles with the print unions. But it's a great pity we weren't able to use all these marvellous new methods while we were still there, in Fleet Street.

Michael Frayn

Most of the journalists who managed to make it to Fleet Street hoped, like Phil Wrack, to remain there for the rest of their working lives. A few sampled the Fleet Street experience for a few years and then moved into magazines, book-writing or television. Michael Frayn is one of the latter; he was in London working for the *Guardian* when I was on the *Mirror*. I met him again in the Waldorf Astoria next door to the Aldwych Theatre where his translation of Chekhov's *The Sneeze* was playing to packed houses.

Michael Frayn went straight from university to the *Manchester Guardian* where he worked as a reporter from 1957 to 1959, when he came to Fleet Street, to write the Miscellany column for the *Guardian* and he wrote a column for the *Observer* from 1962 to 1968. Since then he has become a highly successful novelist and playwright, whose West End hits include *Donkey's Years* and *Noises Off*.

18 October 1988

My memories of Fleet Street are very thin. In 1959 the *Guardian* decided that they wanted a written column, so they sent me down from Manchester to do it. Previously it had consisted mainly of contributions from readers, and it had been going steadily downhill. In London, I was given a completely free hand. The feature page editor was Brian Redhead who later became famous on the BBC programme *Today*, and he frequently saved me from getting the sack. I wrote a terrible column, absolutely appalling. I could never get around to doing enough reported stories and instead I used to write funny little invented paragraphs and gradually it turned into a humorous column.

When I went down to Fleet Street first I had instructions to introduce myself to the London editor of the *Guardian*, Gerry Fay. I found him in El Vino, with Philip Hope Wallace. When he said, 'What will you have?' I automatically replied: 'A half of bitter, please,' because I'd been working in Manchester and up there if anybody asked you what you were going to have, there was only one answer. It was always: 'A half of bitter, please.' Gerry Fay paid not the slightest attention. He simply called out to a passing waiter: 'And another bottle of champagne.' That was my introduction to Fleet Street.

I do remember another story about El Vino. I don't know whether I should mention his name, but what the hell, he won't care. It was Henry Fairlie. And he'd been assigned to cover the summit conference in Paris. By this time Henry had been employed by almost every publication in Fleet Street. He was a brilliant journalist, an outstanding right-wing commentator, but he did have this very bad habit of running up enormous bills and consequently a lot of the newspapers in Fleet Street found it too expensive to employ him.

He finally landed up on the *Daily Mail* and they had arranged to send him to this vital summit conference in Paris. Henry managed to draw a huge advance on his expenses and he got as far as El Vino and there he stuck. He covered the entire conference by telephone, from El Vino. And the funny thing is that his coverage of the conference was perfectly satisfactory; in fact some of the stories he got on the phone were a lot better than the rest of them were able to get, over there in Paris.

He was an extraordinary man, with his own sense of priorities. He went off to cover Washington for the *Evening News*, after he'd run out of all the other Fleet Street possibilities, I think. He'd gone bankrupt, which was one reason why the Washington job attracted him. I went to see him there in 1967 or 1968, and he was still Washington correspondent for the *Evening News* and he was living in this magnificent house in Georgetown and he gave the most expensive dinner parties with enormous fires roaring away in all the grates. Yet when I tried to make a telephone call, I found that his phone had been cut off, for non-payment of the bill. Can you imagine it? A journalist not paying his phone bill. That's what I mean by his priorities. I don't suppose he's changed.

I worked very closely with Brian Redhead. Initially we took an instant dislike to each other. He thought I was a young upstart and I thought he was tremendously full of himself, which I have to say, he is. But we decided that if he was going to be feature page editor and I was going to write for it, we'd better quickly come to some working arrangement, which we did, and after that it was wonderful. He was a very good journalist and turned out to be a very loyal boss. If you were on his page, he'd fight like a tiger for you.

I moved to the *Observer* in 1962 and wrote my column for five years in Tudor Street, in a great warren of little offices, a lot of old houses, joined together. Then they moved into New Printing House Square and had a wing in the then new *Times* building, today occupied by merchant bankers. The *Observer* remained there until the recent move out to Battersea. I think I learned something about writing a column simply by having to do it. In a sense it was easier when I was doing a column three times a week for the *Guardian*, because you never had any time to think.

This place, the Waldorf Astoria, is where David Astor used to bring people to sack them, because it was owned by the family and he always got special rates. It never happened to me, but he brought my predecessor, Paul Jennings, in here and gave him a lunch and then told him that in future they wanted him to do a lot more – travel writing and women's pieces and fill-in bits for the business pages, but of course still continue his very funny column. Paul immediately got the message and resigned promptly. You were never fired from the *Observer*, any more than you were from the *Guardian*; they just made your life so uncomfortable that you had to go.

Haley of *The Times* was famous for sacking people in the bog. If you happened to be having a pee next to him in the Gents, he was quite likely to say, 'Oh, and by the way, we shan't be renewing your contract.'

I think I was young enough to be highly impressed when my name first appeared in a newspaper; it had worn off a bit by the time I'd got into the theatre and had my first play on in the West End. Once I became well-known as a playwright, and started being interviewed myself, instead of interviewing other people, I began to see my old trade from a new angle. For a start, they always got something totally wrong, and it was usually the same thing. That's because they all start by checking on the cuttings. So that if some journalist once interviewed you and got something completely wrong, that mistake would crop up in every subsequent interview, because they'd got it from the cuttings. You wouldn't get any chance to deny it either, and put the record straight, because they wouldn't bother even asking you about it, since it had been in the cuttings. The result of all this was that after a few years there'd be hundred of cuttings in the newspaper libraries all carrying the same mistake, so it couldn't possibly be wrong, could it?

Probably because I've been working in other media I haven't really been aware of the changes in newspapers recently. I guess Harry Evans changed things a lot. He was an old friend of mine. He'd been a leader writer on the *Manchester Evening News* when I was a reporter on the *Guardian*, the same firm. We both used to lunch in the canteen on the top floor every day. I liked him very much; he was a dazzling editor.

I've never felt the slightest bit bitter about the fact that anybody who appears on the television regularly is instantly more famous than the top newspaper columnist or the playwright of the year. People don't really remember what you've done, what you're famous for, when you appear on television, they just remember that they've seen your face somewhere. Usually they think you're someone they've met in private life.

If that's fame, it's a very transitory kind of fame.

Milton Shulman

Michael Frayn now writes mainly for the theatre; for the past thirty-two years, Milton Shulman has been writing about it. When I met him first in the early sixties he was working as a producer for independent television all day and going to the theatre almost every night as critic for the *Evening Standard*. I talked to him in his flat overlooking Eaton Square.

Milton Shulman came to England with the Canadian Armed Forces. Before the war he had been a lawyer. While at the University of Toronto he had edited the university newspaper, which was a daily, and while at law school had edited the law school journal. He decided to stay on in England after the war and after a very brief spell with Reuters, joined the *Evening Standard*. He has written several books and is well-known as a radio broadcaster.

8 December 1988

On the first day I arrived at the *Evening Standard* the editor Herbert Gunn said, 'I understand you're an expert on the German army?' I replied that I was, and he said, 'Well, will you go to Germany and find Martin Bormann?' I told him that to the best of my knowledge Martin Bormann was dead. He replied that there was a great deal of doubt as to whether he was dead or not and added that he thought it would make a very good story, my search for Martin Bormann.

I said, 'Well, it will take a long time, it's not the sort of story I could do in a day or two.' He asked me how long it would take and I said at least two or three weeks. Then there was a long pause. 'Two or three weeks?' he asked again. I nodded. 'Then,' he said, 'if you don't think you can find Martin Bormann inside two or three weeks, would you like to go down to the Palladium and interview Chico Marx for the Diary?' I've always regarded that as the archetypal Fleet Street story.

Equally typical is the fact that Beaverbrook happened to read my book *Defeat in the West* around that time and rang my editor at Secker and Warburg to ask where he could find me.

'That shouldn't be too difficult,' my editor David Farrar replied. 'He works for you, on the *Evening Standard*.'

I had been in Intelligence during the war, and from the landing in Normandy until the end of the war, I was responsible for writing a daily report on German activities opposite the Canadian front and after V-day went around with my Colonel, Colonel Chater – I was then a major – and we interviewed Von Runstedt and other German officers to find out what had gone wrong. This was the basis of my expertise on the German army and also the basis for the book Beaverbrook had just read. When it came out, in 1947 or 1948, I'd decided to stay on in England and try my luck here on the basis of my rehabilitation payment from the Canadian army, the advance on the book, and a job in Reuters which I had managed to con myself into, and which, along with the publicity the book got, led to an offer from the *Evening Standard* to work on the Diary.

When he read the book Beaverbrook immediately got in touch with Gunn, the editor, and said, 'Do you realise you have a writer on your staff, working on the Diary?' As a result of that call I was sent out to do a series of interviews with people like Jacob Epstein, Mae West, Joe Louis, T. S. Eliot and so on; I later collected them all into a book called *How To Be a Celebrity*.

After I'd done four or five of these, Beaverbrook sent for me and asked me if I knew anything about films. I said not very much, and he said, 'Just what we want. A fresh mind on the subject of films. Have you ever heard of Darwin?' 'Darwin, *Origin of Species*?' I asked. 'No,' he replied. 'Bernard Darwin, golf correspondent of *The Times*. I don't play golf myself, but it doesn't matter whether you know anything about golf or not, he's such a good writer that I love to read everything he writes about golf. That's what I want you to do when you write about films.' So I became film critic of the *Evening Standard*, and my salary went up from fifteen to twenty-five pounds a week.

Within a couple of weeks I was on the front page because I had attacked *No Orchids For Miss Blandish* as a tasteless and violent film. Then I wrote a review saying that I couldn't stand the boring British starlets from the Rank Charm School and adding that any day I could find, on the Central Line, six more attractive girls than Margaret Lockwood, Patricia Roc, Jean Kent, and the rest of them. Rank challenged me on this, so I stationed myself at Bond Street on the Central Line, where all the model girls get off to go to work and picked six girls, on a wet Monday morning, and they all were given screen tests. One was a girl called Caroline who used to advertise Craven A cigarettes, you used to see her picture all over the place. Another one, Eunice Bailey, turned up on the cover of a lot of magazines and one of the six married one of the richest men in the world. None of them ever made it as film stars but the point was that it was a good stunt and it made my name.

A few years later all the Hollywood film companies withdrew all their advertising from the *Express* group newspapers and said that they wouldn't advertise in the Beaverbrook papers again until I was fired. They didn't like what they called my 'anti-film' approach. It was probably the first time that Columbia, MGM, 20th Century-Fox and all those film studios ever got together over anything. The thing became an international scandal. *Time* magazine wrote about it; it was in *Newsweek, Paris Match*; there were editorials in the *Sunday Times* and the *Spectator* about it, asking how dare these American companies try to put pressure on a British newspaper proprietor? Of course Beaverbrook revelled in all this sort of thing. At the time the papers were tiny and he didn't need the advertising, so he could appear as a great defender of the freedom of the press without it costing him a bean.

This was 1963 and I was suddenly famous. A year later Kenneth Tynan was fired because he threatened to sue the paper for the letters they were printing about him and I became theatre critic. There are about sixty theatres in London and I've been drama critic of the *Evening Standard* for about thirty-two years, and it gets a bit like a dentist facing an impacted tooth every day; it's just a job, boring most of the time.

I've met all the theatre people socially in their houses, or they've been here. They rarely if ever changed anything as a result of my notices. They will do something totally stupid and when you point it out to them, they hardly ever change it, even when, as I sometimes found out later, they thoroughly agreed with me. They hate changing things because of something some critic has said. They don't like the critics a bit despite the fact that the critics are an absolutely essential part of the business. After all, what is a critic? A critic is free publicity, thousands and thousands of pounds worth of free publicity they wouldn't get in any other way. I remember when we had an eleven-week newspaper strike, the management of the theatre, or one of the principal players, would step forward in front of the curtain and say: 'Our friends the critics can't write about us at the moment so will you please tell your friends all about this play?'

They couldn't afford to take big advertisements telling the public what the play was all about, and for the most part what the critics write is the life-blood of the theatre; they can scream and yell as much as they like about criticism, but in the end it's just as essential to them as it is to us. And in London we have nine or ten major critics, and we hardly ever agree, so there's hardly any play where you can't find a quote from one or two critics who have said it was marvellous, so that it's 'Scintillating . . .' on the billboards despite the fact that half of the critics described it as a waste of time.

As a critic, I want to be read by people who don't ever go to the theatre. The number of people who do go to the theatre is very limited. I try to remember that I am writing for an audience which has never had the experience about which I'm writing, and I try to make it interesting for them. As to how often I've been wrong, the three examples I'm always being attacked about are *The Birthday Party* by Harold Pinter, *Waiting for Godot* by Sam Beckett and *Look Back in Anger* by John Osborne. As far as *Look Back in Anger* is concerned, I did write: 'This man has tremendous promise' although I did think that particular play was a great whine. But of those three plays, I'm not even sure that the verdict is in yet as to whether or not they are great plays.

I once said to Harold Pinter: 'Do you realise that there haven't been forty great playwrights in the English language since Marlowe, if you cut out people who are now living and try to write down forty names?' Yet all sorts of people wrote plays. Dryden wrote plays, Shelley wrote plays but none of them have survived. No doubt they were greatly admired in their day, no doubt they were the Becketts and the Pinters of their time. There's no evidence that a hundred and fifty years from now we're going to be reading Beckett or Pinter or seeing their plays. We may be, we may not, we just don't know. When people ask whether I was right or wrong about *Godot* on the first night, the point is most people didn't know what the hell it was all about. It is easy enough now because it has become O-level reading and you have teachers analysing every phrase, but on that first night even the cast hadn't the faintest idea what it was all about.

I'm far more interested in how many times I've been right. I've seen about four thousand plays and I would think the number of mistakes I have made was minuscule.

I'm rather sad about leaving Fleet Street. I loved El Vino, when Philip Hope Wallace, who was a kind of Samuel Johnson, ran his own table and we all sat around. There's a little plaque in El Vino to mark the table and of course, because it was the *Guardian*, they had to get his name wrong; they spelled it with two 'l's'. Philip Hope Wallace held a nice court; Paul Johnston, George Gale, Perry Worsthorne, they all used to gravitate to his table. It would have been wonderful if only we'd had a tape recorder in those days.

But what I miss most of all, now that the new technology has come in, is copy paper. There's no copy paper around any more. We're moving tomorrow to Kensington, and there'll be nothing to take a note on. Paper doesn't exist any more. Carbon doesn't exist any more. To my mind, that's the biggest change . . .

Keith Waterhouse

One of the plays that Milton Shulman did not pan was *Billy Liar*, a comedy by a young journalist, Keith Waterhouse. I had known Keith when I was on the *Mirror* in the early sixties and met him again in the Wig and Pen, another of the famous old Fleet Street haunts.

Novelist, playwright and one of Britain's best-known television scriptwriters, Keith Waterhouse came to Fleet Street determined to take over what was probably the toughest job Fleet Street had to offer: he wanted to succeed Cassandra as *Daily Mirror* columnist. He achieved this ambition in the seventies. He left the *Mirror* shortly after it was taken over by Maxwell and now writes a column for the *Daily Mail*.

31 October 1988

Let me start backwards. I've just come from the Sydney Jacobson memorial service at St Bride's, and I've been sitting in the church with all my old Fleet Street mates around me and in a way we were saying farewell to Sydney and looking back on his life and I was looking back on my own life too, but really we were all saying farewell to Fleet Street because it's probably one of the last of the Fleet Street goodbyes before the remaining papers move out too.

When I left school I started sending articles off to the local paper, the *Yorkshire Evening Post*. When they didn't get published, I had to earn some money so I took a job as an undertaker's clerk. I worked for a firm called J. T. Buckton and Sons: We Never Sleep. But after they'd read a few more of my pieces, the *Post* offered me a guarantee of a job when I'd done my national service.

When I thought I'd had enough experience on the *Post* I went down to Fleet Street. I'd been there once before as a kid and I'd stared at the plaque to Edgar Wallace, Reporter, and my head was full of books like Philip Gibbs's *The Street of Adventure* and *I Laughed in Fleet Street* by Bernard Falk, the uncle of the present BBC man, and I could picture Edgar Wallace criss-crossing the street from Reuters where he worked. My head was full of it and I wanted to be a part of it.

The first newspaper I tried was the *News Chronicle* and I was so confident that I was going to work for them that when they didn't offer me a job I walked down to Waterloo Bridge and leaned over the parapet sobbing with rage because I knew I ought to have got that bloody job, but they'd said that I didn't have enough experience.

The next paper I tried was the *Mirror*. The news editor there, Kenneth Hord, also told me that I didn't have enough experience. But on my way out of the building, I took the wrong corridor and found myself outside a door marked Features Editor. I banged on the door. I've always been dealt with kindly by madmen, and James Eilbeck, the features editor, was certainly a madman – he killed himself later, as you know, threw himself under a tube train. Being mad, he took me on, on a month's trial.

In those days on the *Mirror* you had to fill in a form which had all kinds of warnings on it like what sort of clothes you were supposed to wear in the office and so on, and also a number of questions you had to answer. One of the questions was: What do you ultimately want to do on the *Daily Mirror*? And I answered: To succeed Cassandra.

The first big job I was sent on was a news story, the flooding down at Canvey Island. It was no great honour; it was such a big story that everybody including the copytasters were sent out on it. But I had the great good fortune to find a honeymoon couple stranded on the roof of a prefab. They were spending their honeymoon up there on the roof of this prefab with the floods lapping around their feet. It was a good tabloid story and it made page one with my byline. My head was so swollen it was brushing both sides of all the corridors.

The next thing that happened on this story was that I was sent back to find this couple and offer them a decent honeymoon in the Dorchester or one of those big hotels in Park Lane. So I went back to find the buggers. The bride was still there on the roof. I told her that the *Mirror* wanted to put them up in a swanky hotel for their honeymoon. 'Oh, I don't know about that,' she said. 'I'd have to talk to my husband first.' I asked her where he was. 'Down the buses,' she said.

So I went down to the bus station and the first thing I saw was a big poster announcing that the *Daily Mirror* had adopted this marooned couple and were giving them a slap-up West End honeymoon, and I hadn't even found the bridegroom yet. I told an inspector that they'd just have to get this man off the buses in time for the next day's *Mirror*.

In the end, they did get him off the buses for me and I took the pair of them to the hotel as arranged, but I was very naive in those days. I'd been told to give them whatever they wanted and what this extremely smart couple did, as it turned out, they went straight to Selfridge's and furnished their entire home, putting it all down to the *Mirror*. Well, good luck to them.

I don't know if Cassandra ever got to hear that my ambition was to succeed him. I blush a bit when I think about it, though I'd no chance until he was dead. George Gale did it for a bit, but he wasn't right for that column, as he would probably agree now himself. In the end, I just drifted into it, as one always does, in Fleet Street.

I'd been running a back-page column on the ill-fated *Mirror* magazine for about a year when Hugh Cudlipp called me into his office and said something like, 'Now you're doing this great column in the *Mirror* magazine. But supposing it were to happen that the magazine should come out twice a week, so that we'd want two columns from you, one on Monday and one on Thursday, what would you think about that?' I got the message: what he was really saying was that they were going to kill off the magazine and he wanted me to write a column for the *Mirror* itself. It's funny in Fleet Street, they don't ever come out straight with what's in their minds. They talk in overtones which you're supposed to understand.

When the *Mirror* magazine was killed I had some eight or ten columns in hand, and I had to run this stuff because I'd already written it, but it wasn't until I'd used it all up and had nothing at all left that the adrenalin started to flow and everything was all right. Once I was on the tightrope with a great hole in the paper to fill and no safety-net under me, then it all began to work for me.

I find writing a column is demanding, but not difficult. It's demanding because it demands you for the whole of the previous day. I suppose there were times when I could have given up journalism because I was earning enough from novels and plays and television, but I was hooked on Fleet Street, hooked on the *Daily Mirror*.

I think the dispersal of the newspapers out to Wapping and the Isle of Dogs is bound to affect the quality of Fleet Street journalism in time. I've been trying to get this together because it's a question that's often asked. Again I find myself thinking back to Sydney Jacobson, when we all used to work there together, and at the end of the day we'd all go over to the pub, and I'd have written the leader, taking the policy dictated by Jacobson, he was the *éminence grise* behind the policy of the paper, and I'd say: 'Well, all right, Sydney, I've done it, but I don't totally agree with it.' And then we'd have a great, wonderful, vicious argument about it and get pissed and we'd almost come to blows, and then Sydney would come home with me and we'd continue the argument, and maybe it would end up with Sydney lying in the fireplace and all the time, while we're still arguing about it, the presses are thundering out the leader I wrote.

The continuing debate was an essential feature of Fleet Street, the awful pubs were the forum where people talked and a lot of the talk was rubbish but we learned a lot from it too. This just doesn't happen any more. Now I have a computer, my stuff goes straight from screen to screen; I no longer need go anywhere near Fleet Street.

The people who made the greatest impression on me were Sydney Jacobson, Cassandra, and Hugh Cudlipp. Sydney Jacobson educated me politically. He was my governor, as indeed he was Hugh's governor, politically. Cassandra's great quote was: 'Don't let the bastards tangle with it.' It being your copy. And Hugh Cudlipp taught me how to put it across, presentation in fact.

I left the *Mirror* when Maxwell took it over, but not because of that. When he bought the paper, Maxwell started sending for the people who worked for it to check them over. I was working as a free-lance, on contract, and I had to explain this subtle difference to Cap'n Bob. I said, 'I don't work for you, Bob. I perform at your place. I'm an act, just like an act in a theatre. Now, let's say you're the Palladium. If for some reason the Palladium doesn't want to book my act next week, there's always the Coliseum.' He laughed: 'Ho, ho, ho!' that famous, Santa Claus laugh. But in due course I did go to the Coliseum.

And whenever I meet him these days, he always says: 'Ho, ho, ho! Well, Keith, I know that you're playing Her Majesty's at the moment but if Vere isn't happy with you, there's always the Lyceum.' I find it all rather endearing, especially the way he always gets the names of the theatres wrong.

I was very sad to leave the *Mirror* at the time, but looking at the paper now, I can't say that I'm sad to have left it. I miss the romance that Fleet Street held for me long before I ever arrived there, but that doesn't exist anywhere any more.

Lord Snowdon

During the time I worked on the *Daily Mirror*, one of the nights that sticks inescapably in my mind is the night when we heard that Princess Margaret was to marry Anthony Armstrong Jones, who was described in some of the reports that came in as a Fleet Street photographer, though it would have been more accurate to refer to him as a distinguished theatrical photographer who had had a number of his pictures published in Fleet Street newspapers, principally the *Daily Express*. Two years after he became Lord Snowdon, he returned to the newspaper world.

A nephew of Oliver Messel, the theatrical designer, Anthony Armstrong Jones became one of the leading West End theatrical photographers in the late fifties. In 1962 he became Artistic Advisor to the *Sunday Times* and subsequently did a number of photographic assignments for the *Sunday Times* all over the world. He is one of the most sought-after portrait photographers in the UK and has published photographic essays on London, Malta and Venice.

22 November 1988

I did Natural Sciences at Cambridge for about ten days but I didn't like it much, so I changed to architecture and did three years of architecture and then failed my exams, came down meaning to go back the next year, and then never went back. And so I suppose I started as a failed architect. I had taken some photographs at Cambridge and just drifted into photography as a profession, probably because of my uncle. Through him I met Peter Hall and Peter Brook, and I just happened to be around when there was a movement against romanticism and the theatre was becoming more and more brutal and realistic with the arrival on the scene of people like Brendan Behan and Sean Kenny.

I started taking photographs during rehearsals and they used to blow them up enormously and exhibit them outside the theatres to get people off the buses and into the box office to buy tickets. And then I sold a picture to the *Weekly Sketch*; it was a full-page picture of Alex Guinness in the play *Hotel Paradiso*, and there was a terrible row because it appeared in one of the Fleet Street dailies long before the *Weekly Sketch* came out. I was asked to explain it, but I couldn't. I discovered later that what had happened was that the dramatic critic of the paper concerned had seen my photograph of Guinness and had liked it, so he'd borrowed a screwdriver from the stage-door keeper, had unscrewed it and had taken it down to his newspaper office and had it copied. He apologised in the end, but that was the first picture I had published in a Fleet Street daily.

Harold Keeble of the *Daily Express* then came to see me at the studio. He was just starting *Photo News* and it was the first time that newspapers started using big theatre photographs; previously they had just used tiny photographs along with the theatre notices. Harold Keeble had a Yorkshire accent but he was very grand. He never filed photographs; he'd just hide them under the edge of the carpet in his office where nobody else would find them.

In those days I used to go to Stratford and drive back later that night after I'd photographed the play, and I found that if I printed them beautifully, and dried them properly, quite often Keeble wouldn't use them because he didn't think they were hot news. On the other hand, if I didn't bother to finish them properly, but simply took them down to him wet, between two bits of blotting paper, at about two o'clock in the morning, he'd always use them even if it meant tearing out a whole page and redesigning it around the wet picture; he liked that kind of immediacy. I got tremendous excitement out of going down to Fleet Street with photographs and I got a huge kick out of seeing pictures I had taken appear in the paper next day. I sometimes used to hang about in Fleet Street until two o'clock in the morning to get the first copy off the presses.

I had done some magazine work with Mark Boxer and Jocelyn Stevens and when the *Sunday Times* colour magazine started, I joined it as a photographer. I think I'm the oldest member of the *Sunday Times* colour magazine.

I did several assignments abroad with David Holden; I

enjoyed working with him very much. We were in India together and in Yugoslavia. One day he suddenly got a cable in Yugoslavia to say that Roy Thomson was coming out to do an interview with Tito, so David quickly did a set of questions for Roy to ask Tito. Roy came across on the boat to Brioni, just reading a detective novel and not even glancing at the questions. And when he got there, Tito was expecting all those deep intellectual questions about world affairs, and Roy simply said, 'Look, I'm a capitalist and you're a communist. Now, you've got this island here, and you live alone. You could fit a hell of a lot of beds and hotels on this island, so shouldn't we do business together?'

And Tito was so amazed by this approach that everyone became very relaxed and the interview went very well; they got on frightfully well together. I loved Roy Thomson. He used to send for me to ask me what his children would like for Christmas. He never used to come near the magazine and I once said to him: 'Why don't you come down to see the magazine?' He replied, 'Wouldn't they mind?' I told him that they'd be thrilled to bits, and so he came down and said hello and everyone loved it.

I got arrested quite often. I was arrested in Detroit. As you probably know, nobody walks in Detroit. If the police see you just walking round, they get suspicious. I was standing at a street corner, just wandering around as I always do and suddenly I see somebody getting arrested, so I start to take pictures. I'm immediately arrested for taking pictures. They asked for my papers but my passport was back at the hotel and to make matters worse they found on me a policeman's card; I'd been photographing a policeman's funeral the previous day. I was locked up in a cell for two or three hours, I suppose, being pushed from one policeman to another until eventually I was being questioned by the head of police in Detroit and the whole affair ended by him asking me whether I'd like to photograph his grandchildren. He couldn't have been nicer.

On another occasion when I was in India with David Holden I took some pictures from a plane and immediately afterwards the steward came and asked me to go and see the captain who confiscated the camera and the film, the whole lot, and when we got to Bombay we were the last off the plane and I was arrested by a sergeant and taken off to a cell. After I'd been there for a few hours, I started to get a bit bored and said, 'Would you like to see the pictures?' He said that he would, so I opened up the back of the camera and pulled out the undeveloped film and he said, 'They're not very good, are they?' I was then released and went back to my hotel.

We were staying at a very grand hotel on this trip and the next morning at about six o'clock a frightfully important head of police knocked on the door, absolutely covered with pips and epaulettes, and said, 'Oh, Tony, how nice to see you again!' in that grand Indian voice. 'I believe I was at Trinity while you were at Jesus and I'm extremely sorry that one of our boys was a bit over-enthusiastic last night because what came through was that you had been photographing the fleet. Anyway, we'll now make certain that you have a police escort wherever you go.' Which of course was the last thing that David or I wanted. I said, please, please not, but he insisted and from then on, until we managed to give the police car the slip, every time we came to a village and got out to do some photographs, the police escort would say: 'Look at the camera now, and give a big smile.' It destroyed the whole thing.

I've never been to Wapping – to get to Wapping from here would take all day. I used to have a room in Rotherhithe which I loved. But now I can project things from here. I don't like cameras with a motorised drive. I just use an ordinary camera. Cartier-Bresson never used a motor and I reckon that if an ordinary camera without a motor drive is good enough for Cartier-Bresson, it's good enough for me.

If I were starting out all over again, I'd certainly want to include the Fleet Street experience. The immediacy is good, the discipline is good and the rough and tumble is good. The sad thing is that if you work only for the glossy magazines, your pictures may not be published for sometimes a year, three months at the earliest, and by that time you've lost interest in them. Whenever I do a book I try to get them to get it to press as quickly as possible; if I finish it in May, it's out by October.

I don't consider it an invasion of privacy to take pictures of people in public places but one could very easily be guilty of invading privacy when, for example, you take pictures in a hospital or a mental home. The patient in bed might not even be aware that you have taken a picture, but I would still regard that as an invasion of privacy and would make every effort to explain to them that I had taken a picture and ask if it was all right to use it. Taking pictures of people in the public eye in public places is perfectly all right, even if they don't want to be photographed. Where it becomes an invasion of privacy in my view is when a photographer intrudes on someone's private property with a long focus lens in an effort to steal a shot. That's trespassing, anyway.

Anne Scott-James

Another journalist who has affectionate memories of Harold Keeble is Anne Scott-James who appeared on the Fleet Street scene just after the war when newspapers were realising, perhaps for the first time, just how important their women readers were. She had married Macdonald Hastings, another distinguished journalist – their son, Max Hastings, is now the editor of the *Daily Telegraph* – and she is perhaps best known for her daily column in the *Mail* between 1960 and 1968. In 1967, she married Sir Osbert Lancaster, the *Daily Express* cartoonist.

Anne Scott-James (Lady Lancaster) joined the editorial staff of *Vogue* in 1934 and she worked there until 1941 when she became women's editor of *Picture Post*, the Hulton Press weekly news-photo magazine. She edited *Harper's Bazaar* from 1945 to 1951, and worked for Beaverbrook until 1960 as women's editor of the *Sunday Express* and as women's adviser to the group. She joined the *Daily Mail* as a columnist in 1960.

9 November 1988

I got started on magazines when I was pretty young, with a job on *Vogue*. I had answered an advertisement in *The Times* for a copy-writer, but as soon as I started to learn something about sub-editing and caption-writing, I became very involved in it all. I loved *Vogue*.

Later, when I switched to *Picture Post*, I found that as a woman, you had to fight for your chances. *Picture Post* was very progressive but all the time I was there, it was also a very male-oriented place. I wasn't an active feminist; I just thought that as an individual I had to look after myself. I don't think I would ever have been militant, I wouldn't ever have put bombs in letter-boxes or things like that. But I would have felt very much on the side of those early Suffragettes.

The *Picture Post* offices were in Shoe Lane, so it was physically in the Golden Mile. It was very stimulating and exciting. After I left *Picture Post*, I edited *Harper's Bazaar* for five deadly years and I despised myself for it, because it was really going backwards. Happily I then got a golden job on the *Sunday Express*, under Harold Keeble who was a great editor, and I knew nothing about newspapers at that stage. I wasn't even looking for a job. He had asked me if I would write, in an emergency, a free-lance article about Queen Mary who'd just died, and I wrote it and they liked it enormously and asked me if I'd do another and then simply clutched me to their hearts.

I had my own page for many years, that was keenly competitive. But I did sometimes just scrape in before other people. When Nancy Mitford wrote that famous article about U and non-U, for example, I tore off to Paris immediately and got hold of her before anybody else had thought of interviewing her. I also went to New York and did an interview with Grace Kelly before anybody had cottoned on to her either.

I thought Chris (Arthur Christiansen) was a wonderful operator, he had such flair, such instinct. He also used to pick such good people. After all, he hired Osbert, didn't he? My page on the *Sunday Express* was called Anne Scott-James, and the articles were all angled towards women. And to a very large extent, they let me do whatever I wanted to do. I did go to Russia, for instance, to do a page from there, which went down very well. And at the time of the Hungarian Uprising, I went to Vienna and got interviews with a lot of the refugees coming over the border.

I can't claim that I ever had any of the Noel Barber type scoops, but to have your own page on a popular Sunday newspaper, well that's pretty well the fulfilment of any journalist's dreams. I never had any ambitions to edit a newspaper; I wouldn't have wanted that kind of life. John Junor who became editor of the *Sunday Express* after Keeble always said that my copy was not to be touched; if there were any queries after I'd left, the subs would have to ring me at home before they changed a line, although I usually stayed and saw my page to press. I used to go out with them all on Friday night, just for the company; I didn't drink at all in those days.

But I was very interested in politics and social problems and when I went over to the *Daily Mail* in 1960 my column was a column of comment. I shared an office and a secretary in the *Mail* with Bernard Levin for several years, which, when you come to think of it, is an amusing way to spend your time. At that period he was writing four or five columns a week for the *Daily Mail*. I was writing one a week, and we had an agreement that on the day I was writing my column, I would have the pick of the stories, and most of the time he played the game utterly fairly.

One day there was a marvellous story about Lord Shawcross who was opening a new hotel in Manchester when the ceiling fell in. I thought, marvellous. And at eight o'clock Bernard rang and said, 'Of course, Anne, you're not a bit interested in that boring story about Lord Shawcross, are you?' And I replied, 'Bernard, it's my day, and yes, I am.' And that was the end of that.

I didn't spend a lot of my social life in Fleet Street. I had two children, after all, and any spare time I had, I always spent at home. Indeed I wasn't even employed full-time in Fleet Street. I had a desk and a secretary and I had two very full days but otherwise I was pretty free. I went into Fleet Street at the age of forty, with an editorship behind me, so my status was pretty high. I didn't ever have to do anything I didn't want to do. I wasn't a cub reporter.

Today there are some very good woman feature writers on serious subjects. I think the fashion writing is worse than it used to be because women don't want to be bothered with fashion any more. You won't find a clever woman doing fashion in these days. At one time it used to be the only way into Fleet Street for a woman, however bright she was, but these days they've got the whole world at their feet. There are even a great many women writing about economics, which used to be strictly a male preserve.

But I think standards generally have disimproved. The *Daily Express* was a marvellous paper in its day, but it's rubbish now. On the other hand, you've got some good new newspapers like the *Independent*. I would say it's all swings and roundabouts really. However, I doubt if the nation's opinion of the press has ever been so low as it is at present and it's all the fault of perhaps about four newspapers, and it's very unfair. Look at all these recent libel cases, they're so ridiculous; the juries are just trying to punish the newspapers for overstepping the bounds of decent behaviour. I think the press generally is hated, and I feel it's very unfair that the whole press should be tarred with the same brush. All the same, I wouldn't like to see any tighter control of the newspapers. I think it's for the press to sort itself out.

When the newspapers were all in one place, Fleet Street was a bit like a university town. Every time you went out you met someone you knew. You'd have a drink, or a cup of coffee, and chat about what you were doing, it was a very socially attractive place to work.

I think something is going to be missed by the dispersion. My son Max edits the *Daily Telegraph*, and he's got to go out practically to the sea every day to do his work. The other thing is that most of the staff hardly ever go to the office. They go in about once a week, instead of every day. It's too far, they can't. So they just type their copy on those VDUs from their homes, straight into the office.

I remember Harold Keeble and I used to bump into each other in the corridor and he once said to me: 'Every time I bump into you in the corridor, one of us has an idea.' I don't know how they get their ideas now. The sparkle must suffer. Indeed there isn't much sparkle in any of the newspapers now, not even the best. They get such sparkle as there is by hiring funny men to write funny columns.

I still bank in Fleet Street, but I don't enjoy going there any more. I used to, until quite recently, but not any more. It's lost the village atmosphere it used to have.

John Edwards

John Edwards has been a Fleet Street journalist all his life and yet he has hardly spent more than a few days at a time in Fleet Street, or even in England. I first met him a week after I joined the *Mirror*. He was then Tommy Steele's PRO. About three weeks later I met him again in the features room of the *Mirror* and he told me that he'd just been appointed a feature writer on my staff. It was the first I'd heard of it, but that was the way things happened in Fleet Street.

John Edwards started in the *West Wales Guardian* and worked in Dublin for the *Evening Herald* and in Liverpool for the *Daily Post* before joining the *Daily Sketch* as a reporter. He then worked briefly for Tommy Steele before joining the *Mirror*. He spent several years in America, and on his return rejoined the *Sketch*. When the *Sketch* was merged into the new *Daily Mail*, John Edwards became one of the *Mail*'s star feature writers.

20 October 1988

I went on a visit to China with Prime Minister Heath when he was considered a good friend of the Chinese, towards the end of the Cultural Revolution, while Mao was still alive. I was at a banquet held in the Great Hall of the People. They had a drink called Mao Tai, which is basically a rice spirit, and they toast each other in it and the toasts come fast and furious. Deng Xiaoping went from table to table, toasting you and you had to match every toast. I still think that the Mao Tai we were drinking could have been marketed in the West as lighter fuel. But I knew he was coming towards our table and I also knew that you always had to have a phrase from the little Red Book ready.

Deng Xiaoping went from table to table, toasting everybody, and I had been reading this book and I knew the language. What they would all say was: 'I am so and so. Dig tunnels deep, store grain, and never seek hegemony.' He had a white-gloved waiter with him who carried a stone jar of this Mao Tai and an interpreter, and eventually he came to us, and I thought, 'This is it. He's going to toast us.' I was practically unable to stand: my ankles were melting from the amount of Mao Tai I'd drunk. So, I thought, I'll repeat that phrase to him; it seems to be the most acceptable one since all the government people appear to use it. I picked up my glass which had been recharged by this white-gloved waiter and said, 'Dig tunnels deep and store Mao Tai and never seek hegemony.' I realised fully what I was saying, but I couldn't stop myself, and I thought: that's it. Either I'm in prison in China for the rest of my life, or I'm executed at dawn. All this was interpreted into Deng Xiao's ear, whereupon he burst into hysterical laughter and filled the glasses again and kept looking back at our table and laughing.

Shortly after I joined the *Daily Sketch*, I left it to become Tommy Steele's press agent, and it was the time of the first film festival in Moscow after the war, and Tommy was picked to represent the British film industry. So I got in touch with Pat Doncaster of the *Mirror*. I'd never met him before but I knew his name from the record reviews. And I asked him whether he'd be interested in Tommy Steele's impressions of Russia, so this was a genuine proposition and Pat Doncaster put it to Jack Nener, the editor, who said yes.

We did a centre-spread on Tommy on the Friday, and then Jack Nener got in touch with me to ask if they could have another piece, so I got Tommy on a terrible line from Moscow; I could hardly hear a single word, but it all went in on the Saturday and on the Monday I had a telephone call from a man named Reg Payne who wanted to know if I could come and see the editor and I was on the *Mirror* staff by the Monday morning.

A few months after I joined the *Mirror*, I was sent to America. At this period, the late 1950s, and early sixties, America was still the kind of place where correspondents were half-expected to put their messages to Head Office in a bottle and cast it on the waves. You couldn't pick up a phone and dial London from New York in those days; you had to book your call. It seemed very far away. Anyway, I was sitting in the old *Mirror* features room and Reg Payne sort of swept me out, in the general direction of the Printer's Devil. He said, 'In there, there's a man called Ralph Champion. If you play your cards right, you could be on your way to the States.' This was dream stuff, such a short time after I'd joined the *Mirror*. I asked Reg afterwards, 'Why me?' and he said that Jack Nener had told him to find a replacement for the New York office and I was the only person in the features room whose name he could remember at that moment.

Two weeks later my wife and I were on the plane. And since then, I've been travelling constantly. It would have to be millions of miles. I've made over sixty crossings of the Atlantic, mostly by Concorde. When I started, the international terminal at Heathrow was actually one Nissen hut plus a few tents.

I was in the States for the whole of the Kennedy era and for me it was mind-boggling. I knew Martin Luther King very well. I remember the first time his name ever appeared in the English newspapers, we were there in the old Baptist church when it was bombed, and the National Guard had their tanks ringed around it.

When I first went to Cape Canaveral, the facilities consisted of a mound of earth where the press were supposed to stand, surrounded by a rope about six inches in diameter. I didn't know it at the time, but that rope was there to keep out the snakes, which apparently won't crawl over a rope six inches in diameter. There were literally only two phones, and Werner Von Braun was standing around with us.

Probably the biggest story I was ever on was the fall of Saigon. By this time I was working for the *Daily Mail*. I decided to stay on when the Americans pulled out. It wasn't bravery, I just wanted to see what it would be like after the Americans had gone, and I wasn't alone, anyway; there were about eight of us in the British press corps who decided to stay on. It was in any case far less frightening than clambering over those gates and being helicoptered off the roof of the American Embassy. Filing copy that day was quite exhilarating. We were all filing from Reuters and it was right beside the Presidential Palace which had been under heavy attack. And there was this little South Vietnamese guy who was tapping out the copy, and I went in and handed over all my money, some hundreds of dollars to send out four or five hundred words: 'Dunkirk of the Air', I think I called it. This was probably the last copy sent out from Reuters. Then the lines went down, and that was the end.

But after we'd been there for about three weeks a senior North Vietnamese officer, a Vietcong, came to see us and asked who was the head of the press unit which had been left behind in the Caravelle Hotel. Sandy Gall of ITN went down and asked, 'Do you want us to disband our communications?' And he said, 'What do you mean? We've had three operators on duty since the day the city fell and not a soul has come near us.' The post office had been open from the moment the Americans pulled out but nobody knew. That was a typical Communist thing to do, to re-establish communications and not tell anybody about it.

The most embarrassing thing that ever happened to me was during the presidential election of 1976, when I was travelling with Governor Carter of Georgia, who was not generally regarded as a particularly charismatic character, and I'd drawn the short straw and was accompanying him on his presidential tour. He'd been asking me about Dylan Thomas, and I was ashamed that I knew so little about him, and then suddenly he stopped the car and said, 'Look, he's a neighbour of mine, and he's being lucky again.' I'd just been telling Jimmy Carter that I was from a farming community in Wales, and I took one look at this field and said, 'Well, he's only going to be lucky if he's in the business of growing weeds.' Carter said nothing, but got out of the car slowly, stepped over the ditch, and pulled one of those weeds out of the ground. It was the first time in my life I'd realised that peanuts grew on the ground.

I'd learnt on the *Mirror* that you had to think quickly and that the story is the most important thing. If you lose a hand, be sure it's not the one you need to dial the office. Editors are not interested in your problems, only their own. On one occasion I went out to cover a coup in Liberia which had been organised by a master-sergeant, John Doe, who had elected himself president. We were taken to the palace, and it was pretty terrifying. There were people there in war-paint – the real Africa you're always reading about.

The principal event had been the murder of the previous president, so I went to one fellow who claimed that he'd killed the former president and I asked him how he'd been killed. He said, 'I killed him myself, I stabbed him.' He had his walkie-talkie with him and another man came down instantly and said, 'He's saying he killed the president. That's not true. I killed him.'

And for the next ten minutes we had a succession of people all claiming that they'd killed the president. Finally, the man who seemed to be in charge said, 'All right, we're coming to collect you at your hotel tomorrow morning at nine o'clock.' We asked why. 'Well,' he said, 'because at nine o'clock tomorrow morning we're going to execute the cabinet.' But something went wrong and we weren't called out at nine o'clock though they did take about nine people down to the beach and tie them to stakes and kill them for the edification of the few members of the press who were there.

Master-Sergeant Doe by this time had become a particular friend of ours, mine and the cameraman. And he came to us one night and said, 'I'm going to see my mother because she wants to congratulate me on my great success in politics.' So we got into a car and went down in convoy to the jungle where there was this awful corrugated-iron emplacement with chickens running around under our feet. I was introduced to his mother and I said, 'Mrs Doe, you must be terribly proud of your son.' We were conducting this interview by oil lamp while all the time he was on the radio-telephone to the capital, ordering the execution of about another ten former ministers, while his mother was telling us what a marvellous son he was.

When the Pope was shot in Rome I went out on the Alitalia plane they'd laid on for the press, and got there at about eleven-thirty that night. I wondered where I ought to go. St Peter's Square? No point. It was bound to be full of nuns lighting candles. I reckoned everybody would be covering that, so I thought, to hell with it, I'll go straight to the hospital. And when I arrived there, there was nobody else there at all. Nobody else seemed to have thought of it, it was absolutely extraordinary.

By now it was about one o'clock in the morning, and it wasn't until about four a.m. that the police came and sealed the place off. By that time I was well established inside and knew everybody. And then about six o'clock in the morning the surgeons came out of the theatre with blood all over them, and there was a balcony on the floor where I was and they went out on to the balcony and started to light up cigarettes and breathe the morning air. These were the very people who had just been conducting the hours-long operation to save the Pope's life and several of them spoke good English, and they told me precisely what had happened, how long the incisions were, how close to death he had been, the facts indeed that very few people in the whole world knew unless they'd read my piece. The Pope had been in the operating theatre and while he'd been there, a victim of a road accident had been brought in to the next theatre. So the Pope of Rome was being operated on and immediately next to him – which, if you think about it, is exactly what he would have wanted – there was another operation going on, on a man who'd been involved in a road accident. And I had it all to myself. I knew that it had to be accurate because whenever I didn't understand something they were saying, the head surgeon would take my notebook and draw in for me the actual operation as they had done it, precisely where they'd made the incisions, where exactly they'd tied his intestines up and all the rest of it. And there was nobody else there.

The next morning when the Cardinals started to come to the hospital in their Mercedes cars in their scarlet robes, I was the only reporter inside. It was a fantastic sight and I still think it was the best piece I've ever written. I got it by simply taking a chance.

For my money, that's what Fleet Street is all about.

Katharine Whitehorn

I first met Katharine Whitehorn in 1959 when she was writing a column for the *Spectator*, then edited by my friend, Brian Inglis. We met again when her husband, the novelist Gavin Lyall, appeared on an independent television programme I was editing in the early sixties. And we talked after Christmas in her elegant house near Primrose Hill.

Katharine Whitehorn joined the staff of *Picture Post* in 1956 and was with it until it folded in May 1957. She then worked for *Woman's Own* before joining the *Spectator* in 1959. She went to the *Observer* in 1960 and has been writing a popular weekly column ever since.

11 January 1989

I remember doing a profile of Mrs Thatcher when she was Minister of Education. She gave me about an hour in her office and I turned up with one of those miniature tape recorders which were quite new to us then. Half-way through the interview I realised that it wasn't working, but I was far too intimidated by her, even in those days, to say so, and so I simply went back to the office and told them that the story didn't make it.

I've always felt that mine was basically a serious column – the G. K. Chesterton view that a comic illustration illustrates something just as seriously as a serious one, and makes people remember it.

The first real job I had in journalism was sub-editing true life love stories for *Home Notes* but that didn't last very long and luckily I got a job on *Picture Post*, where I got a proper training. I was really a reporter, but because I was the only girl on the staff, I also got to do the fashion stuff.

The great thing about *Picture Post* was that you always went out with a photographer, and they were frightfully good, very gnarled old hands, canny as anything – people like Bert Hardy and Slim Hewitt. Because, if you think about it, if you're a journalist, and you're out on your own, it's rather like being a learner motor-cyclist. But on *Picture Post*, going out with these very experienced photographers, it was rather like learning to drive in a car, with an instructor by your side. They were wonderful people and although the journalist was technically in charge, just as the conductor is technically in charge of a bus, those photographers would point you towards the story you had to get, half of the time. One really had more fun on *Picture Post* than at any time since, not quite, but jolly nearly. I started doing a column for the *Spectator* in 1959 and it was so pleasant that I really didn't want to leave.

Then around that time the *Observer* decided that they wanted to have two women's editors, one doing the frocks and one the gravitas (a very *Observer* word, that) because they thought that anybody who could do the fashion couldn't possibly have enough gravitas to do the rest. They actually advertised, and we all had to do a sort of examination; I did a couple of specimen pieces, one on tipping and one on careers, and I think the original idea was that they would have me doing the gravitas and Anne Scott-James doing the frocks. She had the wit to pull out at the last minute, and George Seddon, who had just arrived down in London from the *Manchester Guardian*, rang me and said, 'You won't want to do the gravitas because you don't want to leave the *Spectator*, do you? So how about doing the fashion, part time?' I didn't know much about fashion but I knew a lot about clothes and it seemed to me that only a few women are interested in fashion, but all women are interested in clothes.

To begin with, I got a lot of very hostile correspondence and the advertisers absolutely blew up because in those days fashion was frightfully stately, it all emanated from Paris, and the *Observer* readers were supposed to shop at Harrods and Harvey Nicholls and I started featuring garments from C & A Modes and Marks & Spencer and this was considered horrible. But my point was that to write as if everybody had enormous sums of money to spend on clothes, which they hadn't, was quite ridiculous.

One of the things I tried to do was to stop Englishwomen from wearing cardigans over everything. Every country in the world has things that they simply cannot see. The Americans have boxes of Kleenex all over the place, which they never see. In the Japanese No-plays you're simply supposed not to see the little chaps who pass them the fan and things and in the same way, the British don't ever see cardigans. I also wrote an article on 'Why not trousseaux for men?' The point being that women always get lots of lovely trousseaux things but the men used to get married with two trunks of out-dated RAF equipment. And I did a piece on 'Clothes for Other People's Houses', on the grounds the other people's houses always seem colder than your own.

Then I stopped doing fashion altogether and started writing a column. In the sixties, if I wrote anything serious in the column, they always hoicked it on to the leader page. I objected very strongly to this on the grounds that by hauling my column on to the leader page every time they thought I was dealing with an important subject, then by implication this meant that the rest of the time it wasn't important. I believed that all the things I was writing about, the things that occupy people when they're not at work, their emotional life, their leisure time, their family, home decoration, all these things are just as important as anything else.

I was completely supported by George Seddon who at that time was conducting brilliant pages, the stop, look and listen pages, women's pages that weren't really women's pages at all. And he had a very good theory that if you muck people's copy about too much, it may make it better this time, but you'll do such awful things to their confidence that it will be worse the next time. He was very good at giving you your head and letting you find your own length.

I didn't know a great deal about what was going on in the paper, but I did sense that we were getting into the doldrums around 1975 when the paper was losing an awful lot of money and all sorts of desperate expedients were being tried out and the unions kept saying: Open the books, open the books. And when they did open the books they found that the Astor family had put in more than seven million pounds over the last few years and there was nothing left in the coffers and we were losing money like anything and were just about to sell out to Murdoch when over the hill came, gallop, gallop, on a white charger, ARCO, who seemed at that point to be the perfect proprietors – very idealistic, very rich and very far away. When ARCO pulled out, it was incredibly difficult. With Tiny Rowland, as everybody knows, we don't care if he sells us, it couldn't be much worse.

I think the middle of the road and the popular papers from the *Express* downwards have got unquestionably worse in recent years. The *Daily Mirror* used to be brilliant, it used to be something you could use as an index to all the other papers, but the *Mirror* ruined itself by trying to compete with the *Sun*. The *Sun* replaced the old *Daily Herald* which was of no interest to any human being. I think what one misses today is something which is down-market but good. I think the *Mail* is probably the nearest, but it's so right-wing. I buy the *Mail* when I'm going to the office by tube for Keith Waterhouse and the Money Mail. At home I take the *Independent* and the *Guardian*.

George Seddon

Katharine Whitehorn's mentor and champion at the *Observer* was George Seddon, features editor of the paper in the sixties. He is now retired and writing books; I met him in his house in Hammersmith.

George Seddon started on the *Northern Daily Telegraph* as a reporter. He graduated to the *Manchester Guardian* as a sub-editor, finally becoming number two on the foreign desk. He joined the *Observer* in 1959.

20 January 1989

When I joined the *Guardian*, it didn't have a foreign editor; the editor simply refused to delegate. After I'd subbed for the newspaper for about eighteen months I was put on the foreign desk, the third foreign chair as they called it. Then I got up to the second foreign chair but I couldn't get any further. The *Guardian* was quite unbelievable in 1934. Everybody was known by his initials, I was GMS and the editor was W. P. Crozier but you couldn't call him WPC, it had to be WPC, Esq.

I was given an enormous amount of responsibility and I stayed on until after the war started. I was a conscientious objector, so I spent the war working with the Quakers, with maladjusted children in a hostel.

After the war I went back to the *Guardian* in charge of the foreign desk, and I was so convinced that the world was about to come to a nuclear end, and the outlook generally seemed so alarming that I decided to buy a farm in the Lake District so that we could get away from it all. I had a young family then and packed up journalism altogether for ten years. Then I went back to the *Guardian* as a sub under Alistair Hetherington, and came down to the *Observer* in 1959 as assistant to William Clarke who wrote a marvellous feature summing up the past week, and known as The Week.

The atmosphere on the *Observer* was entirely different from the *Guardian* in the sense that it wasn't in the least like a newspaper. There were no conferences, we spent most of our time talking, and David Astor was like a Renaissance Prince, with favourites; one man would be his chosen advisor until one day he'd meet another of equal brilliance, and he would succeed to the post of advisor.

The talking started on Tuesday and went on until Thursday and no decisions were ever made, or if they were, they were overturned by David Astor after he'd taken some member of the staff out to lunch and had discussed it.

There were great outings to Cliveden for the staff, big bonuses and dos at the Cafe Royal, but by then, of course, after Suez, they'd started to lose out to the *Sunday Times*, because of the public's reaction to their condemnation of Suez. That really hit them.

Around this period I was made features editor, a thing the paper had never had before. I had two instructions: to find a new fashion editor, and to find a women's editor, another thing they'd never had.

They had tried to find a women's editor the year before I became features editor, and what they had demanded was two one thousand word essays along with the application, and this put most of the big names out of the running because there was no way they were going to compete. The articles were on tipping and on women's role at work.

This second topic was a very crucial one with David Astor. The reason the *Observer* had never had a women's editor was because he didn't believe that any working woman journalist was fit to write about women, on the grounds that only a wife and mother could write about women faithfully. On the other hand, he also believed that if a woman journalist happened to be a wife and a mother, then she should be at home looking after her family and not working in a newspaper office. So this became a total impasse.

Among the hundred or so applications, I found Katharine Whitehorne's, and they'd taken no notice of her. I immediately got on to her and asked her if she wanted to be women's editor. She didn't, so I made her fashion editor and continued to be women's editor myself, as well as features editor, for several years.

Brian Inglis

Brian Inglis succeeded Patrick Campbell and preceded me as Quidnunc of An Irishman's Diary, the daily column in the *Irish Times*. He was editor of the *Spectator* when I came to London and we have kept in fairly close touch ever since.

Brian Inglis is probably best-known as presenter of the television programme, *What the Papers Say*, though he has written about a dozen books. His first, *The Freedom of the Press in Ireland 1784–1841* was published in the early fifties, based on the thesis he wrote for his doctorate at Trinity College, Dublin, and since then he has had absorbing interest in newspapers.

5 December 1988

I got into Fleet Street in the most extraordinary way. A man called Stuart McClean ran the *Daily Sketch*, which had been in existence for years, but was a very genteel publication rather like the *Lady* and he wanted to turn it into a popular tabloid like the *Daily Mirror*. He had the idea that Fleet Street had become inbred, that it needed an infusion of new blood from outside. So he wrote to all the local representatives of the paper, the stringers and correspondents, looking for ideas, and one of them was Bobby Childers in Glasgow or Edinburgh. And he apparently replied, 'Well I don't know about around here, but my niece is being courted by a man in Dublin called Inglis who I believe is quite bright.'

So McClean sent for me to come across from Dublin. He had a copy of that day's *Irish Times* under his arm and he asked me whether I had written anything in it. Well, as it happened I had written the third leader that day, plus a long book review, which was signed, and what we used to call a 'special', a feature on some aspect of the news which carried the byline (they usually did in the *Irish Times* in those days) 'By a Special Correspondent'.

He said, 'You wrote all this in one day's copy of the newspaper?' and immediately invited me over to London to sit in on an editorial conference. The only two things I remember about that conference are that the chief reporter, who eventually became stringer in Paris, endlessly kept repeating, whenever he mentioned a story, 'Well, we're digging, we're still digging,' and another man, I think he was an associate editor, kept saying, 'Yes, that's ideal! An old man and a pair of tits on the front page.' The old man was looking down at something, and the model with the big tits who was wearing a tight sweater – this was long before the days of the Page Three girls – was so positioned in the page, that it looked as if he was eyeing her saucily. It was meant as an eye-catching gimmick. Designed to make people stop in the street and look at the front page of the *Daily Sketch*.

I was then offered what by Irish standards was an astronomical salary to join the *Sketch* as a leader writer – I think it was a thousand a year plus five-hundred expenses, and in 1953, that was a lot of money – and you were expected to put in your full expenses; it was a way of paying people well and of avoiding tax at the same time. For that money I was expected to write one leader of about 500 words in length every day. It used to take me about half an hour to write it, though I tended to spend a lot of time hanging around the office because you never knew when something was going to crop up. Also old Herbert Gunn, the editor, liked to have someone around to whom, or at whom, he could talk.

I'd made up my mind that I'd leave the *Sketch* after one year and I did so. I still had a five pounds a week retainer from the *Irish Press* and nine pounds a week from Radio Eireann which tided me over until I got into the *Spectator*. I got the job through the *Guardian* people, Gerry Fay, the London editor who used to drink in The Clachan. I went as assistant editor and became editor in 1959.

I started *What the Papers Say* on Granada Television in 1956 and went on doing it until 1973. I also did another programme about news, *All Our Yesterdays*, until about fifteen years ago. I read all the newspapers every day over all those years; well, I was very bad about the *Financial Times* and the *Daily Worker*, but I read all the others. And when you read all the papers every day like that, you don't notice the changes. It's only when you come back to them after a long interval, after a year or so, that you really notice the changes.

One change I have noticed in the papers since I stopped doing the programme is that today most of them hold the same point of view. This could be due to Maggie Thatcher's tendency to give knighthoods to editors while they are still in office. *The Times* used to have an absolutely rigid rule that members of the editorial staff could not accept an honour, even after they had retired. The feeling was that if you were allowed to accept an honour, you might well be expecting one, and that would affect the quality of your work, it would make you less impartial, to put it at the very lowest.

When I started *What the Papers Say*, you'd have one paper saying that the Queen was wearing blue and somebody else saying that she was wearing purple, glaring inaccuracies like that. That sort of inaccuracy doesn't occur any more but while I think papers today are more accurate, they are in general less truthful, particularly the Royal Family watchers.

People love to read beastly stories about, say, Koo Stark, but they love it equally well when the papers are taken for vast sums in the court for publishing stories which they enjoyed reading. Cheque-book journalism crept in insidiously and increasingly and so was difficult to stop. So did the invasion of privacy. But the problem is, how do you frame a law to stop it? I would say that probably the press is in some need of control, but how do you go about it? If you think in terms of photographers, you may be able to control the photographers in Fleet Street, but there are photographers all over the world, and how are you going to control them? It's exactly the same as the *Spycatcher* thing. If the pictures are being published somewhere else, it's ludicrous to say that we should stop them being published here.

I doubt if the *Sun* lost one reader over the Koo Stark story. And there's another aspect of it, the follow-my-leader aspect; in the sense that other papers picked the story up and ran versions of it.

If I had it to do all over again, I wouldn't go back to Fleet Street. I was never a newspaperman in the sense that I was even glad to get out of the *Spectator*, which was a nice, quiet place. I don't miss Fleet Street a bit. In a curious way, I miss television more because it only took up one day a week. To have to go into an office five days a week is my idea of hell. But I do think it's going to make a difference to a lot of people when the last of the papers move out of Fleet Street; the kind of people who flourished in Fleet Street's great days, political correspondents and people like that who got all their ideas and information from gabbing and chatting in places like El Vino. They're going to miss it.

Deirdre MacSharry

Deirdre MacSharry is another journalist who doesn't miss Fleet Street a bit. I met her first shortly after she had left university in Dublin and was trying to decide whether to be an actress or a journalist and we arrived in Fleet Street at around the same time, although she had been in the States in the meantime.

Deirdre MacSharry was an editor on *Women's Wear Daily*, the American daily fashion paper, at the age of 23. In 1959, she came to London to work for *Woman's Own*. She was women's editor of the *Daily Express* from 1962 to 1966, fashion editor of the *Sun* from 1966 to 1972 and editor of *Cosmopolitan* from 1973 to 1985. She is now editor-in-chief of *Country Living*.

5 January 1989

I really hated Fleet Street. When I left university I thought of acting and did quite a bit of it. I think a certain amount of drama is needed for journalism, which is why I found it so debilitating in Fleet Street; they were all so middle-class.

I used to write pieces for the *Irish Press* and the *Irish Times* while I was acting in Dublin. I suppose it was in my blood. My mother had been editor of a very successful women's magazine in Dublin, and I think the first journalistic trick I ever learned was when she serialised the novel *Rebecca* and put the circulation up enormously.

I toured with the Dublin Gate Theatre Edwards–MacLiammoir Company in Egypt and America when I was about 23 and it became clear to me that working in the theatre was going to be very difficult. So I did what any sensible 23-year-old would do, I went to see Eugenia Shepphard who was, until she died about a decade ago, one of the great New York journalists, and I showed her a piece I'd had published in the *New York Herald Tribune*. She sent me to *Women's Wear Daily* where, after a bit, I became the youngest editor ever of the only daily fashion paper in the world, a giant, and that sorted me out.

I discovered that you couldn't come to work with holes in

your stockings, which we wore in the days before tights, and you couldn't swan about the place, you had to get it right. I hadn't realised until then that the largest business is the fashion business, that the rag trade is far bigger than anything else, and if you say in a paper like *Women's Wear Daily* that skirts this year are going to be short, millions of people could be out of a job: less fabric, less labour, less everything. You had to be very careful.

When I came to London in 1958 I used my New York thing of picking up the phone and ringing the two people I'd heard of: Hugh Cudlipp and James Drawbell. They both offered me jobs, but Drawbell offered me five pounds more, i.e. twenty-five pounds a week. It was great money at the time and it allowed me to have a small flat in Chelsea. Drawbell was very charismatic, very much the editorial director. He didn't do anything common like sitting in the office and actually doing the work, as I do. He sat in a grand office with a rose on his desk in honour of some member of the staff who'd been killed in a plane crash on a job. That was *Woman's Own*.

When I first arrived I thought Fleet Street was very glamorous and Jimmy Drawbell believed that women's magazines had a very important role to play in women's lives, which is something I still believe to this day. Newspapers, in my view, have not assumed this role. I remember when I first joined *Woman's Own*, they were talking about decorating. I mentioned bathrooms and was told that they never showed bathrooms. I asked why not, explaining that in America they had wonderful bathrooms, and think about all the things you can do with a bathroom I suggested, and so on, but what I didn't realise was that in those days three and a half million people in Britain didn't have a bathroom of any kind.

After two and a half years I decided that I wanted to do something else and Jimmy Drawbell arranged for me to see the editor of the *Evening News*. When I got there, I found it all extremely fuddy-duddy; the previous fashion editor had been there for fourteen years and they thought it amazing that I wanted to spend money on photography. They were very sweet, but it was incredibly dull. After I'd been there six weeks, Bob Edwards offered me a job on the *Daily Express*. I liked him enormously. At the interview I was very nervous and talked about culture shock; I was full of all the American psycho-babble at that time. He listened to it patiently and then said, 'By the way, what we want is a women's page with people wearing nice, short clothes.' I believe a lot of people on the *Express* thought it a great mistake on his part to hire a complete unknown.

In the beginning, I loved it. I loved having the giant byline with a diamond built into the 'I', designed by Ray Hawking, the art editor. I loved having a huge budget to spend on photography.

In my first story I thought I would try to illustrate an emotion and attempt to convey the idea in clothes. I used the Sydney Smith quote: 'Bliss is eating caviar to the sound of trumpets.' I hired a trumpeter and a Rolls Royce, and we went to White City with models and greyhounds. I thought the whole thing was fantastic and I wrote a piece about clothes which give you an enormous lift, bliss, caviar to the sound of trumpets, and we photographed a model with the greyhounds and the trumpeters in the background. I went back to the office, and had the whole thing laid out and went home to bed absolutely exhausted. At ten to eight the phone rang; it was the editor, Bob Edwards. 'You'll have to come back to the office,' he said. 'I'm afraid this won't do at all.'

I got a taxi to Fleet Street and couldn't find the key to my office and it was just coming up to edition time. Eventually somebody found a key and happily I had another set of photographs of models wearing three vests and three bikinis, so we removed the Bliss layout and put in the three bikinis instead.

It was a lesson well learned. I'm talking now about twenty-five years ago. They don't treat readers like cretins any more, not even in Fleet Street, but it was the stone age then. The editors were fine, but the people I was dealing with, subs and features people, they really had crawled out of the stones.

There were subs there who were brilliant subs, but they'd never been anywhere, they'd never seen anything, or met anyone. They went home at two o'clock in the morning in a taxi and didn't even sleep with their wives. And when you came back from Paris, say, with a terrific story – I discovered the whole Yeah-yeah business, pop stars wearing couture clothes, short skirts and so on – they would have the temerity to say: 'Well, my wife wouldn't wear that sort of stuff.' It was so lowering, it was such an insulting attitude to the public.

And it wasn't just fashion. It was everything to do with what appeared on the women's pages, which after all was my job. Their attitude was simply antediluvian. Happily, it's a period that's now dead. Fleet Street deserved everything that's happened to it. They were their own worst enemies, so bloody awkward, so macho, so class-ridden. I think Ann Leslie who was the star feature writer then felt it even more than I did. Bob Edwards was very encouraging but quite soon he was replaced by Derek Marks, who was terrified of women. He hated me. But Harold Keeble was there too, and he was absolutely brilliant. I think I learned all that I know about lay-out and photography from him. He had an odd habit of putting any copy you left with him under the carpet. He was terrified of women, though he'd had several wives. Whenever you went into his office, he would always pick up the phone and pretend that he was talking to somebody.

I never socialised in Fleet Street. I read afterwards that they objected to this. I never went to the Stab in the Back or any of the Fleet Street pubs, and I only went to El Vino to meet my lawyer friends from Dublin, never to meet journalists. I didn't have any friends in Fleet Street. But I did like the power of the press. To be able to pick up the phone and say, 'This is the women's editor of the *Daily Express*', in the days when the *Express* was selling more than four and a half million copies a day, that was really fantastic.

After the *Express*, I went to the *Sun* under Hugh Cudlipp. This was the old, pre-Murdoch *Sun*, and it was obviously dying. They were all such nice people, but they were getting out such a feeble paper. They were mostly old *Daily Herald* people, another branch of the stone age. They would congratulate each other every day on how they were getting through to the people when they clearly weren't getting anywhere. They didn't even know who their readers were. Some of them hadn't been on a bus for years. They hadn't the remotest idea what butter cost, they'd never taken their clothes to the cleaners, they'd never stood in a line at a shop, they were all male, male, male-orientated. Women came in as secretaries and if they were lucky, they came in to do the women's pages. I was there as fashion editor. It was all very lonely and depressing. I learnt then never, never to isolate yourself from your staff and your readers, which is why I still operate in a big office with all the rest of the staff. I've never had an office of my own, because I've seen what it does to people.

I worked on the Murdoch *Sun* with Joyce Hopkirk, who was women's editor, Angela Lambert and Maggie Goodman. I used to help shoot the Page Three girls. By then I'd been beaten about the ears so strongly that in fact I quite enjoyed some of the sessions with the Page Three girls. They were all rather tasteful girls in those days. After that they began to look like whales. We used to shoot actresses and people like that and mind you, they were wearing rather more than they wear now.

It was fun that first year, working for Rupert Murdoch, who seemed then to be a rather shy and diffident Aussie in shirt sleeves. When Joyce, Maggie and I left to go to *Cosmopolitan* he gave a very nice party for us and told us there'd always be a job should we decide to come back. In those days he did actually take his coat off and work on the stone. Mind you,,those were his beginning days. People become sacred monsters after a while but no one is born a sacred monster. You start off a teddy bear, really, or, as they say in New York, a pussy cat. He seemed to me quite pussy cattish.

I became editor of *Cosmopolitan* in 1973 and we changed attitudes, gave women the weapons, made it smart for women to have jobs instead of cringeing about it, preached power dressing and all the rest of it: nothing wrong with that, no need to apologise, it was a very important revolution in my own lifetime. I'm so pleased that I was involved.

I'd never have been able to do it if I'd stayed in Fleet Street.

Jean Rook

Jean Rook, who also worked for Hugh Cudlipp as fashion editor of the old broadsheet *Sun*, disagrees with Deirdre on almost every point.

Jean Rook, star columnist of the *Daily Express*, began her career in Sheffield before coming to London to work for the IPC magazine, *Flair*. From *Flair*, she went to the *Sun* under Hugh Cudlipp and then moved to the *Daily Sketch* to write a column. She remained on as columnist for 18 months after the *Sketch* was absorbed into the new *Daily Mail* and, in 1973, joined the *Daily Express*, a newspaper which bestowed upon her the title of the First Lady of Fleet Street.

18 January 1989

The First Lady of Fleet Street?

I didn't invent that title, contrary to what people think. I was lying in bed one morning, when my husband read out: 'She's formidable, she's fearless, she's every other adjective you can ever think of beginning with an 'f', she is in fact the First Lady of Fleet Street.'

I started to say: 'Well, she's got to be a bit of a . . .' when he interrupted me and said: 'It's *you* they're talking about, you chump.' One of the assistant editors had done it without any reference to me. I never said it myself. If I'd thought of it I would have, though, believe me.

The first time I walked down Fleet Street I was walking into things, I was so excited. This was the street in the Christmas card, with the *Telegraph* clock and St Paul's down there at the bottom of it. The *Daily Express* looked so swanky. I was a *Daily Mail* reader then, so I wasn't so terribly grieved that I hadn't started on the *Express*.

Actually it was Godfrey Smith who got me started on journalism. I had written a few tiny bits for the *Sunday Times* when I was at London University and he helped me to get into what was then Kemsley's training school in Sheffield, and although I'm Yorkshire, I hated Sheffield. I married my deputy news editor in Sheffield, Jeff Nash, and he used to tell me that I had an absolutely great future in Fleet Street and that I'd have to get to London. Of course I thought that everybody in Fleet Street had been reading what I was writing up there in Yorkshire and that I'd soon be discovered. But of course they hadn't and I had to come to London via an IPC magazine, *Flair*.

Then Hugh Cudlipp, with whom I was desperately in love – what woman wasn't? – sent for me one night and asked me if I'd like to be fashion editor of the *Sun*. Naturally I said, 'Yes, please.' I became fashion editor under Amy Landreth who was the Mistress of the Memo. They used to fall on my desk like snow. God, did I mess it up, the only way to get rid of the load was to junk half of them in the bin. She sent me to Neasden to cover something, and there was a fashion show on there featuring a girl called Leslie Hornby. She had said, 'Go and have a look at her,' but I didn't bother. Deirdre MacSharry, who was on the *Express* at that time did, and within twenty-four hours they'd renamed her Twiggy, and I'd lost the best scoop of my life.

When I was on the *Sun*, Princess Margaret came out in some terribly old-fashioned patterned black stockings and I wrote a piece about it. It made *What the Papers Say* and everything else and was probably the innocent start of ceasing to look at the Royals as if they were wax dummies in glass cases. I never thought of it as Royal bashing at the time. It was an amusing and realistic comment. I think if Royalty is going to last, there's a great difference between making a comment like that – or like every man and woman in the country has made, about the Queen not going to Lockerbie – there's a great difference between that and printing a line like A LOON AGAIN when all Charles wants to do is spend a short time in the Highlands.

Being from Yorkshire, I've always said that whatever success I've had has come from being ordinary. All I do really is reflect what people think, but it gets them going. It's what they've all been talking about, over tea, over dinner, in the pub, so whether they agree with me or not, they've seen something about it on TV and they can then look in the paper to see what Jean Rook has to say about it. My talent is to stimulate and to amuse and to vent the readers' feelings. I know I can't change anything, any more than Mrs Joe Soap can, but on the other hand, she hasn't a platform from which to say it, so I can say it for her.

I hated working for women. I did it twice and I'd never do it again. And when Dixie Scott, who was features editor of the *Daily Sketch*, rang me one night and asked me to come over, I leapt at it, even though there were rumours that the *Sketch* was going to close. Dixie got me to write a column on the *Sketch*, instead of the fashion stuff I'd been doing.

The night the *Sketch* was amalgamated with the *Daily Mail*, I was having my baby, Gresby, called after my great, great grandfather Edward Gresby Rook, who drove a stage coach between Horncastle and Boston in Lincolnshire.

I think the *Mail* was a fairly unhappy ship at that time – the problem was that there were two people for every job, and everybody resented everything you managed to get into the paper – and although I adored David English who was a marvellous editor, I was tempted when the *Express* offered me better money, better quarters (a lovely room overlooking Fleet Street), a car, etc. But as soon as I announced that I was going to the *Express* . . . Wow! The *Mail*, who had not displayed my stuff terribly well and had kept me on miserable commons, came back with a ridiculous offer. They zapped back with money untold, a seat on the board, a trust fund for the eighteen months old baby, and an hour in Vere Harmsworth's office, drinking innumerable cups of coffee out of Royal Doulton cups.

Not only that, but at four o'clock in the morning, they sent Harold Keeble round to convey this counter-offer to me. My husband opened the door, and I came down in my bathrobe. I bet Harold nearly fainted when he saw me without make-up, and when he offered me all this stuff on behalf of Harmsworth, being a mercenary little soul, my eyes were beginning to ring up strawberries.

But my husband said, 'You can't do that. You've gone all the way to the church door with the *Express*. If you take this offer, you're only going to make them look like fools and you'll make your own name stink in Fleet Street. Also you'll become a slave to Associated Newspapers, from which you'll never be able to move, because nobody will ask you.' So I turned down the goodies and joined the *Daily Express*. The most dreadful period of my life was under Larry Lamb. Looking back on it now, it was funny, but at the time it was terrifying.

I was on holiday when my secretary rang me, and I thought this is rare, my secretary disturbing me on holiday. Then she said, 'I thought you ought to know before you return. Larry Lamb has just walked in here as editor.'

Mount Etna was exploding at that moment, and it couldn't have been more symbolic. Because I had met Lamb once before when he had called me and asked me to come and see him at the Soar-away *Sun*. He offered me less than I had been getting at the *Mail* and when I refused his offer, he was so mortally, totally offended that I thought he was going to explode. I knew that he couldn't bear so-called 'stars'. He had to be the star though I don't mind betting that if you went round to thousands of readers and asked them to name the editors of their favourite papers, they wouldn't have a clue.

I never spoke to him at all during the last six months he was there. After he had gone I heard that he had told someone that I was indispensable to the *Daily Express*. However, the point is that I held on and the most wonderful moment in my life was the afternoon when someone came in and said, 'Larry Lamb has got the chop.'

But having said that, I must admit that I admired him as a journalist. I think his Soar-away *Sun* was a brilliant conception. And although I've never worked for Murdoch, I think he's the most fascinating of the lot. I've never even met him, but he fascinates me totally because of his super success. At the same time, I still think the *Sun* is the junkiest paper in Fleet Street and that it has done a great deal of damage to our profession.

I'll miss Fleet Street. I won't miss the pubs or the socialising because I don't socialise, but I'll miss St Paul's and the *Telegraph* clock and the Edgar Wallace plaque, the whole feel of it.

If I had it to do all over again and I was young, I'd be very tempted to take a telly job, to try to do a Wogan, but I'd have to remember that I'm only asked on TV because of the platform from which I'm writing. The only person I could never interview was Dame Anna Neagle. She couldn't answer any of my questions, she had absolutely nothing to say. That's easy enough to cope with when you're writing a column, but if it had been on the telly, I don't know what I'd have done.

I only had one libel on the *Express*, and it was a fairly nominal one. I go to a lot of trouble to verify my stories. For example, I would never take an exclusive from the *Sun* and run a piece on it because I know that the chances of it being untrue are 80 per cent plus. I believe the Royals are fair game. Either we get at them a little bit, or, come the revolution, they'd better watch out and not say that they haven't been warned.

Nigel Ryan

Nigel Ryan and I worked together briefly in the mid-sixties on a short-lived experimental independent television company known as Television Reporters International. We had previously met when we both worked for Independent Television News around 1963, and I wanted to meet him again and talk to him because he started in Reuters which was a very important element in the Fleet Street experience at that period and later became an even more important element in the move to Fortress Wapping.

Nigel Ryan joined Reuters in 1954 and became one of their foreign correspondents in 1957. He went to Independent Television News in 1961 and was editor-in-chief from 1968–71. He has since been vice-president of NBC News in the United States, and director of programmes for Thames Television, and is currently a director of TV-AM News.

8 November 1988

I'd just come down from university in the early fifties and everything in England was terribly gloomy and the only thing I really wanted to do was to live abroad, anywhere abroad. I managed to get an interview with Christopher Chance of Reuters through my old school Ampleforth, and the father of one of the boys there, who knew Christopher Chance, and it worked. To my amazement, I was offered a job.

For a long time my job was to look up and check background facts in all the stories that came in to us on the teleprinters, and it was tremendously good training of a type that is no longer mandatory, with the result that there are far more mistakes and more sloppy editing today generally than there used to be in the old days. What I did was called subbing, but it was only after a few years I was allowed to take a piece of copy and adapt it for use in different parts of the world, which was real subbing.

Finally I was sent out on a job: to report on a Miss World beauty contest. I remember Miss France threw a tantrum and I reported that 'she stamped her pretty foot' and when I got back to the office there were long faces all round.

'You've no right to describe her foot as pretty,' they told me. 'We are in the agency business, we're in the business of objective journalism. Whether her foot happens to be pretty or not is an opinion, which has no place whatever in factual reporting.'

Then I was sent to Rome. I didn't really want to go to Rome. I wanted to go to France because I was in love with France, and I spoke French well. In fact I had discovered a secondary source of income translating Simenon novels. But the first offer of abroad I got was Oslo and I certainly didn't want to go there, and the second was Rome, so I took it. It was the beginning of three magical years for me.

For a start, I was now a millionaire. For the first time in my life, I was earning real money, about a thousand pounds a year, in those days, plus a Rome allowance on top of that which was tax-free, so that I had over a hundred pounds a month to spend on myself and I felt richer than I've ever felt in my life, before or since.

Rome was staffed by six Reuter correspondents because in those days it was the main take-off base for Africa and the Middle East. I spent half of the first year in the Middle East, and it was 1958, the year when the uprising in France brought de Gaulle to power; it was the period of the beginning of all the upheavals in the Middle East, the assassination of King Feisal, and I was sent to Baghdad and then the Pope died and in one way and another I made my mark as a foreign correspondent. Then I was sent to the Congo.

This came as a bit of a shock because I had been having such a sybaritic life in Rome. I'd become accustomed to spending a couple of months in the Middle East and then I'd be back in Rome and it was the easy life again.

But the Congo wasn't a bit easy. It was the time when Lumumba had just come into power in a country with thirteen doctors, four university graduates and no army officers, and it was about to be given its independence. Reuters sent me out ahead of Independence Day to see what would happen. I remember one particular day when the army mutinied. We heard rumours that a convent of nuns had been raped and that the army was on the pillage and that the Belgians had pulled out altogether, and it was a most disagreeable sensation down there on the beach where you take the ferry across to Brazzaville. You could almost smell the panic.

I remember a guy with two guns who came up and pointed one of them at me and said something. I replied, 'It's all right, I'm English,' or something equally ridiculous. I produced my passport and he spat into it. I remember being rather glad that he had the two rifles because he couldn't point either of them at me effectively without the other one getting in the way.

I turned round and walked away and felt a very nasty sensation as he kicked me while I was turning my back on him. I thought the important thing was to stay on my feet so I walked slowly back to the American Embassy and took sanctuary there for a bit.

I went back to my own flat later that night when things had started to quieten down, but there were still a lot of people lurking in the shadows, mutineers with loaded rifles, and it was very scary indeed until my colleague Sandy Gall suddenly appeared on the far side of the square and shouted 'Hi, Nigel!' totally unaware that every eye was glued on him and every gun trained on his back. Anyway he got across the square safely and came up and we finished a bottle of Irish whiskey together. But it was very frightening.

The most important difference between working for a news agency and working for a newspaper is that if you worked for a news agency, you were nobody's friend. Because although, for example, the *Daily Express* took the Reuter service, the correspondent on the spot wanted to beat Reuters, so he wasn't going to give you any information, although naturally he expected you to give him all the information you had. A certain amount of trading inevitably took place and one did a deal, sometimes working with the *Daily Express* correspondent against the *Daily Mail* and sometimes the other way around. One *Daily Mail* correspondent who shall be nameless once told me that his standard practice on arrival anywhere was to sit down and type: 'I stood on the roof of the Baghdad Hotel or the Conga Hotel, the whatever hotel . . . as Kassim's, or Nassar's or Lumumba's air force flew over or as their tanks rolled away into the bush or whatever.' But that opening sentence 'I stood on the roof as . . .' was absolutely vital because it enabled him to put his byline at the top of all the Reuter material.

If you worked for an agency, every hour of the day and night was a deadline for one of the newspapers which took the service and so you had to file as often as you could. The great thing was that we were all young and underpaid and hungry to succeed; we were all under thirty, none of us knew what the word tired meant and we simply went on filing right round the clock.

I think TV started to make a real impact at the time when I was a foreign correspondent for Reuters, but there were really two phases in the television take-over as the prime source of news. The first was home news, when it suddenly became demonstrably clear that the prime minister live on television was far more immediate and credible than something you'd read in the newspaper the next day, but television didn't start to dominate foreign news until well into the late sixties. In the early days, it couldn't touch the newspapers when it came to hot news stories from foreign parts: if you worked for television, you had to get the film to an airport, get it on a plane, have it flown to London, where it had to be developed and the quality was never all that good, but the worst thing about it was that it was always about thirty-six hours late. So it didn't even start to be competitive until first the jet plane and then the satellite, combined with electronic cameras and video-tape recordings, made transmission more or less instantaneous and then the situation was totally reversed. In '67 during the Six Day War in the Middle East, television had been able to boast that its viewers could see that night the same events that they had read about in their morning newspapers. By the time of the Yom Kippur war, thanks to the newly established satellite station in Tel Aviv, ITN's *News at Ten* had the first pictures the world was to see of that war. This marked the end of newspaper dominance in foreign news.

I didn't consciously decide that I wanted to be a television journalist. What happened was that when I was out in the Congo, Robin Day turned up to interview Lumumba and said to me, 'You're the Reuter man out here. Do you know a chap called Lulumba?' And I replied, 'He's called Lumumba, with an "m" and his first names are Patrice Emerie.' He said, 'Well, my goodness me, how incredible!' I had been out there for three months and it would be very hard not to know his name since he was the Prime Minister. And I not only knew his name but I also had his phone number so I rang him up and made a date for Robin to meet him and Robin was so impressed that it led to an offer from ITN when I was next in London. They sent me straight back to the Congo, as it happens.

I think that television, despite all the criticism of it, has replaced the newspapers, even the quality newspapers like *The Times* and the *Telegraph*, as the prime source of information in most British homes for the last two decades. People do respect it and it has maintained its credibility, in spite of all its vicissitudes, which have been caused mainly by public affairs and documentary programmes and not by the news bulletins.

So far as the prospect of increased control over the media is concerned, I think the more powerful a government becomes, the more it will want to control everything, and the tendency will be that it will want to control the sources of information. A free press is a pillar of our society and television ought to be fighting for it. But television cannot look to the press to support it. Fleet Street is if anything more anti-television than it is pro-a free press. But I don't really think that television is biased against the Government, certainly it is completely impartial in its news coverage. It's only anti-Thatcher in the sense that Thatcher is anti-broadcasting.

I immensely enjoyed being a foreign correspondent, and I greatly enjoyed being editor of ITN at that particular time. But if I were twenty again, I think I'd rather be an extremely successful novelist than work for any of the news media.

Fleet Street in the days when I worked in Reuters had very much a family atmosphere in which the cousins may have squabbled a bit, but it was all still very much a family affair, and, however tough the competition was, everyone had a great respect for the truth, which is not universal today. I think the British public have every right to hold the popular press in low regard, even compared with the popular press of my Fleet Street days. In my day both the *Express* and the *Mirror* were very serious in attempting to inform public opinion. The *Daily Express* was a propaganda machine, but its correspondents were required to be men of substance. The same applied to the *Mirror*. Do you remember the election when the *Mirror* asked: WHOSE FINGER ON THE TRIGGER? That was very serious, and it was taken very seriously. If the *Sun* newspaper came out with something like that today, nobody would pay any attention. The popular papers don't carry any weight any more.

Peregrine Worsthorne

Some journalists went to Fleet Street with the idea of becoming executives, even editors maybe, and wound up writing columns or reviewing books; others started out with the idea of becoming foreign correspondents, and finished their careers behind an editor's desk. That's what happened to the current editor of the *Sunday Telegraph*.

Peregrine Worsthorne, who has been editor of the *Sunday Telegraph* since 1968, began his career on the *Glasgow Herald*. He joined *The Times* in 1948, working mainly in the United States as Washington correspondent, and in 1953, he moved to the *Telegraph* group where he became deputy editor of the *Sunday Telegraph* in 1961.

3 November 1988

To be a foreign correspondent for *The Times* seemed to me to be the very summit of every ambition; it was, I believed, even more influential than being a politician. As a job, I thought it would be very grand. I still do, actually. But I had joined the army in 1943 at a stage when one might otherwise be thinking about a career. I didn't even start to think about a career until I came down from Cambridge in 1946.

I'd always liked the idea of writing for any paper, really, but specifically for *The Times*, although there weren't all that many jobs going in those days. I did get to see the deputy editor of *The Times*, who told me that there was no way of getting into a Fleet Street newspaper without some provincial experience, two years at least.

So I got myself a job on the *Glasgow Herald* and in two years to the very day I went back to him and said, 'I've done what you told me to do,' implying that there was a firm promise of a job there, and he gave me a job as a sub. I was thrilled to get any sort of employment and the pay was about six pounds a week. But I still wanted to be a writing journalist.

The Times, where I worked for eight years when I came down to London, didn't see itself as a part of Fleet Street at all. It was totally self-contained, superior in its own eyes, a sort of collegiate life. We all gathered in Printing House Square, and never went near Fleet Street. We had our own pub, our own little world, and we rarely met other journalists. In those days the newspapers tended to have their own little worlds and ours was a very distinctive, isolated world. Quite different from Fleet Street. It had lots of Oxbridge dons just doing the job as a hobby. I don't think any of us went to El Vino at that period; we all drank in a little pub in Blackfriars Avenue and it wasn't at all a mixing group. We had Henry Fairlie, who has now done a bunk to America. Lots of very grand figures who came in and wrote leaders and then went back to Oxford or Cambridge; they were all professors, Fellows of All Souls, that sort of thing. It wasn't the usual picture of Fleet Street at all.

After about five years I was made junior correspondent in Washington, in the period just before the last days of the Truman administration and the first Eisenhower–Adlai Stevenson election. By chance I got a lucky break. The senior man, my boss in Washington, was convinced that Stevenson was going to beat Eisenhower. He wanted Stevenson to beat Eisenhower, as did most of the British correspondents in Washington. The idea of having a Republican in the White House seemed almost to go against nature.

Stevenson was the liberal crusader and everyone was charmed by him and my colleague was so convinced that he couldn't lose that he allowed his wishful thinking to colour his judgment to the extent that he hadn't even prepared a turnover, as the main article was called, to meet the situation which would arise if Eisenhower should win, which he did. So they got me out of bed and asked me to write a turnover for the leader page. I had a very short time in which to do it, and it was my first big break. The Number One chap in Washington had a nervous breakdown, so horrified was he at the prospect of Eisenhower in the White House, and I was left in charge.

During that same election Nixon was running as Vice-President and he got into some kind of trouble over some sort of a slush fund he was involved in, and he gave that famous television broadcast with his little dog, about his humble antecedents. It was a real tear-jerking performance, very sentimental, very cheap-jack. I was sitting next to the great Walter Lippman, the distinguished American political commentator, on the campaign trail, and the big question was whether, as a result of this television performance, Nixon was going to be dropped from the ticket. Lippman, the great pundit, said, 'It's a disaster, he'll have to be dropped from the ticket.' So I sent a dispatch to *The Times*: NIXON TELEVISION APOLOGIA DISASTER. HE'LL HAVE TO BE DROPPED FROM TICKET.

Needless to say, Lippman, though a great theoretical pundit, had no sense of actuality, and of course Nixon wasn't dropped. Millions of American viewers wrote in telling Eisenhower to keep him on and my dispatch was a disaster. From then onwards I vowed never to be misled by electoral pundits. None of us correspondents knew any Republicans at all. Because of the long years of Roosevelt, the Democrats were regarded as the only sensible party. I remember an American columnist called Joe Allsop, he was very important and he invited me to dinner adding, 'I think I ought to warn you that young Robert Taft is coming to dinner, so you may care not to come,' rather as one might ring one's guests if one had someone coming from the National Front. That was in 1952. Now, of course, they've had to think again.

I was in the States for three years and came back to be a leader writer on *The Times* under William Haley but I wasn't doing anything satisfactory on the leader writing side because I was meant to be writing about American affairs and he wouldn't allow me to explain what the McCarthy business was all about. He just regarded him as an evil man and didn't want anything written about the situation.

Then they wanted to send me to Ottawa as correspondent there and there was a lot of talk about Ottawa being one of the great new centres of news but I was highly sceptical about this. I resigned rather than take up the appointment. The man who went in my stead has been there ever since and, poor man, he became an alcoholic out of sheer despair. He's now retired. I had the feeling that if I went to Ottawa, I'd never escape; it would be like some terrible exile, a sort of Gulag, so I never went. I joined the *Telegraph* instead, as a leader writer, initially. The *Telegraph* proved to be a very different set-up, much more genuinely Fleet Street with a real Fleet Street pub, the King and Keys, a quite dreadful pub.

There was the *Daily Telegraph* upholding all the Victorian virtues, writing leaders against the permissive society and so on and the Keys in those days was an absolutely Hogarthian dump with drunken diplomatic correspondents fighting with drunken leader writers. You were lucky to escape without having your eye blacked, whereas the *Guardian* had a frightfully dull respectable pub called the Clachan and they were all writing articles in favour of the permissive society and yet behaving with utmost respectability, while we Tory people were all drunk out of our minds. It was all very bizarre, but that's how life is.

I was in Africa a lot during this period. It was the time of the Wind of Change, a fascinating period. I went to Ghana several times. I covered the Macmillan Wind of Change tour which was certainly my most interesting foreign assignment. It was quite clear to me even then that democracy wasn't going to work out there.

I don't believe the arrival of television had a profound effect on newspapers. I think at first everybody was frightened that it was going to kill the newspapers. But the only lasting effect it had was on political coverage, because of the statutory obligations imposed on the television companies to ensure impartiality. People suddenly became accustomed to seeing, as part of their news diet, a Tory minister facing a Labour shadow minister, and vice-versa, the habit of strict impartiality. In those early days of television, you either took the *Daily Herald* or you took the *Daily Mail*. There was no question, before television, of looking at both sides of the question. Nowadays, because of television, everybody increasingly has to do just that.

My first job as a sub on *The Times* involved making sure that the spelling in Arabic of the members of the Sudanese cabinet was correct because *The Times* had to worry about all those people in the colonial office who ran the Sudan. You couldn't get away with spelling any of the names wrongly. Today, that's all gone by the board. Nobody gives a damn if you don't even get the names of the American cabinet right. It's indicative of what's happening. Obviously, if your readers don't mind, you don't have to be so careful. However, you'll notice that there's been no decline in the accuracy of sports reporting nor any lowering of standards in the reports about the stock exchange. That's because people still care about sports and money. You wouldn't last a day if you got any of the sports results wrong, but if you get something wrong in the political or diplomatic field, relatively few readers even notice, so there isn't the same pressure for accuracy.

I find it very unsatisfactory to be situated here in the Isle of Dogs. I think journalists should be in the centre of affairs. I don't mean all journalists, but writing journalists certainly ought to be. It's a waste of time travelling to and from this place and you never meet any of your colleagues from the other newspapers. But I don't think that the newspapers are going to change fundamentally as a result of this diaspora. It will be a slow business and I don't know how one will be able to measure the change. I think you'll get less lively journalism, as a result of the lack of excitement and the exchange of ideas, and it won't be nearly as much fun and one likes to be in a profession in which one is enjoying oneself.

I would certainly go back into journalism if I had it to do all over again, absolutely. I didn't really choose Sunday journalism, it chose me. I was working on the daily and the deputy editorship of the *Sunday Telegraph*, when it started, seemed an exciting job. But I think on the whole working on a Sunday newspaper is less exciting, less fulfilling. On a daily, you have six outlets a week, and the more you have, the more excitement there is. It's not even that a Sunday newspaper, only coming out once a week, really gives you a chance to stand back and take a measured view. That's not what newspapers are about. That's what books are about.

Mary Kenny

Mary Kenny was only 15 when I left Dublin for Fleet Street. I met her in London in the mid-sixties when she was working on the *Evening Standard* Diary.

Mary Kenny joined the *Evening Standard* in 1963, and then returned to Dublin as women's editor of the *Irish Press* from 1969 to 1971. She came back to London to the *Evening Standard* as Fleet Street's first woman features editor in 1971, when she was 25. After about a year she went back to feature-writing and is now a freelance, working for the *Daily Telegraph*, the *Daily Mail* and the Catholic press. She has also written several books. She is married to Dick West.

27 January 1989

Fleet Street was my university. I was expelled from school when I was sixteen and didn't have any further formal education after that. I did a year as an *au pair* in Paris and while I was there I wrote a few pieces for the *Evening Press* in Dublin. I also wrote for the *Irish Times*, and in that way I collected some cuttings that I could use when I came to Fleet Street, but I worked for a bit as a secretary on the *Guardian* before I got hired by the *Evening Standard*, by Charles Wintour who was very good at hiring mavericky sort of people.

What I principally learnt in Fleet Street was that you can find out about anything in life simply by asking questions. I know you should read books but you can find out an awful lot if you're sitting next to someone at dinner, with absolutely nothing in common. You can have a wonderful conversation by just asking questions. Fleet Street taught me how to talk to people, how to get on with people, above all, where to find things out.

I was the only non-Etonian on the *Evening Standard* Diary when I joined the paper, except for Max Hastings, who was a Wykehamist. At that period, the middle to late sixties, there

were lots of clever, glamorous women in Fleet Street like Anne
Sharpley, Anne Scott-James, Jean Campbell, Drusilla Beyfus
and Clare Hollingworth who was always jumping out of
aeroplanes and doing things like that. There was a sort of
tradition of the girl star reporter and Fleet Street in comparison
with most other worlds was a very liberated place, the BBC
and other worlds seemed very stuffy by comparison.

What most sticks in my mind from my young years on the
Standard are the Paris events of 1968, the *événements* of the time
when Charles Wintour was convinced that there was going to
be another revolution in France, that capitalism was going to
collapse and everybody thought it was all terribly exciting. I
had no experience at the time, but I thought that something
extraordinary was happening. Most of what I wrote in those
days makes me cringe now.

Despite the very liberated atmosphere in Fleet Street, the
one field in which women hadn't made much headway was in
the area of editorial responsibility. Being made executives, that
sort of thing. I don't suppose a lot of women wanted that sort of
responsibility. Maybe they were conditioned not to want it, or
maybe they had too many other things in their lives to want to
be saddled with such responsibility. The question of what was
called the Night Turn on the *Evening Standard* did become a bit
of an issue and there was a sort of feminist stirring at the time –
a feeling that the women should be included in the rota. It was
actually a very tedious job, boring and uninteresting. One had
to sit there and take calls during the night, fires in Chelsea,
things like that. Most of the women reporters were very glad
not to have to do it, but there were the feminists who felt that
they should be treated in exactly the same way as men.

I think I was the first Fleet Street woman features editor. I
did the job for a year from '71 to '72, and looking back on that
year, I don't think I was very good at it. I was far too young and
I was not technically good enough to give me the confidence I
needed. One of things that I did learn from being features
editor is that it teaches you how to handle writers; above all,
their insecurity, and their need to be constantly helped and

reassured and massaged. I didn't think I was doing the job properly, so I quit it after a year and went back to writing features. I wasn't happy doing it, because in a place like the *Evening Standard* anyway, a lot of the job had to do with budgets and things like that, it wasn't particularly creative. I'd have done it far better ten years later.

The popular papers have given women lots of opportunity, they have been very enlightened in that. And the women they have produced have not been the sort of gung-ho sisters, they have been very down-market ladies who just want to maximise sales. Women today are doing much more in areas like financial journalism than they did formerly, the doors are much more open now. But some papers are still nervous about hiring women executives and I think one reason for this is the sort of gallantry that still exists. Some editors like to conduct pretty rough editorial conferences, and they don't really feel free if there's a lady present.

These days I'm a free-lance. I work for the *Telegraph* and the *Daily Mail* and the Catholic media, so I'm pretty spread around. I won't miss El Vino's because I've sort of grown out of it really. Sitting around having drinks is a young people's pursuit in a way. If I had it to do over again, I think I'd drink a little less.

Although I was mixed up with the Women's Lib movement in Dublin when I went back to be women's editor of the Irish Press from '69 to '71, I wasn't involved in the storming of El Vino's. At the time it happened, I was going through a very priggish socialist stage, and I thought it a very trivial issue.

Christopher Mitchell

It's not possible to talk for even a few minutes about Fleet Street without the name of El Vino cropping up. It's usually wrongly referred to as El Vino's, and it's the capital of the principality; a wine bar which serves sherry and spirits, but no bitter beer, and it's situated roughly opposite the end of Fetter Lane on the south side of Fleet Street.

El Vino was run, until 1973, by Frank Bower, a tall, courtly, white-haired gentleman who wore a morning coat, a flowered waistcoat and cravat, and who remained convinced to the end of his days that it was his duty and his privilege to exclude from the pub all those people who were not, in his opinion, quite right for El Vino. It is now being run by his cousin, Christopher Mitchell.

23 November 1988

I've been here for about thirty-three years.

Frank was my grandfather's brother's son, actually a cousin once removed, always known as Uncle Frank. He died about fifteen years ago, I think maybe because fifty years behind the counter in Fleet Street drove him round the bend in the end. El Vino was a wine bar. In 1879, my grandfather started an order office, that's an ordinary off-licence, in Mark Lane, where you could order anything you wanted delivered. In 1915 he bought these premises which he operated as a free vintner, so we really have been concurrent with the great days of Fleet Street.

My grandfather died in 1952 and left the business to my mother, who was an only child. When she died, she left it to my brother and me, between us, but until his death, my Uncle Frank always ran the place. I was terrified of him. He was very autocratic. He encouraged and cultivated the upper echelons of Fleet Street. He was only interested in the top people. Lord Northcliffe used to come in here regularly at half-past eleven for a glass of Madeira and a sticky bun. I remember when I came here first, Harry Guy Bartholomew, who was a very big, strong character, was a regular customer. Hugh Cudlipp didn't come here so often; he wasn't a favourite of Frank's.

I remember Michael King, Cecil King's son, he was a regular, and the cartoonist Vicky. Until one day Vicky had the temerity to take Frank's hat down from its peg and try it on. It was far too big and came right down to his shoulders. Frank kicked him out and he never came back after that. I don't suppose Frank would have let him in. Frank was very particular about letting people in. Often, when the place has clearly been three-quarters empty, he's been known to say to a customer he didn't like the look of, 'You can see there's no room in here. Why don't you go somewhere down the road?'

We became very famous for our stand against the Women's Libbers. A lot of it is myth of course but essentially what happened was that Fleet Street had always been strictly a man's province until the war. When the men all went off to the war, that created a vacuum and women started coming into journalism in a big way, and some of them started to come in here. Frank, for purely chivalrous reasons, didn't like to see them standing up, so he provided stools for them at the bar. They could also sit at the tables to the side in the front bar or in the back room. But as more and more women started to come in, quite clearly the bar area is very small and women are apt to have handbags and shopping and umbrellas and so on and they tended to spread these out on the bar and on the floor with the result that the men couldn't get near the bar to order a drink. So Frank made a rule banishing women to the back bar and the side tables. They couldn't stand at the bar drinking, or use the stools at the bar, those were the only rules we ever had about women.

But when the Sex Discrimination Act came in we got a horde of the most dreadful types, they weren't even from Fleet Street, they were from the *Daily Worker*, I think, and they came storming into the place demanding to be served at the bar. My manager at that time had to fight them off with soda syphons. The upshot of it all was that they took us to court, the Westminster County Court, where a fine old judge, Judge

Riddle, an Irishman who is actually a teetotaller, heard the case and we won it.

Three years later they were back again. This time they took us to the Mayor and City of London and they lost again. Then they wanted to appeal and they needed money for this and tried to get Legal Aid but were refused on the grounds that their case was frivolous and a waste of the taxpayers' money.

Eventually they got the money from the Equal Opportunities Commission to launch an appeal and in 1982 the Court of Appeal found against us. So now we are obliged to serve women standing at the bar, not that many women do. They were people who never came here normally, and I don't think I've seen any of them in here since.

The characters I remember? Well Derek Marks, larger than life, a legend in his own lunch-time, as someone put it. He drank pink gin when he was on the *Standard* and graduated to champagne when he moved to the *Express*. Wentworth Day, a free-lance with the *Mail*; Philip Hope Wallace, the famous drama critic of the *Guardian*, that's his chair over there with a little plaque over it. He was one of the old school; he could go straight to the phone after a show and phone in his review, dictating the piece without a single note, he was marvellous, a first-class character. And Pat Murphy, who did promotions for the *Daily Mail*, he had a great gift of the blarney, he's retired now and living in Ireland. I remember Reg Willis, the longest-serving editor of the *Evening News*; when he was with the *Evening News* it had the largest sale of any evening newspaper, and when he left the circulation went down. Noel Monks, a very famous war correspondent, Noel Whitcomb, Donald Zec and John Cope, editor-in-chief of the *News Chronicle*. David English used to come in but now of course he's too high up; he's architect of the *Daily Mail* really. Editors don't come in here any more, nor proprietors either.

We still get a smattering from the *Mirror*, the *Express* and the *Mail*. The *Evening Standard* is going to Kensington in a fortnight but the *Express* is only going over to the other side of Blackfriars Bridge. Many of our old customers still come up from Wapping and the Isle of Dogs to meet their friends here. El Vino was always regarded as neutral ground; all the newspapers had their own pubs near their offices, but the executives and the star reporters and columnists all used to come here. These days Fleet Street is becoming the centre for the legal profession, barristers and solicitors and accountants too, expanding out of the Temple because of the shortage of office space there.

But don't forget the real Fleet Street characters haven't been around for about fifteen years. Today's newspapermen and lawyers are not the characters we used to get in here. There are very few real characters around today. I remember a chap called Scott Watson who used to drop in here for a gin and tonic every night on his way home. One night Frank swapped his gin and tonic for a plain tonic water and Scott Watson drank it down, without batting an eyelid. Then, just as he got to the door on his way out, he turned round and said, 'Think I'm a bloody fool, do you?'

The real reason behind the move from Fleet Street was the feeling that the proprietors couldn't get out of the union problems which they had created for themselves but what finally gave them the spur to go ahead and do something about it was the sale of the City of London School for Boys, just off Tudor Street. That site was bought for £96,000 by the Morgan Guaranty Company of America. That made all the owners of the Fleet Street papers realise what they were sitting on, in terms of the site value of all their premises. Once the move started, it all came together and they'll all be out of the street within another year; it has all happened inside three years.

But we'll still be here and El Vino will continue to exist as a wine bar for journalists, if they choose to come back here, male or female, for lawyers, for accountants, for everyone and anyone in fact who is properly dressed and well-behaved.

Richard West

When I joined the *Mirror* in 1959, it had two daily selections of letters, one edited by the Old Codgers, and the other by a tall, serious-looking young man with glasses and an austerely humorous air: Dick West, who was later to marry Mary Kenny.

Dick West claims to have failed in a number of other fields before trying journalism. Before working on the *Daily Mirror*, he had been given three months' trial by the *Guardian*, and had simply stayed on for years until they offered him the job of agricultural correspondent, when he decided it was time for a move. He became editor of the letters column for the *Mirror* until one of his headlines (WHY CAN'T WE HAVE A TEENAGE POPE?) upset Hugh Cudlipp and he was forced to move on again. He boasts that he has never had a staff job in his life; he has always been a casual free-lance. He has worked as a foreign correspondent for the *New Statesman*, the *Daily Telegraph* and the *Spectator*. He also writes for *Private Eye*.

24 November 1988

I've often thought it was the abolition of the death penalty which destroyed Fleet Street. Edgar Wallace built his fortune on gallows drama. Right to the end, the crime reporters were kings in Fleet Street. Now they scarcely exist. Even after the most horrific murders, of children, for instance the Moors murders, newspapers cannot whip up much excitement about the pursuit of the murderers, because they are only going to end up with a prison sentence.

The journalist, if that is the right word, who suffered most grievously from the abolition of hanging was Frank Ross. He was a life-long con-man, who had been in prison in France and England, including Dartmoor. His last conviction, in the forties, was for selling fake health certificates to Cypriot restaurateurs. When he came out he decided to go straight, by flogging stories about murderers on trial or awaiting the gallows. Getting in to see them was easy. Sometimes he posed as a priest – I have seen him wearing a dog-collar in the Feathers in Tudor Street, another casualty of the years. Sometimes he would pose as an old acquaintance, confident that people would think that they remembered him.

There was a murderer called 'Guardsman Mick', a kind of homosexual rent boy who suddenly turned on one of his patrons. Frank wrote to him saying that he remembered him from the days when he (Frank) ran the canteen at Caterham Guards depot. Guardsman Mick gave him a full story as well as some compromising letters from well-known homosexuals, which I suspect Frank sold back to the writers.

Frank was a bald, portly man and in his fifties and sixties might have passed as a clergyman to someone dim and credulous. He was especially interesting on Christie, whom he saw on the day before his execution. All Christie was worried about was his income tax, Frank said. I met him on another occasion after he had been to see a convicted poisoner in Manchester. He showed me the letter the woman had sent him, starting 'Dear Rev. Francis' and ending 'I know you will be on your knees and praying for me this evening.' 'Silly cow!' was Frank's only comment.

Frank's interviews and observations about these murderers used to appear in the Sunday newspapers, especially, I seem to remember, the *Scottish Pictorial* (if that's what it was called) where Frank was billed as 'Britain's top psychiatrist'. I think someone ghosted a book for him about his life as a con-man. I wanted to do a book with him about the murderers, using the many letters he had. Unfortunately he would only let me have a letter or two at a time, for the price of an evening's drinks. I soon got fed up and dropped the idea. But he was a Fleet Street curiosity, in a grisly way.

I last saw him in the Feathers about the time of the abolition of hanging. 'I'm all in favour, as a matter of principle,' he said, 'but it's the end of my profession.'

What abolition has done for murder, permissive customs have done for the sex crime. Adulterous or homosexual vicars are no longer news, now that they openly boast about what they have been up to. This may be why the *Sun* and the *News of the World* now go after the kind of people, like actors and politicians, who in the past had never set themselves up as figures of rectitude.

It's interesting to compare what's happened in Britain with the United States, where an old-fashioned moral code has returned and where the death penalty has been restored in many states. In Florida, one of the death penalty states, the crime reporters are kings and queens of the press once more.

Everyone now agrees on the awfulness of restrictive practices by the print unions but people still do not see what a disaster the National Union of Journalists was for journalism. During the fifties and increasingly into the eighties, it had a stranglehold on Fleet Street newspapers, with dire results for free-lances and for journalism generally. Bright young people from university simply did not want to go into journalism if it meant having to do a kind of apprenticeship with a local paper. And good local papers did not want to take them. The only people who got union cards without any difficulty were boring young Trotskyists who had entered the union through the political network.

The NUJ made it difficult to hire and fire people, which was one of the things which had made Fleet Street such a lively place. It put a premium on cautiousness, particularly in reporting subjects like strikes and racial trouble. It also led to terrible feather-bedding and idleness, the four-day week and not working 'antisocial' hours. All this encouraged the dullards and depressed the enterprising.

The NUJ was especially bad for free-lances. There was, maybe there still is, an NUJ 'Free-lance Branch' which is simply a contradiction in terms. It was dominated by Trotskyists and feminist harridans, the kind of people who actually prefer to sit in a meeting rather than in a pub. Among the officials of the Free-lance Branch were a member of BOSS and reputedly two members of the KGB.

Another effect of the NUJ was to grab all the available

money for themselves. The newspaper chapels grudged any money spent, for instance, on foreign travel, and the management didn't have the guts to overrule them. Editors had to conceal from their own staff the fact that they were paying outsiders. Once, Bill Deedes asked me to do a story for him in India, a couple of leader-page pieces. The *Telegraph* gave me a ticket but no money. On the day before I was due to leave I rang Bill up in some desperation and he said, 'Meet me at the King and Keys at six.' I went along there and while we had a drink at the bar, he slipped me five hundred quid in cash with strict instructions not to tell anybody on the *Telegraph* that he'd given it to me. In return, I scribbled my signature on a beer-stained receipt.

Free-lancing used to be the best-paid as well as the most exciting form of journalism, if you were any good at it. Foreign correspondents got all their stories reprinted (and paid for) in dozens of papers at home and abroad. A Crimean dispatch written initially for *The Times* by William Russell Howard, describing the gratitude of wounded Russian prisoners whose case he had taken up, appeared in Scotland with the conclusion: 'Thank God and the *Inverness Evening Advertiser*.'

Sue Arnold

Another journalist who very early in her career was made aware of the harmful impact of the abolition of capital punishment upon her chosen profession was Sue Arnold. She now writes for the *Observer*.

Sue Arnold went straight from university to become a trainee journalist in Thomson Newspapers in Blackburn, Lancashire. She joined the *Evening Standard* Diary at the time that Mary Kenny was working on it, and, since 1977, she's had her own column in the *Observer*.

6 February 1989

I went into journalism straight from Trinity College in Dublin. Why did I go to Dublin? No particular reason. No Irish family background, nothing like that. And I'd no thoughts of going into journalism at this stage. As a child I'd wanted to be a ballet dancer. Most little girls do but I'd actually gone to a serious ballet school until I was seventeen, and I can still dance on the tips of my toes, up to a point.

I very nearly went into advertising. While I was at Trinity, I won a competition run by J. Walter Thompson to find the ten most ingenious undergraduates in Britain. I was the seventh most ingenious undergraduate in Britain and the ten of us were all given fifty pounds provided by Cassandra, the *Mirror* columnist who had worked in J. Walter Thompson, and they offered us jobs as copywriters.

But I'd been writing things for the Trinity magazine, *TCD* and by this time I'd decided that I wanted to be a journalist. I was so ignorant that I didn't know that there were different sorts of journalists. But I became a trainee in the Thomson Newspapers and was sent up to Blackburn, to the *Lancashire Evening Telegraph* to get some provincial experience as a reporter.

My first interview was with the Lady Mayoress. She didn't impress me, and the editor didn't impress me. In fact the only thing that impressed me was seeing my own name in the newspaper the next day. I had to go to the courts and I found that fascinating. There was an old chap there called Cyril who'd been reporting the courts for about a hundred years and he told me that there was no fun in court reporting any more, once the death penalty had been abolished, nothing dramatic any more, like the judge putting on the black cap and condemning someone to death.

After three months I became a columnist which gave me aspirations, and that's why I didn't stay with them for the stipulated two years, I ditched them after six months because I wanted to go somewhere more exciting than Blackburn. I could see that if I stayed in Blackburn I would go mad inside those two years. So I wrote round to all the newspapers and I used to go down to Fleet Street as often as I could to try and see people.

Eventually I got a job as holiday relief on the *Evening Standard* Diary, under Magnus Linklater. That was a time in Fleet Street when I was the happiest person in the whole world. I still think that it was the very best time of my life. I was so pleased, so conceited: I used to burst into rooms and say 'I work for the *Evening Standard* Londoner's Diary'. I was thrilled to be in Fleet Street and to be a part of it. Mary Kenny was on the Diary then, and I found her very scary, she was so much a woman of the world. She used to come in, in the morning, wearing the evening dress she'd been wearing the night before and tell you all about the people she'd been with.

Then the editor in Blackburn complained to the NUJ that I'd broken my indentures, which wasn't true because I hadn't actually signed anything, but Charles Wintour wouldn't back me up, I believe because I'm half Burmese, and sacked me, despite the fact that none of the other people on the Diary had been anywhere near a provincial paper.

The nicest thing that ever happened to me was much later when Charles Wintour was forced to present me with the IPC Magazine Writer of the Year Award.

As a result of the complaint, I had to go before an NUJ Tribunal and I was fined twenty-five quid, and I was looking for a job again. I got one in the London office of the *Manchester*

Evening News, and after that I was on the *Daily Sketch* Diary, the nastiest job I ever did in my life. Jean Rook was there and Jeremy Deedes was on the Diary.

I stayed about six months with the *Sketch* and then went off to Persia and worked on an English-language paper out there called the *Teheran Journal*. How this came about was that at that time I had a very rich American boyfriend and we had a row and he gave me, as a joke, a one-way ticket to Timbuctoo, which is in the middle of nowhere, but I traded it in for a return ticket to Persia, because I had an aunt out there. This was long before the Ayatollah, and it wasn't a very newsworthy place in those days.

When I came back to London I got another holiday relief job on the Pendennis column in the *Observer*, to replace Polly Toynbee who had gone off to write a book. They took me on for a month and I stayed and stayed and stayed, doing the briefing column, doing a bit of news reporting.

The thing that really made them keep me on was a story I did about the hippies living in Piccadilly Square. I went and spent a night with them and wrote about it and it appeared on the front page with my byline. And at the same time as I was writing for the *Observer*, I was also subbing for the *Sunday Times*, the late Saturday night subbing shift, because I was about to get married at that time and we needed the money.

I was useless as a sub. I was actually subbing on the *Sunday Times* when the first edition of the *Observer* came out with my piece on the front page, and I was immediately sacked from the *Sunday Times*, for working for the opposition, I suppose. After my front page story appeared I was offered a staff job on the Pendennis column under Edward Mace.

I got my own column in 1977. It was supposed to be funny, that was the only instruction I got. I don't make things up, I try to see the funny side of things that really happen. I mean things that are meant to be funny very often aren't but you could go to a funeral and it could be hilarious.

I don't use the new technology, I can't because of my bad eyesight. I use a very old portable typewriter which has lost a lot of its bits and pieces and has to be tied together with my dressing-gown cord. And I either give this typewritten copy to my secretary and she feeds it into the computer, or I phone it in and they do it for me.

My husband says I must have the very best job in the whole world, because I like writing and I can write about anything I like. That's the up-side of it. The down-side of it is that sometimes you just don't feel funny and you can't think of anything funny to write about.

Margaret van Hattem

I met Margaret van Hattem through Brian Inglis in London, and she confirmed what I had always heard but never really believed about the *Financial Times*: that it is not a bit boring or dry and only about money.

Margaret van Hattem was an Australian journalist who worked for Rupert Murdoch in Australia before coming to Fleet Street to join first Reuters and then the *Financial Times*. She died in July 1989.

5 December 1988

I came to Fleet Street in 1974 via Rupert Murdoch's *Australian*. This was to have been the Australian version of the *Guardian*, and indeed it was quite liberal at the time, and Murdoch was known in Melbourne as Rupert the Pinko, until the 1975 election when things went against us, and anybody with any scruples left, if they hadn't already done so.

I was into political reporting at this period. I'd written to all the Fleet Street papers I'd ever heard of, though I missed out on several opportunities because I didn't understand the language. I thought when people said we don't have any vacancies but do come in and see us anyway, they really meant that there wasn't a job going and so I hung about Reuters economic section in Fleet Street, waiting for a posting, but in those days Reuters never posted a woman anywhere, and in the end I got sick of waiting and applied to the *Financial Times*.

Before I went there, I'd always thought it would be an awfully dry and boring place and that you'd have to know a lot about economics and finance and business, about which I knew very little. But the *Financial Times* was bliss. They let me write all sorts of things and I was sent off to Malaysia within a month to do a special survey. They sent me off to India, they sent me off to Singapore, they allowed me to write anything I wanted to write.

I was initially interviewed by Freddie Fisher. I remember he sat me down at a much lower level than he was seated at, and kept peering down at me and saying, 'I can see that you are literate, but tell me, are you numerate?' He had me there, because although I'd taken a degree in English and French at Western Australia University, I didn't know what on earth he was talking about. But he took me on, and put me on the foreign desk, filling in on Asia for the Asia correspondent.

Then they offered me a posting in New York which I thought would be very boring, I didn't want it at all. They were rather surprised when I refused New York and offered me Brussels, which I also thought would be very boring, but I accepted it and went off there to write about the Common Agricultural Policy and had an absolute ball. It was very easy covering the CAP at that time because the *FT* were first in the field and nobody else was doing it. I worked in Brussels very happily for two years from 1978 to 1980, when I came back to London to work as a Lobby correspondent. That was very cliquey indeed and nobody bent over backwards to help me.

The office told me to get into the Irish story because nobody else was doing it from the Westminster end. So I went across to Northern Ireland to see if I could find some Protestants that I really could like. I did meet some, but I had a horrible experience when I was manhandled at a Paisley rally, actually kicked to the ground and thrown out of the meeting.

Paisley and Molyneux were up on the platform in front of all these people, it was like a weird sort of family ritual. There were mothers and fathers who had driven for miles through the snow to bring their sons to this rally; nobody brought their daughters. It was about half-way between a prayer meeting and a political rally. A funny little clergyman from the floor of the hall started with a prayer which was the most irreligious thing I'd ever heard in my life; calling on Hell Fire to come down and swallow up their enemies, followed by a standing ovation for Paisley and Molyneux. They wound up by singing The Sash.

I was sitting throughout the entire thing when someone came up to me and said, 'On your feet, lassie!' I said, 'I'm press,' and then suddenly there was this splintering sound as my feet were being kicked from under me, and I was on the floor being kicked on the backside and wondering what I should do about it. Then they started singing 'God Save the Queen', and Paisley said: 'I see a woman here who will not stand up for the National Anthem. I knew there was a Fenian amongst us, they always send one to spy.' I didn't know how I was going to get out without being lynched. But they made quite sure that I did get out. I thought Paisley was evil.

It's great fun working for the *Financial Times*. It's very free, I sometimes think I'm working in a Golden Age. They let me write all sorts of things, but one of the difficulties is to stop yourself from writing for your sources, who happen to be diplomats, politicians, and so on. It's difficult to gear yourself to write for the Birmingham businessman. We go for a section of the market, we don't want sales of two million, we're not trying for that.

I think you're shaped by the institution you work for and I don't think there's any other newspaper I'd rather work for.

Raymond Jackson (Jak)

Several of the journalists to whom I talked referred to newspapers as an addictive drug and Rupert Murdoch's principal objection to strikes – apart of course from the fact that they lost him money – was that they forced people to break out of the habit of buying one particular paper every day. If it is true that newspapers are habit-forming, then surely one of the most powerfully addictive ingredients must be the daily cartoon. I talked to Raymond Jackson, 'Jak' of the *Evening Standard*, shortly after he had moved into the Associated Newspapers' new offices over Barkers in Kensington.

Jak has been the *Evening Standard*'s principal cartoonist for thirty-eight years, under three proprietors (including Beaverbrook and the third Lord Rothermere) and under at least half a dozen editors.

26 January 1989

I wish I'd thought of a family, like Giles, because if you're ever stuck for an idea, there's always Old Grannie, and everybody laughs at her. I work for the *Mail on Sunday* now as well as the *Evening Standard*, and I used to do cartoons for the *Daily Express* on Saturdays.

Max Aitken, Beaverbrook's son, obviously liked my stuff, because when the old man died, he gave me a new car, plus another five hundred quid a year, and all the rest of it. I never met the old man, the Beaver himself, which is just as well because somebody told me that if I did, my money could have been doubled, or I could have been out in the street, according to the mood he was in. I'd had a couple of telegrams from him when I'd done political things he approved of. But he was principally a political animal and the purely funny stuff just wasn't his cup of tea.

I was an art student at Willesden School of Art which is now defunct. This is only the third job I've ever had in my life. The first was as a general artist at Link House in Store Street. I did everything there, including retouching pubic hairs out of photographs for magazines like *Health and Strength*. I started drawing cartoons while I was there, and after a year I went to an advertising agency which was part of Benson's. I'd had a few cartoons accepted by *Punch* by then. In this agency, one of the jobs I had to do was roughs in the style of Ronald Searle for advertisements and if the client liked them, they sent the roughs on to Ronald Searle for him to do the finished drawings. Then I broke my arm doing judo, so I couldn't work for three months, so I decided to spend the time walking around Spain and when I came back I went to the *Evening Standard* looking for a job in publicity. The guy I saw, Bruce Lockhart, showed my cartoons to the features editor and I was offered a job on the spot and I've been there ever since. I loved it instantly, the *Evening Standard* in Shoe Lane, which was in the Fleet Street area.

I'm in the office by seven o'clock every morning, but have been listening to Radio Four for at least an hour, at home and in the car. I'm a belly politician and there's no way of knowing where the ideas come from. I've usually formed a few in my mind by the time I arrive in the office, and even at seven o'clock in the morning, some of the early birds will already be in there ahead of me planning the features. I sit in the features department with a huge layout pad in front of me, and go through all the papers with them, and sort out my ideas and sketch down a few roughs, so that by nine o'clock, I'm ready to march to the editor with four or five suggestions. Mind you, this is for the next day's cartoon; I always work one day in advance. I get approval at nine o'clock in the morning, and it takes me most of the rest of the day to finish it off and then I come in the following day with a fresh set of ideas.

The big worry these days is that your ideas might be libellous. Today, for instance, my ideas included Nigel Benn the boxer, who was in the news for his belligerence outside the ring, but he's suing everybody these days. Another idea was about that waiter at the Savoy who bit one of his rival's fingers, that's absolutely made for a cartoon. Then there was the business of the barristers having to mix in more with the solicitors and the banks and that. And finally, there's the business of the Guardian Angels on the tube trains, all good cartoon ideas.

So what I normally do is a couple of sketches on each idea, with suggested captions, and I go in to the editor around nine o'clock, and he may have a lot of other ideas, but there's no aggro, there's no argument, most of them have been good at their job, and can spot a good cartoon idea as well as I can. If he's worried about the possibility of libel, he'll tell me to go and see the lawyer. Charles Forte, for example, though I like him, and he's an old friend of mine, he's a suer.

Sometimes I try to get an idea past the editor that I've tried on him before and had it panned. But I don't really have much to do with the editors. I see them perhaps for about three minutes a day when I bring in my roughs, and after all, I've been here for thirty-eight years so presumably they, or the readers, like my stuff.

When I started on the *Standard* it was about four pages and there was doom and gloom all round, we were all in the same boat then, but nowadays everybody seems to be pretty happy. I think the whole atmosphere is a lot better, though I do miss Fleet Street. I miss the company. You used to walk out there and go into any hostelry and find friends and people you knew from the other newspapers, like a village. Coming from there to Kensington is almost like moving to another country. We're still busily finding out about all the new dumps and clubs and things.

I could never draw well enough to be anything other than a cartoonist, but I love cartoons. I think my early drawings were appalling. I can't see what anybody else saw in them, but maybe everybody else was also drawing badly at that time.

I've been banned for life from El Vino, which is sad. I could never find out why. It could have been because of the day when I was in another restaurant in Fleet Street, boozing and joking with the staff when in came Christopher Mitchell of El Vino who said: 'Who is that awful person?' And, when he was told who I was, replied, 'Not the sort of person I'd like to have in my establishment.'

Next time I went to El Vino, and I only went there about twice a year, they said, 'You're barred', and wouldn't let me in. They may have mixed me up with another Fleet Street cartoonist who used to take his clothes off all over the place, in the law courts, in the office, anywhere. Vicky was banned because he dared to put on the former proprietor's hat. Financially it's their loss because I probably spend more on champagne alone than any other six journalists. When do I finish work? Pass. When I'm not drinking, I'm back home very early, like a wonder child. Otherwise, I suppose you could say that I work as late as I have to.

Ian Wooldridge

From a cartoonist, to a sports columnist. I have never taken the slightest interest in sport of any kind, and when I came to Fleet Street first the only sporting journalists I knew were Peter Wilson and Jack Hutchinson, who were at all the *Mirror* parties. Later, I met Ian Wooldridge of the *Daily Mail* and when I started to do this book, thought he would be the ideal man to explain what it was like to be a sports writer in Fleet Street.

Ian Wooldridge worked on the *New Milton Advertiser* and on the *Bournemouth Times* before joining the *News Chronicle*. Just before the *Chronicle* folded, he moved to the *Sunday Dispatch*, and when it in turn folded, moved to the *Daily Mail*. He has been with the *Mail* as a sports reporter and columnist ever since.

10 January 1989

I remember the first time I ever came to Fleet Street. I was staying in some hovel in Chelsea, and I came in on the bus. All my life I'd wanted to work in Fleet Street, and so I got out of the bus a little bit short of Fleet Street. Just to be able to walk down there and look up at the old street names. I thought at the time, I've worked so bloody hard for this, that this has got to be my day.

I'll never get over that feeling. I still feel exactly the same now, even after all those years.

I was a good school-boy cricketer and I wanted to be a professional, but when I played one match against top professionals I was disabused of this notion and joined the *New Milton Advertiser* as a general dogsbody. After six months in the printing room getting my hands filthy, I was moved to the editorial, where I did all the usual funerals, weddings, local events. I tried to dodge National Service, but I couldn't, so I went into the Navy and learnt Russian, which I don't speak at all now.

After two years in the Navy, I went to a weekly in Bournemouth, the *Bournemouth Times*. I used to come to London every Friday afternoon on my day off and walk round the newspaper offices in Fleet Street, literally banging on doors and the only guy who listened to me regularly was Jack Hutchinson, the famous sports editor of the *Daily Mirror*. He advised me to read Peter Wilson, the *Mirror*'s sports columnist, and that's what I wanted to be, a sports columnist. I saw an advert for a sub in the Manchester office of the *News Chronicle* and applied for it. However, when I went to see them, they offered me a job as a sports writer in Manchester, and after a year I managed to get down to London as a sports writer on the *News Chronicle*.

Six weeks before the *Chronicle* folded I went to see the editor, because I'd been offered twice as much money to go and run a column on the *Sunday Dispatch*. We all knew at that time that the *News Chronicle* was going to go under, but he actually attempted to stop me from going to that other newspaper down the road. I've never, ever forgiven his memory for that. It was awful. But I left anyway and went to the *Sunday Dispatch*, and after a year it, too, went bust. So I moved one floor up or one floor down to the *Daily Mail*, whichever it was, and I've been there ever since.

Sports reporting differs from ordinary reporting in that you are so close, particularly in cricket terms, with the people you are writing about, that it becomes a sort of a club. The one big thing that happens all the time in sport is the introduction of the new sports reporter who doesn't give a damn what he writes about the players and this has caused a big change in sports reporting because every moment they're away from the game, the players are being watched and peep-holed by certain newspapers; and once they write something, then everybody else latches on to it, so that the life of a player becomes impossible. That happened last year when Mike Gatting was sacked from the English captaincy for being caught with a barmaid in his room. If those rules had applied when I was going on cricket tours in '62 or '70, England would never have fielded more than five players, and the press box would have been empty. After all, you're away for five months on one of these tours.

I really despise that sort of reporting. There are plenty of real stories at the back of sport – political aspects, who's going to be fired, who they are about to appoint, what's going to happen about South Africa? There are always plenty of scoops available. The D'Olivera scoop was about the only one I ever got in my life, but that was a big one. D'Olivera was offered a huge bribe by Rothmans, the tobacco company, to declare himself unfit for a tour of South Africa. It was about 1968, and he turned it down. I got to hear about this bribe, which was made in a lavatory in one of the M1 service stations, and we blew the story. I did get another scoop on the Packer affair, when the whole cricket world split down the middle. But I wouldn't cross the road to run one of those scoops reporting on people's private lives.

My training for sports reporting was five or six years hard slog of straight news reporting. There are some ex-sportsmen coming into sports reporting these days, and there are some good ones, but they haven't had the training that you and I have had in the district courts, the council meetings. I do an awful lot of travelling, and in fact it broke up my first marriage. I was away for five months every winter on a cricket tour, I was probably away from home more than seven months in every year. I won't make the same mistake again. I still travel a lot, but these days they are all short trips.

I've been doing this column for the *Daily Mail* since 1972. Basically I can write what I like and it doesn't ever get changed, it's a bit like reviewing a play or a film. The only upset was over the Moscow Olympics when the editor, David English, didn't want me to go, he took the Thatcher line that we shouldn't go to Moscow and I was writing at the time that we should in fact go to Moscow as a team, and we went as a team. I went as a journalist, and although there were rows every day about what I was writing, when we all came back, English said: 'Well, we printed everything you wrote.'

During that period there had been a ridiculous agency story that every time a Russian javelin thrower was in action, they opened the gates of the stadium and he got the benefit of the updraught. Well, if you know anything at all about a stadium, you know that this couldn't be true. The *Mail* insisted that I write this story and I refused. As a result of my intransigence, they then wrote a leader saying that the big difference between the Soviet Union and Britain is that in the Soviet Union the journalists are not allowed to write what they want to write, whereas this arsehole, writing at the back of the paper, is allowed in Britain to put forward his own views and defy his editor. I thought it was all rather sweet.

The arrival of television certainly changed sports reporting in one way. Going back to the great sports writers, the greatest cricket writer of all time, Sir Neville Cardus, would go to a match and write, in the most wonderful prose, the most awful bollocks, a total load of rubbish, but since nobody had seen the actual match on television, nobody could say a word against him. In the old days, the newspaper reporters would go to Brazil and report crocodiles in the streets, and nobody could say that it was nonsense because nobody'd ever been there. Television has changed all that. It has made sports reporting far more accurate as opposed to more honest.

Will I miss socialising in Fleet Street? It's decimating, it's crucifying. If there's any reason to, I'll come back, but it would only be to meet my mates. No one is going to come back to visit bricks and mortar. There has of course been another big change, even without the move, and that is that the new generation has stopped this socialising thing. Before I was married, in my early days in Fleet Street, every night was spent in the Press Club in Salisbury Square. You didn't finish work when the last word was written, you went straight to the Press Club and you started all over again. You never left the Press Club, only for a few minutes to pick up the first edition.

When they gave me this new machine, this word processor, the only person in the house who knew how to use it was my eleven-year-old stepson. I have no technical ability at all. It's taken me six months to learn how to use it confidently. If I dropped dead tomorrow, I'd be very pissed off but I wouldn't feel that I'd been cheated. Let's take one example. All my life

I've been obsessed with the Red Arrows. And I just simply arranged to do a flight with them. I had to do a few medical tests, I'd never had a medical test in my life until I wanted to go flying with the Red Arrows, but I've had it and I've done it, I've done five flights with them actually, and I ask you, in what other job in the world except in journalism could you establish a contact with the Red Arrows and say: 'I wouldn't mind going up with you lot, tomorrow,' and they'd say sure, and that's it, you're up there, with them. For my money, that's what it's all been about.

Sam (Sydney Mervyn) Herbert

Sam Herbert was also on the *News Chronicle* when it folded in 1960; but he had experienced a similar situation over twenty years earlier when the *Morning Post* was incorporated in the *Daily Telegraph* in September 1937, and was prepared for it.

Sam Herbert, who always wrote as Sydney Mervyn Herbert, started in provincial journalism before joining the *Morning Post* as a reporter. When the *Post* folded in 1937, he worked for a time as a free-lance agricultural correspondent, and then went to the *News Chronicle*. During the war he worked for the Foreign Office, returning to the *News Chronicle* as foreign editor in the mid-fifties. By 1960, he was in charge of the publishing side of the *News Chronicle*, a job which included publishing the very popular 'I Spy' series of books and a number of regional television magazines, as well as the Michelin guidebooks. After seven years with the Dickens Press, as the *News Chronicle* publishing division was known, he took over Frank L. Crane Ltd, International Publishers' Representatives, and is now chairman of the company.

7 October 1988

What happened in Fleet Street couldn't have happened until it did, because before the time of Roy Thomson and Rupert Murdoch, nobody ran daily newspapers primarily for profit. It was a superlative game for very rich men; they could think that their newspapers gave them popularity and even political influence. They ran their papers for fun, for prestige, which meant that they weren't primarily concerned with making profit. They didn't want their papers to lose too much money, but they didn't want too much trouble with the unions either. Added to that, they never got together. The Newspapers Proprietors Association was a most extraordinary affair; I don't think they ever worked together on anything. Nobody ever showed any leadership and they never stuck together.

The present lot are in it purely for the money, and that's the big difference. Though I still can't see why they've had to take all the editorial offices out of Fleet Street. We'd already demonstrated to them with *Lloyd's Register*, that you could still have your editorial offices in London and print miles away in Colchester. We demonstrated that away back in 1971/2.

After a few years of provincial experience on the Isle of Wight and in Surrey, I went to the *Morning Post*, and was there when it closed. Then I went to the *News Chronicle* as a reporter. One of the first stories I covered was a semi-Irish one. Do you remember a young American avaiator called One-Way Corrigan? When I joined the *Chronicle*, he had just arrived at the airport in New York announcing that he was going to fly single-handed across the Atlantic. The federal aviation chaps all examined his plane and pronounced that it wasn't fit for the transatlantic journey. He said that it didn't matter, he was going to beat the transcontinental record back to California. And he took off into the clouds and the next thing anybody heard of him was that he was circling an airport in Dublin. I was sent there, and I met Corrigan whose first words, as the Irish heard them over the intercom, were: 'California was never like this.'

During the war I had a whale of a time. I was sent to Lisbon as a sort of liaison officer between the services and the Foreign Office. And when the war ended, I was sent by the Foreign Office to liquidate all the paramilitary organisations which had been looking after information in the liberated countries. This meant trips to Paris, Brussels, The Hague, Rome and, finally, Athens. I had a marvellous time, setting up press attaché offices in all these places. But I still wanted to be editor of the *News Chronicle* more than I wanted to be anything else, and when they offered me the foreign editorship in the early fifties, I went back to Fleet Street. And I was still in the *News Chronicle*, and I still hadn't become editor, when it folded in 1960.

What went wrong? Well the Cadburys had the best intentions in the world, no question about that, they never took a penny out of the paper. Laurence was absolutely devoted to it but until the day he died, and he had been associated with that newspaper for fifty years, he didn't know the difference between a reporter and a sub-editor, and he could never understand why it was that the white-collar workers in the newspaper were so much more trouble than the white-collar workers in Bourneville. It was as simple as that. And of course the *Chronicle* at that time was dogged, like all the other Fleet Street newspapers, with union troubles. Before the war, we installed in the *Evening Star* a baling machine from Canada which automatically bundled up the newspapers. When the *News Chronicle* and the *Star* closed down in 1960, it was still under wraps, it had never been used. And at the machines, one chap was still counting the papers by hand, which the press did automatically anyway, and another was putting the sheets of brown paper down, and a third was getting the string ready, cutting it very precisely, and yet another was pasting on the label of the local newsagent, and so it went on, right to the end.

After the war the *News Chronicle* sent an engineer round the world to look at the latest improvements in design, and settled for a machine which had been developed in Sweden. There were months of delay before they could get the necessary foreign currency, and permits for building and all the rest of it, and when it was all ready to go, then came the discussions with the unions. The new machine was capable of printing at roughly double the speed of the old presses with about half the crew, but we soon found that there wasn't any need for discussions. There was an established figure for the crewing of printing presses which couldn't be altered, so that was settled: the crew would remain exactly the same. The only question at issue was the speed of the new press and it was soon agreed that it mustn't produce any more copies than the old presses had, so therefore it would have to be run at half speed, if at all.

There was a period when the *News Chronicle* tried to operate without an editor. And the next thing that happened was that the managing director, Frank Waters, caught polio in Spain on holiday and died on his way back up through France, so that for a period, near the end, we were without a managing director as well as an editor. And when they brought my very good friend Norman Kerseley (who had been editor of the northern edition) down to London to become news editor and then editor, they didn't even have the courtesy to tell him that they had already decided to close the paper down. None of this bothered me. By this time I'd moved to the publishing division, and I'd managed to separate it from the main company so that if the *News Chronicle* went down, it wouldn't necessarily drag us down with it. We were publishing all the very popular 'I Spy' material and in addition I'd managed to get the publication of the popular Michelin Guides, plus several of the local TV programme journals. In fact I signed a contract with Westward TV the day the paper closed and a few months later, did a deal with Roy Thomson for the Scottish one. By this time I was operating from temporary premises in Puddle Dock, near the Mermaid Theatre.

At this stage the publishing company was known as the Dickens Press. I stayed with it for about seven years after the *News Chronicle* folded, and then took over another company, Frank L. Crane Ltd, International Publishers' Representatives. In this capacity I became a consultant to *Lloyd's Register of Shipping*, then having trouble with the print unions, and making a huge loss. In fact they were thinking of closing it down. Because I knew about the new technology, and because Lloyd's had a deep pocket – the national newspapers couldn't afford the cost of the new technology until the windfall of the Reuters flotation – I was able, years ahead of Eddy Shah and Murdoch, to suggest the remedy. And I moved *Lloyd's Register of Shipping* away out to Colchester, where it was produced by the new technology and non-union labour. But that didn't create a sensation because it wasn't a daily newspaper and there were no pickets and no police. Also we were dealing with a particularly intelligent NGA at that time.

It would have been so easy, once the way had been shown to them by us initially with *Lloyd's Register* and then by Eddy

Shah, for them to have kept their editorial offices in Fleet Street and moved the whole print operation out to green-field sites somewhere. The thing about Fleet Street is that it was one of the great newspaper centres of the world. And it's all been just tossed away . . .

Nick Lloyd

I first got to know Nick Lloyd when he was assistant editor of the *News of the World* under Bernard Shrimsley. In his comparatively short career – he is only 47 – Nick Lloyd has packed in a great deal of Fleet Street experience. He has worked for Rothermere, Thomson, Murdoch and the *Mirror* group, before it was taken over by Maxwell (his wife, Eve Pollard, edits Maxwell's *Sunday Mirror*) and he has worked for papers as diverse as the *Sunday Times* and the *News of the World*.

Nick Lloyd went straight from Oxford to the *Daily Mail* as a reporter in 1964. He became educational correspondent of the *Sunday Times* in 1966 and was deputy news editor and news editor between 1968 and 1970. He became assistant editor of the *News of the World* in 1977, deputy editor of the *Sunday Mirror* in 1980, editor of the *People* in 1982, and editor of the *News of the World* in 1984. Two years later he became editor of the *Daily Express*.

17 November 1988

I became absolutely addicted to newspapers at Oxford. I suppose it was mainly the *Guardian* and the *Sunday Times* then, but I very soon became a student reporter on *Cherwell* and became part of the student press and from that I went straight to the *Daily Mail*. I was never trained as a journalist.

This was during the early sixties period when the number of university students doubled, and the national newspapers suddenly became very interested in what they were up to. It was all part of the Beatles thing, young people were making the news, people wanted to read about what they were doing, tittle- tattle things, gossip, slander, whatever. I think this was a news-desk inspired interest, because the news editors thought that they ought to be targeting their papers towards students.

So what happened was that Fleet Street used to send reporters to Oxford and all the other universities and if you were on a student newspaper and you knew what a good story was, they would very quickly realise this and ring you or come to see you.

This was the time when students were being sent down or rusticated for having girls in their rooms, or being caught having it off in the colleges, it was one of the great scandals of the period. But by actually running those stories, we did put a stop to people getting sent down. The publicity was so awful for the colleges, that they changed their moral attitude and after about a year stopped sending people down for getting caught in the act.

So in a sense I started off in yellow journalism, but I think there's a streak of yellow in every good journalist. I've always had a kind of love affair with journalism and so at all stages of my career I've always found it fun. The old Fleet Street adage is true; it's much better than working for a living. It was true when I was educational correspondent of the *Sunday Times*, it was true when I was on the *News of the World* and it's true now that I'm editing the *Daily Express*. It's all been fun. It makes the adrenalin pump and it's entertaining and it's got a lot of serious bits in it, obviously, as well as lots of tits and bum.

If you work in a newspaper, in a sense you're a part of history, you're in on some of the exciting bits of history, though I can't always bring myself to believe that what we're doing is really happening; I tend to view it all slightly as if I were watching it on a television screen.

I was very closely involved in the 1986 General Election because I happened to be editor of the *Daily Express* at the time. I enjoyed being part of the power process, to be honest. I enjoyed being kept in the picture as to how things were going. And that night when she won again and came down to the Central Office at three o'clock in the morning, that was a great night. You remember those bits you saw on the television, all the people leaning out of the windows, Tebbit and Parkinson, and all the others, well, I was actually in that room, I talked to her for about ten minutes that night. And if you remember that bit where she's making this speech about the inner cities and, as she walked in, her face suddenly lit up and she grinned: at that point she was saying hello to me, she really was. That's the silly bit, you don't talk about it too much, but that's the romantic bit. That's the power bit.

I suppose the most dramatic thing that ever happened to me was that I was shot at. I was in Nigeria for the *Sunday Times* and I was shot at. I found that very revealing about my own views; again, you have an image of what it must feel like to be shot at, but when it happens, it isn't really a bit like that. You just suddenly realise that life is really only about simple things such as food and water and fear and death, and not about any of the things we spend so much of our time making a noise about.

Another thing occurred while I was out there in Nigeria which I've never been able to forget, it was part of the passing mosaic of horror. What had happened was that a second lieutenant and his platoon (they were on the Federal side) had captured a sniper who'd been firing on them. They'd caught him pedalling out of the village on an old bicycle and they pulled him off the bike and shot him through the head, just like that, without any trial, and it was all covered live on television and it became a great *cause célèbre* in the dining rooms and sitting rooms and drawing rooms of the Western world because people were mortified at the thought of this man, trussed up like a chicken, being shot in cold blood, right there, in living technicolor, in the corner of everybody's living room.

The reaction was so strong that the Federal Government felt that they had to do something to redress the effect. I was in Fort Harcourt when the Federal forces court martialled the second lieutenant who had been responsible for the execution of the sniper, and it was all carried out as a public relations exercise. Here we were in this compound, which was gradually being overtaken again by the jungle, and they court martialled this guy and found him guilty, and they took all the press men who were there at the time, about half a dozen of us, plus a BBC camera team, to the playing fields of a Catholic school nearby and tied him to a tree, and in very military, Sandhurst style, read out his death sentence and he kept snapping out 'Yes, sir!' all the time and behaving impeccably.

Then the firing squad came up with their rifles and were just about to shoot him when a BBC man shouted: 'Hold it! We haven't got a sound mike.' Anyway, the firing squad all put down their rifles again and this guy stood there blindfolded, waiting, tied to a sapling in front of the church with a big cross up there in the background. It was all very dramatic.

Then the BBC got their mike working and the firing squad picked up their guns again and shot him, and he quivered and gurgled for a bit, it was all pretty horrific. And when he was finally dead, we journalists all had a fight about it, over that decision to hold it, to wait for the microphone; we fell out over it, we all behaved like animals, it was dreadful. But it told you a lot about, well about everybody, in the end. Because this guy was only being shot so that everybody in the West who was raising money for Biafra or whatever could feel, as they watched the execution on the news that evening, that justice was being seen to be done. And it made you feel that you were only there to record this horrific event which had been staged to appease the tiny political consciences of . . . Yuk. Not very nice.

I followed Larry Lamb as editor of the *Express*. One of the troubles about being editor of the *Express* is that in the days of Beaverbrook, it was the best-selling paper in the country, selling over four million a day. Over the past twenty years, it has lost more than two million of that circulation, because it became old-fashioned and out-of-date, the sort of paper our dads used to read. Then the *Sun* came out and totally undercut it with a very different sort of popular journalism.

I think the *Express* should have gone tabloid a lot earlier than it did. I think not knowing what market they were aiming for was a great mistake. We've been middle-marketed, down-marketed with Derek Jameson, up-marketed with Alistair Burnett . . . God knows what the readers thought; we used to have a new editor every eighteen months. The paper had no consistency, no pattern.

What we are trying to do now is to be squarely middle-market, A, B and C1, hopefully age-group twenty to thirty-five;

we're aiming at a much younger market now. I think the *Express* probably looks more tabloid than the *Mail* because the *Mail* has better print quality, so that it appears to be a bit classier, but that will change when we go over to the new presses.

The *Daily Mail* also has a lower proportion of ads and therefore it looks less cluttered, which helps a lot. But we play a game here, we cut pages from both newspapers and we don't say which is which, and usually people can't tell. They are really very similar in layout.

When we move out of Fleet Street, we're not going very far, only across to the other side of Blackfriars Bridge. But I think the general move out to Wapping and Battersea and Kensington is going to make it a lot more difficult to recruit the right people, because we'll know far less about what's going on in the other newspapers. You won't hear about the rising stars, you won't know who is turning out to be a great new sub, all you'll know is what you'll see in the papers really. So as a market place, it's not going to be nearly as good as Fleet Street was when it was a small village.

One thing that is very interesting is that on nights when a really big story breaks, like the *Free Enterprise* ferry disaster, they all come back here, from the Isle of Dogs and Wapping and everywhere; they all come back from *The Times* and the *Telegraph* and the *Sun* to see what everybody else has done with the story and to sit around and chat about it. That will all change, of course. Another generation will come along who have never done that, so why should they start?

I've worked for Rothermere, Thomson, Murdoch and the *Mirror* group and now I work for the *Express* which is owned by the Provincial Newspaper group. When I was on the *Mail* I was too low down to know much about it but everywhere I've worked has had a different feel, a different management culture, to use a phrase that's fashionable. With Rothermere – that's the old Lord Rothermere, not Vere – you were slightly aware of being owned, in a feudal sense, but that's changed. Vere is engaging, and much smarter than the exterior image you get at first. You weren't even aware of the management on the *Sunday Times* under Thomson in the sixties.

I was with the *Mirror* group in the last days before the Maxwell take-over and that was when the inmates were really running the asylum and although it was a lovely time, the papers were really being run for the benefit of the staffs and not for the shareholders or for the profit of the Reed group. It was a sadly missed opportunity. If the world had been a different place, and the unions hadn't had such a stranglehold, we really ought to have slimmed the company down and got it into shape and gone on to taking over the asylum ourselves. Reed didn't like the *Mirror* group and wanted to get rid of it, but it was a great pity that all the journalists involved were not a bit more businesslike. Together we could all have saved it.

I was longer with Murdoch than anyone else – twelve years – and obviously working in very close proximity. I think Murdoch is a genius. He is Hearst, he is Beaverbrook, he is Sam Goldwyn, and he's his own father too, so when you come to think about it, it's absolutely staggering that he can keep so many balls in the air so effectively.

The present *Daily Express* is run as a public company which is trying to return 15 per cent profit on revenue. There is very little interference editorially, but we're in a very competitive market place with Murdoch and Rothermere and Maxwell and it would be nice to have a bit more money to spend on extra pages and on journalism, on fun, but we just can't do that.

If I have one regret, perhaps it is that I didn't stay in America. I went to America with Murdoch for a year and he wanted me to stay, and I think perhaps I should have stayed. Otherwise I have no regrets . . .

W. L. (Bill) Webb

Bill Webb was literary editor of the *Guardian* for twenty-five years until 1985. I've known him since he spent about seven months or so on the *Irish Times* in Dublin, in the fifties, accumulating provincial experience.

Bill Webb tried to get into the *Guardian* while he was still at Trinity College, Dublin, but although the newspaper published a few pieces from him, they insisted on some provincial experience, which he gained in the *Limerick Echo* and on the *Irish Times*. He then went to the *Guardian* as a reporter, graduated to the arts page and edited the book page from 1960. He was one member of a small group which set up the notorious Booker Prize, and is still with the *Guardian*.

24 October 1988

I started in journalism by walking into the *Guardian* office in Cross Street and asking: 'Could I do anything useful for the paper?' I was then in my second year at Trinity College, Dublin, and had done a bit of university journalism. I was a sort of half-musician and had vague thoughts of writing music criticism.

There was a very nice old Scottish news editor there called Willie Cockburn and he said it had been a long time since they'd had anybody from Dublin; this must have been about 1951 or 1952.

They'd just built a new cathedral in Manchester, so I went out and did a piece about that; after all, I'd been a choir boy when I was a kid. Cockburn gave me little bits and pieces to do during the vacations. I remember I did a piece on the difficulty of finding choir boys for cathedrals which came out as a Miscellany Page lead with a marvellous headline: CHOIR BOYS HARD TO FIND: AN ACTIVITY WHICH HAS LOST ITS ATTRACTIONS. When I finished in Trinity, I did six months as deputy editor of the *Limerick Echo*, and seven months on the *Irish Times*, and then I went back to the *Guardian*.

I didn't know the *Guardian* was planning to move down to London. We began to be a bit aware that it was in the air about two years later when the newspaper dropped the word Manchester from its title; that would have been about 1955. By this time the editor, Alistair Hetherington, was coming down to London regularly and staying in the Mount Pleasant Hotel; in fact he commuted between Manchester and London for several years.

I came down to London when Gerry Fay was London editor, in that lovely room like a ship's cabin, above the post office overlooking Fleet Street. Richard Fry was our city editor; he was born in Vienna and had been educated in Berlin and Heidelberg and he had taken over the city page from Cecil Sprigg, who had been Reuters man in Berlin in the thirties.

I came down initially to see plays when I had stopped being a reporter and was doing the arts page. We used to drink in the Clachan with Philip Hope Wallace, always champagne. Very soon after me came Brian Redhead, though he never edited the page from London, he never worked in Fleet Street.

The foreign editor and his staff stayed on in Manchester until the mid-seventies. I never worked in Gray's Inn Road except when I had to do some overnight stories about the Booker or something like that. Neal Ascherson was without any doubt the best journalist of my generation. He's an old Etonian, and the only kind of Jewish, Scottish, anarchist old Etonian I've ever come across. He knows so much more about Germany than any other Fleet Street journalist and on top of that, he's a sort of honorary Pole.

I got involved in covering the Prague Spring – probably because I had previously been to Czechoslovakia. It seemed very grand, covering world stories like that and coming back to do it from Cross Street in Manchester.

I was literary editor from 1959, and I helped to set up the Booker prize; I was chairman of the judges the first year. I think somewhere between a half and a third of the books we considered were books which should have been on the list.

The *Guardian* has always been out on its own a bit, even in

Fleet Street. Jean Stead, who has just retired, was the second of three women news editors in the history of journalism, so far as I know. She was one of a generation of *Guardian* journalists who suffered painfully from accusations of not really being professional. It wasn't that they didn't know how to do the job, it was just that the *Guardian* was always considered as an amateur sort of paper. The *Guardian* always got the university graduates but that stopped about twelve years ago when the NUJ insisted that people entering the profession had to have provincial experience. How good that was for newspapers, I wouldn't like to hazard a guess. Swings and roundabouts, I'd say.

When I wrote an article in the *Guardian* to celebrate my twenty-five years as literary editor, I gave thanks for a few things. They included being able to catch with my morning rashers as a student in Dublin, the most original newspaper column ever written, Myles na Gopaleen's Cruiskeen Lawn in the *Irish Times*, and the novels he wrote as Flann O'Brien; and my luck in starting in the *Manchester Guardian* reporters' room in what seemed to me the best company in the world – Neal Ascherson, Dick West, Roy Perrott, Michael Frayn, John Cole, Frank Edmead, Geoffrey Moorhouse, Harry Whewell, Nesta Roberts, W. J. Weatherby and, the doyen of 'The Room', Norman Shrapnel.

Marjorie Proops

Marjorie Proops was the only *Mirror* star writer I met before moving from Dublin to become features editor of that paper. She happened to visit Ireland around that time and expressed a desire to meet my old friend, Brendan Behan. Although she was not then, and is not now, a pub woman, I had to explain to her that there was not the slightest chance of ever meeting Brendan anywhere other than in a pub, at any rate during the extremely elastic 'permitted hours' in Dublin. Accordingly we all met at the Brazen Head, and Brendan was totally charming, as he always was, whenever he didn't feel threatened.

Marjorie Proops was a young fashion artist who was hardly out of art school when she was discovered by Hugh Cudlipp and employed by the *Daily Mirror*. Subsequently she worked for Hugh's brother Percy for a time on the *Daily Herald*, before returning to the *Daily Mirror* as a columnist and subsequently as 'Dear Marje', a column in which she answers her readers' letters. She is now an assistant editor of the *Mirror* as well as a director of the company and has been awarded the OBE.

25 November 1988

I had hired a desk in a rickety old room in Wine Office Court and I'd met an agent who carted examples of my drawings, as well as those of other people, around all the newspaper offices. He was fortunate enough to bump into Hugh Cudlipp who saw my drawings and immediately telephoned me and said, 'Come around at once.' And I did just that, all inky and dirty and grubby. Hugh Cudlipp said: 'Stand up. Walk across the room. Sit down.' Then, after a long pause, he said, 'Do you think you would be able to represent the *Daily Mirror* at Ascot?' I was too speechless to answer, but he decided for me. That was my first experience of Fleet Street. From that moment, Hugh and I have remained close friends; he has guided and helped me at every stage.

I had two skills – art was one of them but I also had an extraordinary singing voice. When I was about twelve, I sounded like a baritone. I was a skinny, plain kid, but I had an enormous range. I had nothing else.

When I had been at the *Mirror* for two or three years I had a call from Hugh's brother, Percy, inviting me to join the *Daily Herald* as fashion editor, which meant doing the words and the music, the writing as well as the drawings. I'd never done any writing before. I learned how to do it by doing it, in fact I really learned the trade on the *Daily Herald*. I learned everything except shorthand and typing. I joined the union and for a bit I was even Mother of the Chapel. I was a stone-sub as well, and this was at a time when women were very rare in Fleet Street. They all found it rather amusing and turned it into a game known as 'Educating Marje'.

Eventually I was promoted to women's editor of the *Herald*. That meant I had to go to the news conferences. I was the only woman there and whenever I entered the room Percy and all the other men would stand up. I used to try to get there early, to avoid that embarrassing ritual. Women started coming into Fleet Street during the war, when the men were away in the forces.

I met Hugh Cudlipp at a party after the war and he asked me whether I would like to come back to the *Mirror* as a writer. When I got home, I decided not to ring him back. I reckoned it had all probably been gin and tonic party talk and I didn't want to take advantage of it. But then I got a call from Percy, who by this time had left the *Herald*, and he said: 'Ring my little brother, he's waiting for a call from you. He's getting mad at you.' So I rang Hugh and went back to the *Mirror*.

On my first day, Hugh took me in to meet the editor, Jack Nener, and there was Jack, with his elegant white hair, beautifully dressed as always, he looked far more like a cabinet minister than a journalist. He stood up to shake my hand and then said: 'Fucking glad to meet you.' That was 1954, and that was Jack Nener.

When you're part of the fabric of a newspaper, as I am, you're a bit like the wallpaper. I'm lucky that I get on well with all the people with whom I work. I don't make waves.

I first met Bob Maxwell when he was an MP. I met a lot of people and did a lot of travelling all over the world during my years as a columnist, millions of miles. I think I've been everywhere really, except China and New Zealand. My urge to travel has diminished with the years. When you've done as much as I have, unless it's obsessive, you don't want to do any more.

'Dear Marje' was Hugh's idea; the first one was in 1971. I wouldn't say there's been a tremendously dramatic change in the sort of letters I get, but certainly the balance has changed, it's changed as society has changed. Women are stronger now, they're much more independent. As late as the 1970s, it wasn't unusual to get letters from women who said that they'd had to submit to their husbands sexually, but I'd really be amazed if I had a letter today from a woman who said she'd had to submit – it's not a word that's ever used any more. I suppose, to an extent, I was partly responsible for this change of attitude, from my response to their letters.

If I had it all to do all over again, I believe I'd do exactly the same. Nothing in my life was ever pre-planned; it has all just happened. I love what I'm doing now, and I loved what I was doing at every stage of my career. But I don't think you could ever use the word fun to describe my kind of journalism, it's very much concerned with other people's problems and in no way is that fun though it can be very satisfying.

The satisfaction in this 'Dear Marje' job is that when you get, as I do, about twenty-five thousand letters a year from people in trouble, people with sad, heart-breaking problems, if I can help by just being there, by being someone with whom they can identify, a person to whom they can write, then that's very rewarding to me. We do some telephone counselling here but I don't encourage it. I don't believe in instant counselling.

I decided long ago that I was too old to learn the new technology and I still do my copy in the old way. I have very obliging friends down on the editorial floor. My copy is typed for me – I can't type, I never could – I simply write it all out in longhand and it goes to my secretary who types it out and then it goes into the computers.

I've always been in the features department since my early days on the *Herald*, but I've always been interested in politics and the nights that stand out for me over the years are general election nights.

I've never been one for pubs. I grew up in pubs. My father was a publican in Shepherdess Walk and I've always hated pubs and pub life because I saw so much of them when I was growing up. Also, it's very different for married women. Whereas the men who go to the pubs have mostly got wives at home preparing their dinner, if you're a wife and a mother, you don't want to hang about the pubs, you want to go home and be with your family and get the dinner ready. And that essential difference between men and women will, I think, remain, despite any other changes.

Certainly we've all seen a diminution in standards in the popular press and a lowering of standards all round since I started. We were on to real people and real events that actually happened then, not non-events that never happened to non-existent television soap-opera characters.

But I can't claim any wide experience of Fleet Street. Apart from the last few years, I've only ever worked for the two brothers, Percy and Hugh Cudlipp. But I wouldn't ever have wanted to work for anyone else.

Nigel Dempster

The gossip column, exemplified in its heyday by William Hickey of the *Daily Express*, was one of the features which contributed to the success of the popular papers. Nigel Dempster, the best-known of to-day's gossip columnists, has broken with tradition in that he uses his name, possibly because as a result of various accidents of birth, education, marriage, and career, he happens to be on first name terms with most of the people he writes about.

Nigel Dempster went straight from school at Sherborne to Lloyd's of London. He was a member of the Stock Exchange from 1959 to 1960, account executive of Kimberley Associates from 1960 to 1963, when he joined the *Daily Express*. He moved to the *Daily Mail* in 1971 and has been writing his current column since 1973. He is also well known as a television personality.

17 January 1989

When I started on the William Hickey column on the *Daily Express* in 1963, I was one of an enormous staff, probably about eleven people. In those days they used to have about three editions and a staff going round to all the theatres and clubs in the evenings. It was all highly labour-intensive because Beaverbrook was making such a fortune that he could afford to be lavish with his journalists. Whenever you went on a job, you used to notice that whether it was a war or a wedding, there were at least three *Express* men there to one from each of the other newspapers. Today we have a maximum of four people on the *Daily Mail* Diary.

I discovered when I started on the *Express* Diary, that these people didn't know anyone, they were total strangers to the world they were supposed to be writing about. They only knew each other and they were relying on chauffeurs and maids and butlers for all their information. Consequently, it was all pretty second-hand stuff. The only time they ever came to grips with the people they were writing about was when they'd doorstep a wedding, or a party, or someone would get wind of a divorce, whereupon they'd doorstep somebody's house. That was the sort of business they were in.

I was the first person working for the column who ever actually knew the people, for the simple reason that I'd been living among them for four or five years. I used to go to all the dances and all the parties.

When I left the Stock Exchange, which I joined at the age of seventeen, I worked for the Earl of Kimberley, who was a public relations man in Mayfair. He knew everybody. He'd had about four or five wives and when he decided to take another, the news leaked out and the office was besieged with Fleet Street reporters and I had the job of dealing with them. Through this, I got to know Jack Smeeton who was floating around the *Express* in those days. I used to lunch with him every week and discuss what I'd been doing, and who I'd seen and I'd talk about people I knew and all the stories we'd discussed duly appeared in the *Daily Express* and I got paid twenty-five pounds for a lead item and five pounds or three pounds for the others. I was earning about forty-five pounds a week with Kimberley and I suddenly found my payments greatly augmented by payments from the William Hickey column. I was able to buy a drop-head Alfa Romeo coupé, on the never-never, a Spider 1300, I think it was. I wish I still had it.

After an article in the *Queen* by Penelope Gilliat about journalists in general and columnists in particular, a lot of men lost their jobs and in the early sixties we were suddenly into a new era of columns. Robin Esser was editor of William Hickey and Quentin Crewe, who was the grandson of a Marquis and had been educated at Eton, was editor of the *Daily Mail* column which went under the name of Charles Greville.

It was at this period that I joined the William Hickey column. I was paid five pounds a day and worked six days a week. It was a pretty grubby profession. Journalists, and gossip columnists especially, were held in fairly low esteem following that article in the *Queen*, but I was running out of ideas about what I wanted to do.

William Hickey didn't exist as a person, neither did John

Rolls, nor Charles Greville, nor any of them. When I started my present column in the *Daily Mail*, I used my own name, partly because all the people I was writing about knew me by name, and partly because my television appearances had made my name well-known to the public.

People want to read about the powerful, the privileged and the rich, and always will do. I regard my Diary as a stage on which I wheel people in and out, rather like in a Restoration farce, a little bit of this and a little bit of that. Society is not what it was twenty-five or thirty years ago; it is rich people meeting, it could be pop stars, it could be Mr Kashoggi, it could be casino owners, or racehorse trainers, or Mr Sugar, the Amstrad man, or it could be the Queen or any one of a number of other people. You've got to look at the Diary as a personality page.

I've never been threatened by anybody because they always knew I was going to write about them. We're talking about people who understand all about publicity. Because if you're a duke, you're going to get the publicity, if you're rich, you're going to get the publicity, and you know it, and so we're talking about people who are sophisticated concerning newspapers and their own role in Britain. We're not writing about hoodlums who resort to violence.

As regards libel, I'm a minnow in this business as compared with, say, Esther Rantzen, who has been taken for several millions. The most I've ever paid out is about ten thousand pounds, I can't even remember what it was for. Libel actions in the past have been indefensible for the simple reason that you cannot possibly put your contact in the witness box, because if you do, that is going to be the end of life for them. I know that and they know it and Lord Rothermere knows it, and that's the end of it: there are some people who simply have to be protected. I guess ten thousand quid over the seventeen years I've been doing the Diary is not very much, is it?

We research every piece very diligently, sometimes making transatlantic calls to check Christian names like 'Suzy'. We're a responsible column; everything is checked back and forwards and sideways. Many of the items come in the first place from the people involved. We are dealing with first-hand material, and not with keyhole stuff. You can't run a story unless you've got quotes, and you can't run quotes unless you talk to somebody. I was brought up on the *Express* where you got fired if you got somebody's age wrong.

The present-day journalists, and I mean Mr Rupert Murdoch's employees, tend to print rumours. They're not in the same business as I am. I don't recognise them as journalists and I don't recognise their newspapers as newspapers. They're spivs to put it mildly.

I believe that once you alert journalists to your existence, which you can do by becoming an MP or by inheriting a vast sum of money, you tend to lose your privacy. There are some very rich people and also some very aristocratic people who are never mentioned in the press simply because they've never opened up their houses to the public. Others like Antonia Fraser must be regarded as fair game, because she goes on television, she publicises herself, she tries to sell her books. There are people like that who realise that they have to enter into a contract with journalism. Unfortunately, they, too, are subjected to the lies of the Murdoch press. I'm afraid that I find the people of Britain can't discern any difference between Nigel Dempster and the *Daily Mail*, checking facts for hours on end, and the ludicrous inventions of the *Sun* and *Today*.

The Royal family have always been fair game. They know who I am and I get stories from Royal sources and if they've been hideously libelled in another newspaper, they won't be averse to seeing the correct version of the incident in the *Daily Mail*. They all respect Lord Rothermere, who is the last Fleet Street baron, the inheritor of the great mantle of Harmsworth. The rest of them are all minnows, they make more money, but Lord Rothermere is as great a newspaperman as his grandfather, the first Lord Rothermere, or his grand-uncle, Lord Northcliffe, and the Royal family know that and trust this newspaper.

I think the dispersal of the newspapers away from Fleet Street has done one good thing. It has stopped drunkenness.

There was an awful lot of drunkenness around Fleet Street; it was very easy if you had nothing to do, to go off to the pub and get drunk. Now all Rupert's papers are dry, and it's very difficult to get to the pubs at Wapping. I go to Scribe's to meet my friends and will continue to do so. I don't go to El Vino, I've never done so, and these days it's full of lawyers anyway.

If I had it to do all over again, would I be a gossip columnist? I was briefly New York correspondent for the *Daily Mail* and I have been offered several other jobs, but I went into this business because I found that it was the one that suited me best, if for no other reason than because it's the only way I know of being employed every day. I write more in a day than most journalists write in a week, or even a month. The column appears every day except Saturday. We print about forty stories a week. Out of how many? Out of forty, because every story we work on gets printed. We know immediately if a story is useless; we don't work for two days on a story and then discover that it's no good.

I wish the word processor had come in a lot sooner; it's totally changed our lives. I've worked in America over the years and it's been very frustrating sitting here writing at a typewriter, expending a vast amount of useless energy, then going down to the stone and watching all this rubbish with hot metal when you knew that the whole process could be a lot cleaner and more rapid and easier all round, if it wasn't for the intransigence of the unions. I used to spend every evening of my life on the other side of the stone with a stone-hand. Some of them were good, some were awful, but it didn't matter whether they were good or bad, they all earned a great deal more money than I did.

Fleet Street was a good gathering place, but I can run to my new office in Kensington from my home in six and a half minutes. And there are plenty of good restaurants around, something that was never true of Fleet Street. The sort of people I take to lunch want to go to places that are central and successful like Langan's. Fleet Street has never had anywhere like that.

But at the end of it all, what it's basically about is producing newspapers. A friend of mine who used to be motoring correspondent of the *Daily Mail* and is now vice chairman of Ford in Europe once said to me that Fleet Street would have to go because what it was, really, was a series of factories, manufacturing newspapers, in the heart of London. Can you imagine Ford manufacturing motor cars in Piccadilly? That's how ridiculous Fleet Street was . . .

Marjorie Wallace

Marjorie Wallace is unusual in that she went from television to Fleet Street, instead of the other way round. When I met her first, she had just joined the *Sunday Times* and was a member of the team which broke the thalidomide scandal.

Marjorie Wallace joined Independent Television as a university trainee and worked on one of the David Frost programmes. She then joined Harold Evans's *Sunday Times* and became involved in the thalidomide campaign. Since then she has worked on a number of *Sunday Times* investigative stories, including one on schizophrenia which has proved so important that the newspaper has given her six months off to run the campaign full-time.

3 January 1989

I hated the academic world. I was always lured by the bright lights and I was accepted as a university trainee to go into Independent Television, to work for David Frost. This was one of Frost's first attempts at going serious, and it was all live, three nights a week, the famous trials by television which involved people like Savundra and Ian Smith of Rhodesia and it was all very, very exciting.

I was one of five people who wrote all the background material; the others were John Cleese, Tim Brooke Taylor, Neil Shand, Clive Irving and Tony Jay, who was our advisor.

After I'd been in television for four or five years, I took three months' maternity leave, which was not all that popular at that time. This was long before Esther Rantzen had made it almost obligatory to have a small baby with you at all times. I was at home with a six-week-old baby when Ron Hall, an old friend, introduced me to Harold Evans. They'd been playing tennis together and as they came off the court, Harold Evans said to me: 'We've been doing this investigation into thalidomide. Would you like to do some interviews?'

That was my first brush with Fleet Street and it was also my first big chance: a fortnight's trial.

I worked very closely with Harry Evans and was enormously impressed by him. There were really only five of us working on the campaign and we were all very closely involved; we wrote the book about it together afterwards.

My job when I first started to work for Harry Evans and for the *Sunday Times* for those first two trial weeks – I've now been there for sixteen years – was to try to get some good stories to run week after week, to make a campaign. And I had a list of these children, all the names and addresses and all the details of their deformities, and I just went round the country ringing up their parents or calling on them. Sometimes the parents didn't want to see me, but more often they did.

I suppose the most memorable story I've worked on is the story of schizophrenia. After I'd done all those thalidomide stories, everybody in the country who had a story or a cause wrote to me, and one of the problems which surfaced in this way was schizophrenia.

For ten years I was the *Sunday Times* social services correspondent: I ran a haemophilia campaign, I did the Christopher Nolan story, about that Irish boy who wrote so well, you remember him, mine was the first article ever published about him. I ran a campaign for Nolan which raised forty thousands pounds, and I ran a campaign to raise money for haemophilia, I ran a whole lot of campaigns, supported by Harry Evans who would always back me up if I went to him and told him I thought it was an important cause.

What happened in the case of schizophrenia was that someone wrote to me from Southampton saying that I should come and see what happens to these people when they leave the mental hospitals. I took a train down to Southampton and went round all the doss-houses and the bed-and-breakfast places, and I came back absolutely appalled, saying: 'We must run a campaign about this. This is going to be one of the big scandals of the eighties. In two years' time, this is going to be a major scandal.'

Eventually, after a long time, Bruce Matthews, managing director of News International, Murdoch's company, said to me: 'OK, if you want to run this campaign, you can have six months to see whether you can get it off the ground.' I did it, and I got a lot of response: *The Times*, I believe, had the most letters they've ever had on any home news subject, and it grew from there and I was allowed to set up the charity, based on the articles, called SANE. I've now got another three months to work on this campaign, and I'm working on it full-time.

When we started running these campaigns, I think Fleet Street was ahead of television, and every time we ran a story television would do a follow-up, four or five days later. And it was the same with radio, they always followed our lead.

I think that's all changed now. It's no longer a case of Fleet Street leading the media. Today the newspapers are tending to take their leads from stories they first hear on the radio. In the late seventies, I believe the *Sunday Times* was leading the rest of the media on campaigning stories.

During the year-long shut-down in '78–'79, I went in every day just as if a newspaper was coming out as usual next Sunday. But in a way it was easier for me than a lot of the others because I was working on long-term projects. I was working on the Seveso story, I think, and that was a very long-term project. But a lot of us had the feeling that we had to go in every day, or the whole thing would collapse.

In my early days on the *Sunday Times*, when Roy Thomson was in charge, getting at the absolute truth seemed to matter a great deal more than it does today. Now it seems to be far more a matter of getting the copy in on time, a question of how it fits and when you deliver it. While Thomson was there, we all felt aware of the presence of a benevolent proprietor. He could be criticised perhaps because he was more interested in good stories than in the money-making side of things.

On the question of the invasion of privacy, every day I have to wrestle with the problem of where you draw the line. My particular problem is how you use stories about people who are not really able to judge the issue for themselves. I honestly think most people are grateful, glad for the catharsis, glad to have been able to talk to someone, glad of the release which the interview has offered them. It's almost like performing an actual service for them, though it might not appear like that on the surface. I know this is true because of the hundreds of letters I've received from people who were glad to have featured in an interview, in an article, because it enabled them to see some pattern in their lives, some point in their suffering.

If you can show them that they've played a part, either in a campaign to highlight the disease from which they are suffering, or to tell the world what it's really like to suffer as they do, then you're helping them and not exploiting them. If you can only give them the feeling that all their suffering, all the trauma they've experienced has some point, that it's going to lead to some action, a change in the law maybe, then you've done something useful even for the most hopeless of cases.

Until we ran the schizophrenia campaign Government thinking was that it was far better to close the hospitals and mental homes and try to persuade the people that they would be better off in the community, that independence was the important thing, that everything else was bad. Being in a mental home, being in hospital, being looked after by a psychiatrist, having medication, these were all bad things; being in the community, doing your own shopping, vegetating in a bed-sit, these were the good things. But all the fuss that we've been making about it is beginning to have an effect. They're starting to listen. I've been to Number Ten and I've been to the Department of Health and Margaret Thatcher has my articles and a video-film the BBC made about it and I don't know when she'll get round to looking at them, but I do know that the whole policy is changing. Until recently, the civil servants were still giving the same old stereotyped answers, but now, in the last week even, they're starting to listen to what I'm saying, and I'm certain that things are going to change as a result of the campaign.

That's what campaigning journalism is about.

Jeffrey Bernard

I first met Jeffrey Bernard in the Colony Club, always known as Muriel's, in Soho, a club which we didn't reckon very much in those days, though it has since become famous through television documentaries about Muriel Belcher herself and about some of her celebrated clients like Lucien Freud and Francis Bacon. I met Jeffrey through Michael Nelson, who worked with me on the same team in independent television, and with whom I wrote a column for two or three years for Reg Willis, the famous editor of the *Evening News*; it was known, for obvious reasons, as Nelson's column, and it was, so far as I know, the first column written by a man (or, in this case, two men) which consistently took the woman's angle on all the controversial issues of the day. I met Jeffrey again in his local in Soho.

Jeffrey Bernard didn't go into journalism until he was 31. He then joined *Queen* magazine under Denis Hackett, writing a racing column. From *Queen* he went to *Town* magazine (formerly *Man About Town*), and at the same time worked for *Sporting Life* and the *Daily Mirror*. Currently he writes a column on Low Life for the *Spectator* magazine and a column for the *Sunday Mirror*.

3 March 1989

We all have our deadlines. Mine is opening time. Whenever I have to deliver a piece, I get up early enough to write it, and get it out of the way by the time the Coach and Horses in Greek Street opens at eleven o'clock, because that's where I go at eleven and I usually stay there for the rest of my day.

Until today, I used to send the stuff in to them by motorcycle messenger. However, starting from today, Groucho's in Soho has a fax machine operating, so that I can drop my stuff off there on my way to the pub, and have it faxed to the office.

Before I became a journalist, I'd been everything; I'd worked in the coalmines, I'd been a stage hand, a film editor. I'd done dish-washing, I'd been a boxer, an actor, everything.

I was 31 when Denis Hackett gave me a job writing a racing

column for the old *Queen* magazine; this was before it became
Harper's & Queen.

After that I worked on *Town* magazine, which had originally
been known as *Man About Town*; Michael Hesseltine was one of
the bosses of that outfit which was one of the best magazines of
that time, if not of all time. I also did two columns about racing
for *Sporting World* and a weekly column for Mike Molloy's
Mirror magazine in which I could write anything I liked. I
never drank in Fleet Street in those days, I never liked any of
the pubs or El Vino or anywhere; I always used to jump on a
taxi and come back here to Soho. This is where my home has
always been: the French Pub, Muriel's, the Kismet, all the
pubs and restaurants around here. I never had any family
background in journalism or anything else. I never even
thought about becoming a journalist until I was about 20. I
hated Fleet Street. Journalists become very boring when they
start to talk about all the scoops they've had, as if anybody
cared. Anyway, there are no decent pubs or restaurants in
Fleet Street. There's no atmosphere there, there never was, not
like around here.

One thing I did which caused a bit of a stir was a letter I
wrote to the *New Statesman*, at a time when I was writing a
column for the paper. I'd got extremely fed up with all those
endless letters from serious people who were writing biog-
raphies of, let's say, Jane Austen, and they kept writing to say:
'I'm writing a biography of Jane Austen, could you please send
me any letters you might have which could cast any light on
any period of her behaviour', etc, etc. This was about 1974 and
my letter to the *New Statesman* said: 'I have just been
comissioned by Michael Joseph to write my autobiography
and I'd be most grateful to any reader who could tell me what I
was doing between 1960 and 1974.'

That created quite a stir. It was written about in *Punch* and
several other papers. I never did write the autobiography, and
I don't suppose I ever will now. Nearly everything that I've
ever written makes me cringe. I suppose I must have written
about six hundred consecutive columns for the *Spectator* over

the last twelve years and out of all of those only about 20 are all right by my standards.

I don't very much like what I do. I suppose I became more famous as a drinker than as a journalist about ten or twelve years ago. I don't feel any resentment about that; in a way, I quite enjoy it.

The only journalistic ambition I ever had was that I would like to have been offered a column to do for an up-market paper; the *Sunday Times* or the *Observer*, that sort of thing. I write a column two days a week at the moment; and I could probably manage three. Keith Waterhouse only writes two columns a week in the *Daily Mail*; on the other hand, he does a lot of other things. At the moment he's writing a play about me, based on my columns. It is to be called 'Jeffrey Bernard is Unwell'. Ned Sherrin is going to produce it and they want Peter O'Toole to play me.

When I write for the *Spectator*, I can write what I like. The trouble with writing for the *Sunday Mirror* is that I've got to be very careful not to offend a lot of people like the working-class housewives, who are very easily shocked. People who read the *Spectator* are never shocked by anything.

As far as the new technology is concerned, I don't use a word processor, I don't need a word processor, because I've got one, between my fucking ears, haven't I? It's called a brain, isn't it?

I think *The Times* has declined, but I still take it every day. It's like smoking or drinking, it's an addiction. The nasty ones like the *Sun*, they revolt me, they're disgusting. The *Mirror* is not as good as it used to be, but it's still the best of them, it's better than any of the other tabloids. The *Express* is rubbish. The *Daily Mail* is a woman's paper. I dislike the *Guardian*; there's something very smug about it.

The column I write for the *Spectator* is called Low Life; it's about the way I live, about being in debt, about being drunk and gambling and fast women and slow horses, that sort of thing. I write these columns to pay the rent. I would dearly like to have written a novel that I could be proud of, but I haven't and there's no way that I'm going to do it now. There's no way

I could discipline myself. I dislike writing intensely, and I don't like working any more, so how could I ever write that kind of novel?

We all have our deadlines, as I told you. And mine is opening time here at the Coach and Horses . . .

Chapman Pincher

For as long as I can remember, Harry Chapman Pincher has been regarded as the top Fleet Street expert on rockets, guided missiles, atomic weapons, space exploration and espionage. I talked to him in his beautiful house near the Kennet and Avon Canal, in Kintbury, Wiltshire, where he now spends his time writing books, shooting and fishing.

H. Chapman Pincher, a zoologist by profession, was lecturing at the Liverpool Institute when war broke out. He joined the tank regiment but was transferred to the staff of the Military College of Science, to work on rocket weapons, then in their infancy. He joined the *Daily Express* in 1946 as defence, science and medical correspondent and was an assistant editor of the *Express* and its chief defence correspondent from 1972 until his retirement in 1979. He has written a number of books on various aspects of defence, espionage and treason.

16 November 1988

I was right in on the ground floor of what eventually became British guided missiles, all very top secret stuff. I was posted to the Arsenal, the HQ of all the rocket work in 1943, and I was living in the house of an old friend, Douglas Worth, who worked for the *Daily Express*.

One night he rang me from the *Express* and asked if I could help them with a hand-out which had come from Churchill. Churchill wanted it published to boost British morale which was at a pretty low ebb at that time. The hand-out was all about a new explosive which was going to change the whole course of the war. It didn't of course; it was simply a device to give the public some good news for a change. Douglas had read the hand-out which was absolutely meaningless to him and he asked me if I knew anything about a new explosive known as RDX. I told him I knew all about it but wasn't allowed to tell. But I was able to put him on to the chap who had invented it – a Dr Rotter – and tell him that it was code-named 'Marmalade'. So the *Express* tracked Rotter down and got a far better story than anyone else, the only story, in fact.

The next important thing that happened was the doodle-bug. Everybody wanted to know exactly what they looked like, and the Government took the line that they couldn't keep it a secret since everybody knew about them; they could see them coming over. Well, I knew exactly how they worked because I'd been involved in putting one of them together; we'd picked up bits from several of them and had laid the thing out, on a bench at Farnborough. So when the *Express* asked for my help on this one, I asked my Colonel and he said: 'So long as I don't know anything about it, you can do what you like.' The *Express* got the only drawing of what exactly the doodle-bug looked like, because I was able to show their artist how to draw it. And exactly the same thing happened later, with the V2 rocket.

Around this period, Beaverbrook was desperate to find out what the huge concrete structures which were then being built in the Pas de Calais were for. I knew what they were for, and I wrote the story. There were two lots of structures; one of them was for storing the V2 rockets and the other lot consisted of ramps for the V1s.

When the atom bomb was dropped in 1945, every paper in the street was desperate to get some information about this new weapon, what it was like, how big it was, and once again, the Government was very stupid; it produced a little White Paper that said nothing. I was able to write about it fairly knowledge-ably because I knew a little bit about it, but I didn't know any of the major secrets.

However, I did discover that the Americans had produced a very full report, the publication of which for the moment was held up, and I also found out that the British Atomic Bomb Project (code-named Tube Alloys) had received a copy of this American report in their little office just off Whitehall, and that they didn't know anything at all about the hold-up on its release. So I went over and they let me look at this report, though I wasn't allowed to take it out of the building.

It made my hair stand on end, it had details of an atomic pile, it carried the first reference to plutonium, it had full details of how exactly the bomb worked, all fascinating material. When I got back to the office Christiansen was appalled. 'We'll get run in,' he said. 'We'll end up in the Tower.' Nevertheless they ran the story for several days, and Beaverbrook was delighted and offered me a job on the staff, but I couldn't get my discharge from the Army until 1946. In the meantime, by a stroke of incredible luck, I was posted to the Mansion House, right beside the *Express*, to a different division.

One day, in my in-tray, I found a document which was the beginning of another wonderful story. The government, it was clear from this document, was starting to recruit staff for a whole series of new stations, Harwell, Aldermaston, some rocket stations in Scotland. Nobody had ever heard of these stations before and now they were starting to notify vacancies to people in the services who were becoming redundant. The drill was that the jobs had to be offered first to people already in the services, which is how the document came to be in my in-tray.

I realized at once what this added up to – the start of the British Atomic Authority – and I hurried down to the *Express*, told the news editor all about it, and when I returned, wrote a story and nipped back with it. I did this day after day, as further documents inviting engineers and other experts to apply for various posts arrived in my in-tray, and gradually pieced together the story of the Government's plans for the development of the Authority. Fortunately, they never associated me with these stories.

Through my connections with the Projectiles Division, I had been involved with a lot of officers in the Navy and in the Air Force as well as a lot of the top scientists and consequently I had that one absolutely vital asset for a journalist or an intelligence officer: access to the people who knew all the answers.

Nobody on the staff could ever question any of the stories I brought in because there was nobody with enough technical knowledge to challenge me. The only problems I ever had were with the lawyers getting worried about official secrets. I never signed the Official Secrets Act until after I had retired from the

Express, when I was invited to join a committee on censorship in the event of another war; this was immediately in the wake of the Falklands business. I only agreed on condition they break their standard rule and free me from all obligations under the Act as soon as the committee was wound up.

I got into the spy business quite simply because the first big spy case that came up was that of Klaus Fuchs, and since it involved atomic secrets and I was the only man on the *Express* who knew anything about atomic matters, I was naturally assigned to it. I realised immediately that a lot of the reports which Fuchs had been leaking to the Russians had long since been declassified and could be bought for a few pence from the Stationary Office. So I nipped along there, found about five or six under Fuchs's name; they were stamped SECRET with a line through the word to show that they had been declassified. They didn't mean a great deal to the ordinary reader, they were far too technical, but this material did enable the *Express* to run the headline: THESE WERE THE SECRETS FUCHS GAVE TO THE RUSSIANS.

In 1957, we revealed in what was a world scoop that the first British H-bomb test was to be carried out at Christmas Island in the Pacific in May. The Japanese then announced that they were planning to send a fleet of several thousand small ships into the area to force us to stop the test. The test had been scheduled to take place only a few weeks before a major agreement between America and Russia to end atmospheric tests was to be signed, and since there was no way Britain could do an underground test, this Japanese announcement represented a serious threat. Millions would have been wasted producing an atomic weapon we could never test, and unless it was tested, it couldn't go into production.

One of my contacts – he happened to be chief scientist at the Department of Defence at that period – rang me and told me that they were in deep trouble and wanted to see me. He wouldn't talk over the phone, naturally, but when I went to see him, the gist of his conversation was as follows: 'We need your help. What we're looking for is a piece of deception. If we can convince the Japanese that these tests have been postponed until late June, they won't send in the ships in May; they'll hold them back until June. Now if you were to ring up BOAC and find out that Sir William Penney and a sizeable team of British scientists were booked to fly out to Honolulu on such and such a date in June, it would be quite clear to you that they would be going on from there to Christmas Island, for the test, obviously, wouldn't it? And you could develop that theme, speculate on it, you might even perhaps deduce from it that we must have run into some technical difficulties which have forced us to postpone our test for about a month, mightn't you?'

When I got back to London, I rang Christiansen and explained the entire situation to him. He said, 'If you discover that these bookings have in fact been made, we'll run the story. Speculate as much as you like.'

There was no other big story that night, so we led on it, and it was splashed around the world, and no Japanese junks appeared on the scene in May, and the tests went ahead as originally planned.

The story that caused the greatest commotion and created the biggest political impact was the D-Notice Affair. I've never known a story to run for so long, not even the *Spycatcher* row. The *Daily Express* had discovered that every cable sent out by the post office and the cable companies had to be made available to the security authorities. Incredibly, somebody had just come in off the street and told the newsdesk about it. I checked on it and found out that it was true, and wrote the story. It was very clear that all cables were being scrutinised in a search for spies and we were very nervous that we might be prosecuted under the Official Secrets Act.

Derek Marks, who was then editor, was determined to expose this infringement of personal liberty and privacy. I rang the secretary of the D-notice committee and he agreed with me that D-notices would not apply, but implored me not to run the story. George Brown, who was then Foreign Secretary, got to hear about it and tried to get it stopped by appealing to Max

Aitken, but Derek Marks insisted on running it, and there was one hell of a row.

Wilson called us traitors and set up a committee to inquire into the whole business, hoping they would come up with a decision condemning the *Express* but they didn't, and Wilson was absolutely furious. He rejected the findings of his own committee, and issued a White Paper overturning their verdict. There was a debate in the House, but Labour had a big majority at the time, and the debate went against us. It ruined Wilson's relationship with the press.

I think the spy business will go on for ever because the Russians will never stop trying. People think spying is obsolete because of satellites. If anything, a spy on the ground is more important today than ever. A satellite can tell you what the other side has got, how many long-range missiles, etc, but it can't tell you what they are planning to do with them. You need a man in the Kremlin, or someone who has access to the Kremlin to find out about intentions, which are the really important thing. The KGB set enormous store by it. In fact the KGB has increased its activities since Gorbachev.

I don't really miss Fleet Street. I enjoyed it enormously when I was there, I went everywhere, I met everyone. But I didn't go to the pubs in Fleet Street because I knew I wasn't ever going to get a story from a fellow journalist, and so it was a waste of time, far better to lunch with someone from the Ministry of Defence.

As a result of my connections and the information I was able to get him about long-range rockets and so on in the early days, I managed to get very close to Beaverbrook and I think that during the last fifteen years of his life, I was his closest confidant. He believed in Special Creation, which meant that I was never allowed to refer to evolution. I once wrote a scientific piece about a fossil about four hundred million years old and the Reader wrote on the side of the proof: 'How can this be true when the world was created in 4,000 BC?' I even had a reference to 'ante-natal care' deleted from a story because a child might ask his mother what it meant and this was a family newspaper, and we didn't want to embarrass the parents.

I like to think that I had a hand in changing things a bit, certainly in changing the *Express* attitude to official secrets. They were terrified when I first started bringing in these tales. But the present Government will change things back, and Labour would, too. Peter Wright is entirely to blame for this. The Government was quite happy to deal with each leak as it came along, until Peter Wright.

Harry Henry

Now a dissident voice. Harry Henry is a market researcher who founded Marplan and joined the Thomson Organisation merely because they happened to be one of his clients. He doesn't think much of journalists nor does he hold a high opinion of Fleet Street editors or managers.

An independent consultant, Harry Henry is recognised as an authority on media economics. He has been chairman of the Statistics Committee of the Advertising Association for many years, and was marketing manager of the Thomson Organisation for ten years from 1961.

30 December 1988

I brought the marketing concept to Fleet Street. Associated Newspapers had a market researcher, Mick Shields, who died recently, and he had formed NOP, one of the larger market research organisations, and a subsidiary of Associated Newspapers, but apart from that the concept of marketing was unknown in Fleet Street.

The point about marketing newspapers is that, at any given time, there is a grand total of people in the country prepared to buy and read a newspaper, and it is surprising how little it has changed over the years. There are no gaps in the market, there never have been. Certainly unless you go back to the period when King deliberately went after the working-class reader, there hasn't been a palpable gap in the market.

The point about Murdoch's *Sun* is that Murdoch went after territory Cudlipp had chosen to vacate. When the *Daily Herald* was turned into the *Sun*, Cudlipp believed his own advertising, he believed in the existence of this highly intelligent, blue-collar working man, an animal that just doesn't exist.

The *Mirror* had already started to put itself above its readers, talking down to them and publishing that four-page supplement, *Mirrorscope* or whatever it was called, which actually spat in the readers' eyes by saying: 'This isn't really for you. It's only for the most intellectual among you.' And of course the original Cudlipp *Sun* was a disaster because it was aimed at a market that didn't exist. It was all the result of some remarkably poor market research.

Newspapers are always conducting their own form of market research, but they always make a mess of it. Eddy Shah, for example, believed that people didn't want sleaze in their newspapers for the completely simple and totally wrong reason that they said they didn't want it in a survey. In a survey, people say what they think they should say and not what they really think, and you have to allow for that. The only sensible thing to have done with the *Sun* would have been to close it down and cut their losses, but the unions were very strong in those days and the unions were saying: 'We've got a buyer for this paper. What right have you to take our jobs away? If you do, we'll close down the *Mirror*.' That's all there was to it; they had to sell the *Sun* to Murdoch who had no illusions at all about what people wanted, and he gave it to them; he gave them every day what he had been giving them in the *News of the World* on Sunday, only he did it better, using the old *Daily Mirror* format. The result was that the *Sun* soon wiped the *Mirror* off the map.

The trouble is that newspapers don't know how to interpret readership surveys. The only people who don't ever read a newspaper are people who *can't* read a newspaper; they're blind or they're illiterate and that's it. The total newspaper readership of this country hasn't changed substantially for years, since shortly after the end of the war. You have to be careful about the end of the war because when newsprint came back, you couldn't increase the size of your paper, but you could increase its circulation. The result of all that was a lot of four-page papers with huge circulations; everybody bought two or three tiny newspapers every day.

So for that reason, predictions about newspaper circulation based on the figures just after the war are ridiculous because that was an artificial situation. Since then, everything has been surprisingly stable.

Television didn't in my view make much difference. People who saw the news on TV didn't give up their daily newspapers;

newspapers are an addictive drug. The point here is really that you cannot possibly give a lot of detail in a TV or a radio programme because it takes a lot of time to get information across, so that all those people whose interest was stimulated by a news story on the radio or TV would still buy papers to find out all the details. Newspapers are not nearly so limited in their space as TV programmes are limited in time.

I found it enormous fun working in Fleet Street, although I made enemies everywhere, naturally, because nobody likes being told that what they are doing is wrong.

Marketing means knowing what you are doing. It means doing everything consistently to meet a common policy. Newspapers are no different from any other mass market, low ticket consumer goods, and despite the airs they give themselves, journalists are no different from any other kind of producer; their job is to produce a saleable product, not to consider themselves members of the Fourth Estate.

A year before I took over the marketing of *The Times* group, I wrote a memo to Roy Thomson pointing out that *The Times* must be an elite paper, that you couldn't produce a fat newspaper with all the parliamentary news, all the law reports unless you get a high cover price and unless you get a high advertising rate. You can only get a high advertising rate if you are offering your advertisers an elite audience. At that time, I told him, there were probably too many bishops and not enough top businessman in *The Times*, but nonetheless it must remain elite, or otherwise we wouldn't get the high advertising rate and there'd be enormous run-on losses.

When Denis Hamilton got himself appointed as chief executive of *The Times* newspapers, his main concern was to show Fleet Street how clever he was by doubling *The Times* circulation within a year. Which he did, though the consequences were absolutely disastrous. The losses were horrendous. He put the circulation up from the pre-Thomson figure of two hundred and fifty thousand to four hundred and forty-three by October '69, the losses were fantastic and it dragged the *Sunday Times* down with it.

Now the whole situation has changed. Advertising is more lush, at least it has been over the last ten years, but what is going to happen over the next few years if advertising revenue declines, as it probably will?

The arrival of the *Independent* has done nothing at all to increase the market. It has simply taken sales from *The Times* and particularly the *Guardian*. By the same token, Bingo in all its manifestations has done nothing at all to increase the circulation of newspapers.

We launched the *Sunday Times* colour supplement in 1961, and it lost a million pounds in the first year. Simply because the advertising agents wouldn't buy space in it. All the evidence was showing how wonderful it was: we were selling nearly a million and a half copies a week which were being thoroughly read. Coming up to its first anniversary, in February 1962, we had to do something very dramatic. So what my department did in fact was to organise a visit by a hundred and seventy tycoons to Krushchev's Russia, which was just opening up at that time. We flew them all out for a weekend. A really dramatic gesture to show that we weren't losing confidence. And it was a terrific success. Five of us, including Roy Thomson and myself, had three hours with Krushchev in his office, and although he didn't use the words *glasnost* or *perestroika*, that was the beginning of it all. Krushchev didn't last of course; he hadn't protected his rear. But he was trying to do exactly what Gorbachev is trying to do now.

As far as I was concerned, this was entirely a marketing exercise to establish the colour supplement as a success. In those days it was difficult to get a visa for Russia and here we were, flying out one hundred and seventy top tycoons. I think we had about seven millionaires on board. Lloyd's were worried stiff, because of the life cover involved. Denis Hamilton had refused to come on the grounds that they had imprisoned an innocent British businessman called Greville Wynne, accused of being a spy.

We had a journalist called Tom Stacey with us, and halfway through the discussion with Krushchev, he suddenly interrupted: 'Mr Krushchev, why don't you release Greville Wynne? You know he's innocent.' And Krushchev said, through an interpreter, 'Of course he's a spy. Don't talk nonsense.' And as soon as Greville Wynne was released in 1964, he wrote a book about how he'd been a spy in Russia.

So much for journalists.

Godfrey Smith

Among the party of journalists who went on the trip to Russia organised by Harry Henry was Godfrey Smith, then deputy editor of the *Sunday Times* colour magazine.

Godfrey Smith started as a graduate trainee in the London office of the *Newcastle Journal*. He was Lord Kemsley's personal assistant for two and a half years, and then worked as a sub-editor in Manchester and later as London editor of the *Daily Dispatch*. When it closed in 1955 he joined the *Sunday Times*. He edited the *Sunday Times* colour magazine from 1966 to 1972, and then for seven years edited the Review section of the newspaper. He has been writing a weekly column since 1979.

13 January 1989

I went into the newspaper business to earn some money while I wrote my first book, and I'm still here, trying to get clear of it.

When I left university I got a graduate trainee job in Kelmsley Newspapers, in the London office of the *Newcastle Journal*, but I was plucked out of there within a year to become Lord Kelmsley's personal assistant. I used to write his letters, he wasn't much cop at English. I spent two and a half years in that job, learning a bit about human nature in the corridors of power, but nothing at all about the nuts and bolts of the job. K was a frightful old twit really, but he'd got some good men around him like Leonard Russell, Peter Fleming and Denis Hamilton. When I wrote my first novel, a thriller about the Burgess–McLean case and it was made into a film by the BBC, K realised that I wasn't going to remain upstairs as his PA forever, and we came to a friendly agreement that I should go north and work as a sub-editor on the *Daily Dispatch* in Withy Grove, in Manchester. After about nine months up there, I became London editor of the *Daily Dispatch*, and when it closed in December 1955, I went to the *Sunday Times* in Gray's Inn

Road as news editor for about a year before taking over the Atticus column from Ian Fleming. Fleming actually had been getting the material for his James Bond novels together by doing a huge world trip to write a series on the cities of the world for the *Sunday Times*. He'd been given a ticket for seven hundred and fifty quid, which seemed phenomenal at the time.

I did the column until 1959; it was just the job for a young guy who wanted to be a writer. My predecessors had included Sachèverell Sitwell and John Buchan as well as Ian Fleming. It's a political column now, but in those days it was a gossip column.

K was a very old-fashioned, nineteenth-century, reactionary, leaden-footed proprietor. When Roy Thomson took over, it was an enormous, bracing tonic for all of us. Kemsley had kept absolutely quiet about the fact that he was going to sell the paper and just called in Denis Hamilton, the editor-in-chief, who was still in his thirties and had a young family at school and handed him an envelope, containing a facsimile of the cheque he, K, had received from Thomson for the paper, not a cheque for Denis himself, which gives you some idea how K dealt with his senior men.

Roy Thomson was a breezy, informal, tubby little guy with bifocals who called us all by our Christian names. We all called him Roy and he had a fresh transatlantic frankness and made no bones about the fact that he wanted a title, which of course he got. He did use rather chilling phrases, like that the editorial matter in a paper was the stuff that kept the ads apart, but he released enormous forces of energy and a lot of new ideas. He enabled Denis Hamilton to bring in a new generation of bright young journalists like Ron Hall and Mark Boxer and the Insight team.

The marriage between the *Sunday Times* and *The Times* was a very uneasy one, a sort of shot-gun wedding. There was a bridge across Gray's Inn Road connecting the two buildings, but the fact is that very few people crossed that bridge either literally or metaphorically. Even poor old Harry Evans who did the one brilliantly, was never considered really right for the other one. Quite apart from the actual flavour and attack and intellectual feel of the two papers which differed widely, there was the fact that one was a daily and the other a Sunday, which meant that when Harry went over to *The Times* he faced a very different problem. The sort of brilliant, inspired creative chaos which he used to whip up on the *Sunday Times* didn't work so well on a daily newspaper. It's not the sort of thing you can afford to do every day.

I joined Mark Boxer on the colour supplement in October 1962 when it was still rather puny; it looked revolutionary and strange and lost a million in its first year, in the days when a million was a million. I went on the trip to Moscow with a hundred and something of Britain's top tycoons and advertising men to mark its first anniversary, and the plane that arrived to pick us all up was Russian and didn't look in the least airworthy. Because we were going to Russia, we'd all hired fur coats, and one of the party, looking at the assembled tycoons in their hired fur coats remarked: 'If this plane doesn't make it to Moscow, it may or may not be a serious blow to British industry, but it'll be a total disaster for Moss Bros.'

I edited the colour magazine after Mark Boxer, then I edited the Review section, and since 1979, I've been writing my column. I don't know Murdoch personally. I've met him, I've shaken hands with him, but that's all. I write from where I sit now, ninety-four miles down in the country, with my Tandy 200 computer and I file my column once a week, write reviews and magazine pieces, and so my contact with Rupert Murdoch is zero. The Tandy has been the saving of us old boys; we don't ever have to go into the office any more. I think the British press encapsulates both the best and the worst journalism in the world, and the worst has probably become still worse since the onset of television. The smashing down of the old SOGAT and NATSOPA doors, whatever the human cost, and that was considerable, has released a great deal of energy and produced a lot of new blood.

But I feel uneasy about the concentration of so much power in so few hands. This particular liberation should have produced a lot of new independent papers, but so far we've only had one excellent example. In principle, we should now have much cheaper publishing, desktop publishing, but finding gaps in the market isn't all that easy, and our friend Shah has come a cropper again. It's not an easy business, it's a jungle. They're now calling him Citizen Vain, poor old thing. I think it's extraordinary how David English discovered a new market, and Murdoch found a new working-class one floor underneath the existing one, a totally new class of illiterates. I'm still absolutely astonished at the success of the *Sun*.

Geoffrey Van'Hay

These days, the place where you are most likely to meet Fleet Street's top journalists is Scribe's, a club which is both a restaurant and a drinking den. Its full name is Scribe's Cellars and it is situated in the basement of Carmelite House, one of Associated Newspaper's old premises between Tudor Street and the Thames. Geoffrey Van'Hay, who runs it, learned the difficult trade of catering for journalists under Frank Bower in El Vino.

Geoffrey Van'Hay went to El Vino at the age of 18, and eventually became licensee and a director of the company, before opening Scribe's about sixteen years ago. He is planning to open another branch of the club, Scribe's West, in Kensington in Northcliffe House, the new headquarters of Associated Newspapers Press, which he hopes will become the most important media club in London, a new press club for a city which has been without a proper one for years.

21 February 1989

I started as a cellarman, then graduated upstairs and wound up as licensee and a director of El Vino. I used to work there in the days when the customers included people like Hugh Cudlipp and Vicky the cartoonist, Peregrine Worsthorne, Michael King, Derek Marks, and of course, Philip Hope Wallace. I was actually responsible for putting the plaque up over the chair where Philip Hope Wallace usually sat. I didn't discuss it with Christopher Mitchell, or anybody else, I simply had the plaque made, and of course I got the name wrong. I put it up and put a piece of Elastoplast over it and one day when he came in, I whipped the Elastoplast off and 'This is your corner.'

Later, when I opened Scribe's, he used to come in here because we were open all afternoon, when the pubs were closed. This is a club. We have about 1,400 members who pay an annual subscription of seventy-five pounds a year. We have quite a few editors – Nick Lloyd, Eve Pollard, David English.

I was in El Vino when the Women's Lib made their attack on the place; in fact I was knocked unconscious when the first wave of women came storming in. In those days El Vino was a hierarchy. Ordinary journalists didn't normally go near the place unless they were invited. As a journalist, you would feel that you had arrived when you were able to walk into El Vino and stand at the bar and order a drink. I don't think Frank Bower was that much of an eccentric. I think he was a very clever man who used to feign eccentricity to keep the place exclusive. And it worked. El Vino is a lot more lax these days than it was when I was the licensee.

I think it's a crashing indictment on the country that there's no press club in London. It's probably the most important city in the world from the media point of view, and certainly Fleet Street was unique as the heartland of a great newspaper industry, and we have no international press club, such as they have in places like Hong Kong and Tokyo.

The old press club in Salisbury Square was sold out to Reuters for seventy-five thousand pounds, a nonsensical figure. When it moved to that building behind the *Daily Express*, the top floor of International House, it was run by a committee, most of whom were not associated with newspapers in any way. It was disastrous. And although Max Aitken and Lord Rothermere pumped money into it, it didn't succeed. It was very sad when it folded, but it couldn't have lasted. It was open to anyone who wanted a drink in the afternoon, not just to journalists.

Do you know that when I worked at El Vino there were fifteen pubs between Wig and Pen and Ludgate Circus, and that was on Fleet Street alone? They were all good pubs, too. You could walk in about eight or eight-thirty at night and find the *Telegraph* people in the King and Keys, the *Express* people in the Poppinjay, the *Guardian* people in the Clachan. If you wanted to find somebody, you'd simply go to their pub, and they'd be there.

Scribe's has been going for sixteen years now. We have exactly the same sort of membership as the El Vino clientele;

about 50 per cent journalistic and 50 per cent legal. We have a lot of editors but the editors don't drink in pubs and clubs the way they used to. I can remember times when certain editors would come into El Vino at eleven-thirty in the morning and leave at three, return at four-thirty and drink until eight-thirty. And they were producing good newspapers in those days, they had the capacity to drink and work. It doesn't happen today. The young people coming into journalism don't drink the way the old hands used to. They're very sophisticated, and the competition is far tougher. When I started to work in Fleet Street, there were lots of jobs available and people who had never set out to be journalists were able to get jobs here. They used to say that all the top executives in the *Express* in Max Aitken's day had been chosen because they knew how to sail a boat.

We see much more of Murdoch's News International people than we used to, before they moved to Wapping. They've lost out more than any other newspaper, because they now live in a desert, out there in Wapping. What journalists need is other journalists to spark off. George Gale once said: 'Journalists need other journalists to survive.' I think he's right. Journalists tend to get introspective if they're not constantly meeting one another.

I wish I could write, it's all been so interesting. All the things I've heard. Take the flight to Wapping, for example. I knew it was coming. It was all part of a very clever plan, worked out in detail, all the logistics, like an army man-oeuvre. Murdoch had orchestrated it like a brigadier. But it needed a catalyst. If Eddy Shah hadn't come along at that particular time, the newspaper proprietors would have had to get together and set up some stooge to do exactly what he did. It's like the old saying, if God didn't exist, he'd have to be invented to fill mankind's needs. However, Eddy Shah did exist and he appeared on the scene at precisely the right moment, and while he was making the running, Murdoch made the move to Wapping, and that was it. It was amazing. The big barons could never have done it, though there's really only one baron left in the street and that's Lord Rothermere.

I'm opening a new Scribes, Scribe's West, in Northcliffe House, the new headquarters of Associated Newspapers in Kensington, and I'm hoping it will become the international press club that London so desperately needs . . .

Eddy Shah

It seems to me appropriate to end this anthology of Fleet Street memories with a few words from Eddy Shah, the man who could be said to have ended it all by demonstrating that it was possible to beat the unions and produce a newspaper, using all the most advanced technology, by employing non-union labour or arranging a one-union, no closed-shop, no strike deal. His victory over the NGA in late 1983 and his widely publicised plans to launch a new national daily newspaper entirely produced by non-union labour using the most advanced presses outside London with pages faxed from a headquarters in Vauxhall Bridge, London, proved to be the catalyst which precipitated the flight to Fortress Wapping.

The son of a cousin of the Aga Khan, Eddy Shah had an English mother, was educated at Gordonstoun school, and worked for a time for television in Manchester before moving into the business of free, through-the-letter-box newspapers. In March 1986 he launched a new daily, *Today*, which was later virtually taken over by Rupert Murdoch. In 1988, he launched yet another daily, the *Post*, which folded in a matter of months. He is now back working in independent television.

30 January 1989

I think I really went into the newspaper business by accident. Though it's funny, I always felt as a kid that I was going to become involved in newspapers in some way. I certainly had no ambitions at that stage to become a newspaper proprietor. If I thought about it at all, I suppose I wanted to be a writer, or perhaps a war photographer. My father Moochol Shah had worked for a time as a sub in Reuters – he was on the desk the night those Scottish students stole the Stone of Scone, the Coronation Stone, do you remember that story? Well, maybe that's where that feeling came from, I don't know.

My first job on a newspaper was selling space for the *Manchester Daily News* group. But basically when I started work it was in Manchester in independent television. And it very quickly occurred to me that if ITV could provide programmes and a news service financed basically by local advertising, then there was no reason in the world why I shouldn't publish local newspapers, containing news and information, based on a relatively small amount of local advertising. There had been free, through-the-letter-box papers in the States for years, but they consisted solely of advertisements. I think I was probably the first person in Britain to introduce free newspapers containing news, features and advertising; certainly I was the most successful.

But what I had done only seemed to me the result of a logical examination of what had been happening. If you take a local paper with a circulation of ten or eleven thousand copies, it's pretty obvious that the cover price isn't even going to start to pay for your overheads, it's not even going to pay your rent. So, I thought, why not cut out the cover price altogether – it's not going to make all that much difference – and deliver the paper free, thereby expanding your circulation to whatever you need to attract the advertising, and then rely on the advertising for revenue. All through my life that one phrase, 'Why not?', has dominated my thinking. It's always worked for me.

So I built up this string of free, through-the-letter-box papers and the first real paper I had any connection with was the *Warrington Guardian*. I approached the job of running it by applying simple logic to newspaper production, but I had the very big advantage that I had no traditional upbringing in the old-style, hot metal method of printing newspapers. You may find it hard to believe but I have never once seen a linotype machine in operation. Therefore I wasn't conditioned, as most of the people in Fleet Street are, to accepting all that stuff as an inevitable accompaniment of continued existence. My attitude was very simple: if there was a job to be done and the new technology seemed to be the most economical and effective way of doing it, then why not? That 'Why not?' again.

I may have been partly responsible for the collapse of the old Fleet Street, but the plain truth is that I've hardly ever been there. I never approached Fleet Street, except when I appealed to the *Sunday Times* for help at the height of the Warrington crisis. I approached the *Sunday Times* because they had published a leader sympathetic to what I had been trying to do.

What had happened in Warrington was that we had installed these new machines, and we'd employed people to operate them, and we were happy and the people were happy and then the NGA came along and insisted that all our people join the union. I wasn't against unions as such at this stage. I tended to support the people who worked for me against the NGA insistence that they should join. And it's significant that apart from the famous Stockport Six, who turned into eight, none of the one hundred and fifty people who worked for me left the company. But in the end, when we had all the pickets out, and all hell was breaking loose every night, I appealed to the *Sunday Times* for assistance and went down to London to see Andrew Neil.

I explained the logic to him of production with one union and the new technology and outlined the economics of starting a new national newspaper on this basis. Indeed I even wrote a paper for him, and for Murdoch and all the other newspaper proprietors, on where the Fleet Street newspapers should be going.

At a meeting in the Savoy tearoom, he suddenly said to me: 'Have you ever thought about doing it yourself?' Producing a new national newspaper, he meant, using the latest technology with the total freedom, as I had been advocating, from hot metal and linotype machines and stereo-men and all the rest of it. And I replied that I hadn't, but I would, and I went back and thought about it and decided to launch *Today*.

As soon as they heard about it, the unions threatened to strangle the new paper at birth. So all the decisions I made, all the plans for the paper that were shaping themselves in my mind, were dominated by the need to get the paper out despite all the efforts of the unions. That was one of my mistakes, looking back on it, allowing myself to be hustled by the unions into making hasty decisions. But at the time the whole business of the launch of *Today* became lost in the furore caused by Rupert Murdoch's sudden move to Wapping.

I would agree with you that there were four basic factors

behind the decision to move out of Fleet Street. Number one was the Thatcher legislation against secondary picketing. The second thing was the sudden realisation by the Fleet Street proprietors that they were sitting on top of acres of real estate worth countless millions if they sold out and moved to green-field sites which would be far more convenient and far less expensive. The third factor was the Reuter flotation, which gave them the capital to pay for the new machinery. And the fourth was my stand against the unions at Warrington. What that did was to show not merely the newspaper industry, but industry as a whole in this country, that they didn't need to accept dictation from the unions any more.

The result of it all has been more papers and bigger papers but whether they are all better newspapers, that's another matter. I'm not a sociologist, but they say newspapers only reflect what their readers want and if the readers of the pop papers want lower standards, who can deny them? It's interesting that since the press was deregulated, in the provinces more new papers have been launched and more people are being employed. In Fleet Street, apart from the *Independent*, the ownership of the newspapers hasn't opened up at all.

I've no lingering ambition to get back into newspapers. I sold all the *Messenger* titles for thirty-two million and I only lost about three and a half million on the *Post*. I'm back now in television production, where I started; I've just completed a Capstick's Law series on video for independent television.

No, I've no regrets. I've never regretted anything I've ever done, and as far as your point is concerned, that you only regret the things you could have done and didn't do, that doesn't apply to me because I always did them, or kept them to do later, so how could I have any regrets?

As the man who is widely regarded as having killed Fleet Street or at least having hastened its demise, do I have an epitaph? Well, let's say that it was an archaic, Victorian institution just creaking on, with completely obsolete machinery, an institution that didn't realise how archaic it was. When

I talked to the union people, around the time of the Warrington dispute, they used to say that all their loyalty was to the unions and not to the newspapers which employed them, as if the newspapers could employ anybody at all if they were forced into bankruptcy.

An epitaph? They never saw it coming, and they never saw it going. But it went.

Appendix
A Chronicle of trends and developments up to Wapping

Year

1621	First corantos printed in London.
1621	Proclamation against corantos.
1622	First publication of English newsbooks.
1637	Star Chamber Decree regulating printing.
1641	Star Chamber Abolition Act.
1642	Ordinance regulating printing.
1647	Act for regulating printing.
1649	Printing Act regulating the press.
1660	Parliament prohibits publication of its proceedings.
1680	Royal Proclamation suppressing all unlicensed newsbooks.
1702	Publication of first real newspaper, *Daily Courant*.
1712	First 'taxes on knowledge': Advertisement Duty, Excise Duty, Stamp Duty on newspapers.
1738	Suppression of reports on parliamentary debates.
1757	Increase in tax on newspapers: other increases in 1776, 1780, 1789, 1797 and 1815.
1763	Prosecution of John Wilkes for seditious libel in *North Briton*.
1765	General Warrants declared illegal.
1769	*Morning Chronicle* launched.
1771	House of Commons allows press to report proceedings.
1772	*Morning Post* published.
1775	House of Lords allows press to report proceedings.
1780	*Morning Herald* launched.
1784	*Daily Universal Register* founded.
1785	*Daily Universal Register* title changed to *The Times*.
1787	Separate office for newspapers established by Post Office to distribute newspapers.
1791	The *Observer* founded.

1792 Free distribution of newspapers by Post Office.
1802 Cobbett's weekly *Political Register* founded.
1814 Koenig's steam press first used by *The Times*.
1817 *Black Dwarf* (Sunday) founded.
1821 *Manchester Guardian* founded.
1822 *Sunday Times* founded.
1827 *The Standard* founded.
1833 Advertisement Duty reduced.
1836 Stamp Duty reduced.
     Excise Duty on paper reduced.
1842 *Lloyd's Weekly Newspaper* founded.
1843 *News of the World* founded.
1846 *Daily News* founded by Charles Dickens.
1844 Electric telegraph for news transmission introduced.
1848 Rotary press first used.
1850 *Reynold's Newspaper* founded.
1851 Reuter establishes news agency in London.
1853 Advertisement Duty abolished.
1855 Stamp Duty abolished.
     Daily Telegraph founded.
     Manchester Guardian becomes a daily newspaper.
1861 Excise Duty on paper repealed.
1865 *Pall Mall Gazette* founded.
1871 *Daily Chronicle* launched.
1872 Exchange Telegraph Company founded.
1881 George Newnes launches *Titbits*.
1884 *Financial Times* founded.
1888 Arthur Harmsworth launches *Answers*.
     T. P. O'Connor launches *Star*.
1890 *Daily Graphic* founded.
1893 *Answers* floated as Harmsworth Brothers Ltd.
     Westminster Gazette founded.
1894 Harmsworth buys *Evening News*.
1896 Harmsworth launches *Daily Mail*.
1900 Arthur Pearson launches *Daily Express*.
     Lloyd's Weekly News founded.
1901 William Berry launches *Advertising World*.
1903 Harmsworth launches *Daily Mirror*.
1904 Harmsworth buys *Weekly Dispatch* and turns it into a
     Sunday.

1905   Harmsworth buys *Observer* and becomes Lord Northcliffe.
1908   Northcliffe buys *The Times*.
        Daily Herald launched.
1909   *Daily Sketch* founded (incorporating *Graphic*).
1911   *Observer* sold to William Waldorf Astor.
1912   *Daily Herald* relaunched as left-wing daily.
1913   William Maxwell Aitken lends *Daily Express* £25,000.
1914   Northcliffe sells *Daily Mirror* to brother Harold Harmsworth.
        Sunday Pictorial launched.
1915   Berry Brothers buy *Sunday Times*.
1916   Aitken buys *Daily Express*.
        Sunday Pictorial launched.
1917   Aitken becomes Lord Beaverbrook.
        Astor becomes Lord Astor.
1919   Harold Harmsworth becomes Lord Rothermere.
1921   British Broadcasting Company formed.
1922   Lord Northcliffe dies.
        Major John Jacob Astor buys *The Times*.
1923   Rothermere buys the Hulton chain.
        Beaverbrook buys *Evening Standard*.
        Berry Brothers form Allied Newspapers Ltd.
1925   Press Association buys 53 per cent share of Reuters.
1926   Berry Brothers buy Rothermere's Amalgamated
            Press Ltd.
1928   Rothermere forms Northcliffe Newspapers Ltd.
        Westminster Gazette absorbed by *Daily News*.
        Berry Brothers buy *Daily Telegraph*.
1929   William Berry becomes Lord Camrose; his brother, Gomer,
            Lord Kemsley.
        Elias buys *Sunday People* and 51 per cent share of *Daily
            Herald*.
1930   *Daily Chronicle* amalgamates with *Daily News* to form *News
            Chronicle*.
1931   Rothermere hives *Mirror* group off as separate company.
1936   Television service starts in Britain.
1937   Camrose buys *Morning Post* and incorporates it in the *Daily
            Telegraph*.
        Camrose and Kemsley split – Camrose takes *Telegraph* and
            Financial Times, Kemsley *Sketch* and *Sunday Times*.

1938   *Picture Post* launched.

1939   *Herald* starts circulation war with *Express, Mail* and *Chronicle*.
Odhams take over Newnes magazines.
Telegraph prints news on front page.

1940   Newsprint rationed.
Lord Rothermere dies; national newspapers become
co-owners of Reuters.

1941   Reuters Trust formed.

1945   Astors set up trust to run *Observer*.

1951   Cecil Harmsworth King appointed chairman of *Mirror*
group.

1952   *Guardian* puts news on front page.

1954   *Daily Mirror* tops five million circulation.

1956   Newsprint rationing ends.

1957   Pearson acquires *Financial Times*.

1959   *Mirror* group takes over Amalgamated Press.
Manchester Guardian becomes the *Guardian*.
Thomson buys Kemsley newspapers.

1960   *News Chronicle, Sunday Graphic, Sunday Empire News* and *Star*
fold.
The *Guardian* moves to London.
Mirror group buys Odhams, including *Sunday People* and *Daily
Herald*.
Sunday Dispatch folds.
Sunday Telegraph launched.

1962   First colour magazine issued with *Sunday Times*.

1963   *Mirror* group forms International Publishing Corporation.

1964   *Mirror* group relaunch *Daily Herald* as *Sun* broadsheet.

1966   Lord Thomson of Fleet buys *The Times* from Lord Astor.

1966   News appears on *The Times* front page.

1967   *Reynolds News* closed.

1968   Michael Berry becomes Lord Hartwell.

1969   Murdoch buys *News of the World* from Carr family and the *Sun*
from *Mirror* group.

1971   *Daily Sketch* closed.
Tabloid *Daily Mail* launched.
Vere Harmsworth, third Viscount Rothermere, takes control
of Associated Newspapers.

1975   *Daily Mirror, Financial Times, Daily Telegraph, Daily Express* all
produce new technology plans.

1976   Anderson of ARCO buys *Observer*.
1977   New technology plans rejected by print unions.
        Matthews of Trafalgar House buys Beaverbrook Press from
           Sir Max Aitken.
        Daily Express goes tabloid.
1978   Matthews launches *Daily Star* (later *Star*).
        Murdoch plans Wapping plant, first in docklands.
1978–9 Closure of *The Times* and *Sunday Times*.
1981   Murdoch buys *The Times* newspapers from Lord Thomson.
        Rowland of Lonhro buys *Observer* from Anderson of ARCO.
        Start of Bingo war.
1982   *Mail on Sunday* launched.
1984   Reuters flotation provides many newspapers with cash for
           new technology.
        Robert Maxwell buys *Mirror* group from Reed International.
1985   Stevens of United Newspapers takes over *Express* group from
           Matthews.
        Conrad Black buys *Daily Telegraph* from Lord Hartwell.
        Eddy Shah and Rupert Murdoch make deal with EETPU
           circumventing other unions.
1986   Murdoch moves *Times*, *Sunday Times*, *Sun* and *News of the World*
           to Wapping.
        Eddy Shah launches *Today*.

Acknowledgements

I have referred in the text of my brief history of Fleet Street to most of the books I found most useful; others I consulted during the research on this book included *Fourth-rate Estate* by Tom Baistow, 1958; *Newspaper History: from the 17th century to the present day* edited by George Boyle, James Curran and Pauline Wingate, 1978; *The Life and Death of the Press Barons* by Piers Brendon, 1982; *The Press and Society* by G. A. Cranfield, 1978; *The Voice of Britain: The Story of the Daily Express* by R. Allen, 1983; *Pressures on the Press* by Charles Wintour, 1972; *The Fleet Street Disaster* by Gordon Cleverley, 1976, and *Goodbye, Fleet Street* by Bob Edwards, 1987.

And while I am extemely grateful to all my ex-colleagues and Fleet Street friends who helped me to put this book together, I am particularly indebted to John Edwards of the *Daily Mail* who went to a lot of trouble to introduce me to people I hadn't previously met; to Brian Park, Director of Corporate Affairs in Associated Newspapers; to Brian Inglis, an old friend who gave me a great deal of advice and help when I was initially planning the book, and who has read the proofs for me; to Bernard Shrimsley, who although he would not be interviewed himself, helped me in all sorts of other ways; and of course, to Roger Smith, my editor at Heinemann who was very enthusiastic about the project from the start, and to Richard Wheaton, who ably prepared the copy for setting. I would also like to thank the Editor of the *Daily Mirror* for permission to reproduce Bill Connor's marvellous piece about Fleet Street from his Cassandra column in that newspaper.

Tony Gray
Kew, Richmond, Surrey
September, 1989

Index